# HOW DARWINISM CORRODES MORALITY

This book is extremely comprehensive in scope, dealing with the effects of Darwinism and eugenics in a host of areas. Dr. Bergman has expanded on some of the "facts" that I thought I knew by introducing even more startling and shocking numbers. I learned details, unknown to me before, about the lives of Kinsey, Nietzsche, Sanger, Hitler and even Charles Manson. Darwin left his mark on all of them. I have considered myself to be a theistic evolutionist, but I'm having a harder and harder time resisting Dr. Bergman's teaching. He may have "converted" me. It's my honour to give an enthusiastic "thumbs up" for Jerry's new book. It ended too soon. I was hoping for even more!
**THOMAS B. STOGDILL**, M.D., Bluffton, Indiana

America is seriously ill, and the symptoms are self-evident. Our case of spiritual acid reflux grows worse with each daily news cycle. In his eye-opening book, Professor Jerry Bergman shines a spotlight on the cause of this relativistic malady with remarkable clarity. Our nation's "good idea filter" is occluded; it has been poisoned by generational over-exposure to the falsehoods of evolution-only, particles-to-people indoctrination! What can cure our chronic and debilitating spiritual infection? Only by swallowing the truth can we be saved. The heavy dosage of the morality-reality therapy Dr. Bergman prescribes is civilization's only hope to recover from what has been aptly described as a death struggle between two civilizations.
**JUDGE DARRELL WHITE**, founder and president of American Judicial Alliance

This latest book by Jerry Bergman is extremely important in exposing the true stripes of several renowned Americans, i.e., Margaret Sanger, Benjamin Spock, Alfred Kinsey and Havelock Ellis, some of whom are still unwittingly held up by many today with the highest regard. In his masterful research style, Bergman has sliced through many suppressed layers, bringing to light the facts as to just how deeply involved these individuals were in undermining decency in our society and catering to the basest nature of man, advocating for many outrageous evils, including eugenics, abortion and unrestrained immoral behaviour. At the core is an acceptance and passion for Darwinism. Especially tragic is how many pastors and church bodies, which should be the very sanctuary of truth, caved to Darwinism and were actually in league with those who undermined many foundational truths. This book will force many to stop and think about the ramifications of falling away from "the Way, the Truth, and the Life."

**BRYCE GAUDIAN,** Hayward, Minnesota. development manager for Agilis Corporation

Dr. Bergman rigorously demonstrates the intellectual fingerprints of Darwinism in the eugenics movement, which was surprisingly popular even in egalitarian America. He shows the trajectory of moral decline and loss of religious faith, acceptance of sexual anarchy, abortion and even the next logical step of infanticide, as well as racism and genocide. With the "scientific" justification of "improving the species," unspeakable atrocities can be seen as laudable.

**ROSS OLSON**, M.D. pediatrician

This book describes a spider web—but one not spun by any ordinary spider. A story of evolution's influence is woven through the pages like the spokes of a web and the radiating spirals. The same names keep reappearing as the book traces the influence spiral. Darwin influenced Haeckel who influenced Nietzsche who influenced eugenics and the German scientists and Hitler, thus bringing about the "Final Solution" Holocaust. And from eugenics, the thread branches off to the United States and its policy of sterilization of "undesirables" and its immigration policy that rejected Jews (one of the "inferior races") attempting to escape Europe during World War II, thereby returning them to face the concentration camps and the Holocaust. Sitting at the very centre —the hub—of this web is the spider whose name is "Darwinism." This is a book not to be read, but to be studied. The reader faces the task of following these threads around and through the web, hopefully not to be entrapped.

**DAVID J. OBERPRILLER,** professor, Arizona Christian University, Phoenix

Jerry Bergman provides a tremendous resource for all concerned about the decline of morality in present day society with his newest book on the corrosive influence of Darwinism on morality. In a most thorough manner, this book demonstrates how Darwin's theory has been a lead-in to racism, eugenics, mass murder and genocide. These are not ultimately just Dr. Bergman's claims: his documentation for the chain of events that led some very prominent intellectual and political Darwinists to moral decline and acting on depravity is thorough and convincing. Dr. Bergman's style is relentless in presenting the dark side of Darwin in the lives of many influential and obviously intellectually gifted persons. I highly recommend this book to those who defend Darwin and Darwin's scientific legacy, those who may be riding the fence and those committed to biblical creationism.

**THEODORE J. SIEK**, Ph.D., biochemistry

In this book Dr. Bergman, as he always does, provides a wealth of documented facts to support the thesis of the title. Sadly, I have observed the Darwinian "tooth and claw" way of living, which I grew up with, is now becoming more widespread. The best chapter in the book was a discussion of how the teaching (indoctrination) of evolution has been a major cause of the destruction of government schools.

In his concluding chapter, Dr. Bergman confides that the book was not intended to disprove evolution. That has already been more than adequately done in Dr. Bergman's many other books and articles. This book does do what the title displays—document the damage done by Darwinism.

**KARL PRIEST**, M.A. retired math teacher

Jerry Bergman provides an excellent documentation of what happens when God is pulled out of system of thought and is replaced by ideologies rooted in Darwinism. Some of the consequences are the saddest tragedies in history. The book provides telling examples of ideological manipulation and how harmful ideas can infiltrate cultures and gain support even from unsuspecting people that mean well. As in his other books, Bergman demonstrates outstanding research. You will be surprised to find out that Darwinism influenced our culture today in more ways than you realized.

**ADRIAN CHIRA**, software engineer

Dr. Jerry Bergman has grasped this enormous harm and danger inflicted on humankind by the theory of evolution. He is one of those few scientists who possessed the foresight and honesty to wage the intellectual struggle against this scientific falsehood, the worst there has ever been. In addition to invalidating the theory of evolution, his dozens of books and hundreds of articles have also exposed the damage it has done to society and the dictatorship it has established over the scientific world.

This latest book by Dr. Bergman, of whom I am a great admirer, reveals with numerous examples and quotations how Darwinism has eroded the conscience, moral structure and spiritual values of humankind like an acid. At this time when the world so desperately needs a great moral awakening, this well-researched work by Dr. Bergman will no doubt play an important role in revealing this fundamental problem facing the world.

**ADNAN OKTAR**, Muslim Creationist author

# HOW DARWINISM CORRODES MORALITY

## DARWINISM, IMMORALITY, ABORTION AND THE SEXUAL REVOLUTION

## Jerry Bergman

joshua press

**p r e s s**

**www.joshuapress.com**

*Published by*
Joshua Press Inc., Kitchener, Ontario, Canada
*Distributed by*
Sola Scriptura Ministries International
www.sola-scriptura.ca

First published 2017

Cover and book design by Janice Van Eck

*The publication of this book was made possible by the generous support of The Ross-Shire Foundation.*

*Library and Archives Canada Cataloguing in Publication*

Bergman, Jerry, 1946–, author
     How Darwinism corrodes morality : Darwinism, immorality, abortion and the sexual revolution / Jerry Bergman.

Includes bibliographical references.
Issued in print and electronic formats.
ISBN 978-1-894400-78-7 (softcover).—ISBN 978-1-894400-79-4 (HTML).—ISBN 978-1-894400-80-0 (PDF)

     1. Evolution (Biology)—Moral and ethical aspects.  I. Title.

B818.B47 2017               171'.7               C2017-900424-7
                                                 C2017-900425-5

### To Wayne Frair

Wayne Frair has edited several of my books, and within hours of
completing his review of this book, he passed away.
Dr. Frair graduated from Houghton College with a B.A. in Zoology
and then took a B.S. in Zoology with honours from Wheaton College,
a M.A. in Embryology from the University of Massachusetts and a
Ph.D. in Serology (Biochemical Taxonomy) from Rutgers University
in New Jersey. Dr. Frair was chairman of the biology department
and on the science faculty at Kings College, New York,
from 1955 until 1996. He has authored numerous peer-reviewed
scientific publications in the area of biology, as well as
several books in his field.

## Other books by Jerry Bergman

*Hitler and the Nazi Darwinian Worldview:*
*How the Nazi Eugenic Crusade for a Superior Race Caused*
*the Greatest Holocaust in World History*
Kitchener: Joshua Press, 2012.

*Persuaded by the Evidence*
Edited with Doug Sharp
Green Forest: Master Books, 2008.

*The Dark Side of Darwin*
Green Forest: New Leaf Press, 2011.

*Slaughter of the Dissidents: The Shocking Truth*
*About Killing the Careers of Darwin Doubters*
Rev. ed. Southworth: Leafcutter Press, 2012.

*Transformed by the Evidence*
Edited with Doug Sharp
Southworth: Leafcutter Press, 2014.

*The Darwin Effect. Its Influence on Nazism, Eugenics,*
*Racism, Communism, Capitalism & Sexism*
Green Forest: Master Books, 2014.

*Darwinism's Frauds, Blunders and Forgeries*
Atlanta: CMI Publishing, 2016.

*Silencing the Darwin Dissidents*
Southworth: Leafcutter Press, 2016.

*Censoring the Darwin Dissidents*
Southworth: Leafcutter Press, forthcoming.

*Eminent Scientist Darwin Doubters: Nobel Laureates and Other*
*Eminent Scientists Who Reject Orthodox Darwinism*
Southworth: Leafcutter Press, forthcoming.

# Contents

‖‖‖‖‖‖‖‖‖‖‖‖‖‖‖‖‖‖‖‖‖‖‖‖‖‖‖‖‖‖‖‖‖‖‖‖‖‖‖‖‖‖‖‖‖‖‖‖‖‖‖‖‖‖‖‖‖‖‖‖‖‖‖‖‖‖‖‖‖‖‖‖‖‖‖‖‖

# Foreword

||||||||||||||||||||||||||||||||||||||||||||||||||||||||||||||||||||||||||||||||||||||||||||||||||||||||||||

I had motives for not wanting the world to have meaning; consequently [I] assumed it had none and was able without any
difficulty to find satisfying reasons for this assumption.... The
philosopher...is also concerned to prove there is no valid reason
why he personally should not do as he wants to do.... The liberation we desired was simultaneously liberation from a certain
political and economic system and liberation from a certain
system of morality. We objected to the morality because it inter-
fered with our sexual freedom.[1]

One of the side themes in many of Professor Jerry Bergman's books
over the years has been the serious and detrimental moral implications of Darwinism. In this new book, Dr. Bergman has drawn all
these themes together. By tracing a detailed history of the social
implications of Darwinism, Dr. Bergman shows that the issue is not

---

1    Aldous Huxley, "Confessions of a Professed Atheist," *Report: Perspective on the
News* (Vol. 3, June 1966): 19. Grandson of evolutionist Thomas Huxley and brother of
evolutionist Julian Huxley, Aldous Huxley was one the most influential writers and
philosophers of the twentieth century.

simply one of a difference of opinions, but actually a matter of the soul of society.

The second chapter, for example, headed "Evolution fosters moral decline," sets out the stall admirably. Atheist evolutionists like Richard Dawkins have claimed that they would not want to live in a society governed by a "survival of the fittest" philosophy, without realizing that this is exactly what they have created. All that is good in Western society has flowed naturally from a biblical ethos. All that is wrong in the same society has flowed from the rejection of Christianity as central to everyday lives and its replacement by Darwinistic ideas. Because such a statement sounds simplistic when stated by itself, it is clear that Dr. Bergman has done us all a service by detailing this decline in a large number of different areas and through the lives and works of many people who were influenced in their work by Darwinism.

It is my hope that this book finds its way on to many bookshelves. More importantly, it is my hope that it becomes well read, so that many people start to understand that an evolutionary worldview is not just detrimental to research in biology, but has a negative impact on our everyday lives.

**PAUL TAYLOR**, international speaker, author of *Truth, Lies and Science Education* and director of the Mount St Helens Creation Center, Washington

# Acknowledgements

IIIIIIIIIIIIIIIIIIIIIIIIIIIIIIIIIIIIIIIIIIIIIIIIIIIIIIIIIIIIIIIIIIIIIIIIIIIIIIIIIIIIIIIIIIIIIIIIIIIIIIIIIIII

I gratefully acknowledge the help of Paul Gosselin, who reviewed the entire manuscript, as did Wayne Frair, Ph.D., Clifford Lillo, M.S., Eric Blievernicht and Bryce Gaudian. Also I thank Jody Allen, R.N., Bert Thompson, Ph.D., John Woodmorappe, M.A., MaryAnn Stuart, M.S., Paul Ackerman, Ph.D., Marilyn Dauer, Wilbur H. Entz, George Cooper and John UpChurch for their comments on earlier drafts of this book. Thank you to the various publishers who allowed me to reprint portions of my previous writings. I also wish to thank John Woodmorappe for permission to rely on several of his book reviews in order to complete chapter 12; and most important, Fred Johnson, Ph.D.—without his expert help, this project would never have been satisfactorily completed.

What we need is a truly anti-Darwinian society...we don't wish to live in a society where the weakest go to the wall, where the strongest suppress the weak, and even kill the weak. We—I, at least—do not wish to live in that kind of society. I want to live in the sort of society where we take care of the sick, where we take care of the weak, take care of the oppressed, which is a very anti-Darwinian society.

**RICHARD DAWKINS,** Evolutionary biologist and prominent atheist; in a lecture at Kennesaw State University, November 21, 2014 [1]

1    Eric W. Dolan. "Richard Dawkins on the men's rights movement: Really? That's a thing?" Rawstory (2014); http://www.rawstory.com/rs/2014/12/richarddawkins-on-the-mens-rights-movement-really-thats-a-thing/; accessed August 15, 2016.

# Introduction

IIIIIIIIIIIIIIIIIIIIIIIIIIIIIIIIIIIIIIIIIIIIIIIIIIIIIIIIIIIIIIIIIIIIIIIIIIIIIIIIIIIIIIIIIIIIIIIIIIIIIIIII

**T**his book documents the fact that Darwinism has had a profound adverse effect on morals, not only sexual morals, but also on morals in general, including the mistreatment of minority races, and even the abortion movement. The leading evolutionist of the last century, Harvard professor Ernst Myer, recognized that

> Darwin's great contribution was that he replaced theological, or supernatural, science with secular science…. Darwin's explanation that all things have a natural cause made the belief in a creatively superior mind quite unnecessary. He created a secular world, more so than anyone before him. Certainly many forces were converging in that same direction, but Darwin's work was the crashing arrival of this idea, and from that point on, the secular viewpoint of the world became virtually universal.[1]

1   Ernst Mayer, "What evolution is," *Edge* (December 31, 1999); http://edge.org/conversation/what-evolution-is; accessed August 15, 2016.

As this book documents, the secular worldview has affected few areas as greatly as morality. One example from the United States is that, since anti-abortion laws were ruled illegal by the U.S. Supreme Court, 55 million abortions have been performed in America alone.

The fact is, "the general theory of selection…would apply Darwinism to everything." And in fact, Darwinism has been applied to "explain almost everything about humans beings, from their shape and preference for copulating face to face to their tendency to depression and eating sweets" and, more often, immoral behaviour.[2] Jeremy Rifkin wrote that in our post-Christian secular society today, due to the rejection of the creator, our

> designer [God], humanity is abandoning the idea that the universe operates by ironclad truth because it no longer feels the need to be constrained by such fetters. Nature is being made anew, this time by human beings. We no longer feel ourselves to be guests in someone else's home and therefore obliged to make our behavior conform to a set of pre-existing cosmic rules. It is our creation now[3]

and, as such, we humans

> make the rules. We establish the parameters of reality. We create the world, and because we do, we no longer feel beholden to outside forces. We no longer have to justify our behavior, for we are now the architects of the universe. We are responsible to nothing outside ourselves, for we are the kingdom, the power, and the glory forever and ever.[4]

One result is that Darwin has profoundly inspired the application of the survival of the fittest philosophy on the value of human life, such as the devaluing of human life that has resulted in the murder of many

---

2   Andrew Brown, *The Darwin Wars: How Stupid Genes Became Selfish Gods* (New York: Simon & Schuster, 1999), 9, 16.

3   Jeremy Rifkin, *Algeny* (New York: Viking Press, 1983), 243–244.

4   Rifkin, *Algeny*, 244.

millions of Christians.[5] According to the *World Christian Encyclopedia*[6] and other reliable sources, there were 77 million Christian martyrs since Christ walked the earth 2,000 years ago and 45.5 million in the last century alone, often as a result of communism and Nazism.

Another example of the devaluation of human life caused by Darwinism is racism. Harvard University professor of anthropology David Maybury-Lewis wrote,

> Darwin's *Origin of Species* was followed by a spate of books on the origins of civilization and the history of humankind. These evolutionary theories invariably placed tribal societies at the bottom of the ladder of development.... The theories, then, came to be considered as the "scientific" justification for imperialism [that justified the] stronger and more "advanced" peoples [to have] conquered weaker and more "backward" ones.[7]

Cambridge-trained philosopher Jonathan Sacks, wrote that the world changed with Darwin and his dogma and

> human beings were not even *sui generis*, a class on their own. Not only were they not the image of God, they were just one branch of the primates, close cousins to the apes and chimpanzees. There might be differences of degree between humans and others, but not of kind. Other animals, said Darwin, felt feelings, used language, even had self-consciousness.[8]

Furthermore, then

> came the neo-Darwinians with their assault on one thing humans

---

5    Jerry Bergman, *The Darwin Effect: Its Influence on Nazism, Eugenics, Racism, Communism, Capitalism & Sexism* (Green Forest: Master Books, 2014), chapters 14–17.

6    David B. Barrett, George T. Kurian, Todd M. Johnson, *World Christian Encyclopedia*, 2nd ed. (New York: Oxford University Press, 2001).

7    David Maybury-Lewis, *Millennium: Tribal Wisdom and the Modern World* (New York: Viking, 1992), 20.

8    Jonathan Sacks, *The Great Partnership: God, Science and the Search for Meaning* (New York: Hodder & Stoughton, 2011), 116.

could still pride themselves on, their altruism, their willingness to sacrifice themselves for the sake of others. Not so, argued the sociobiologists. The human person is, after all, just a gene's way of making another gene. Whatever stories we tell ourselves, our apparently altruistic acts are only ways of ensuring our genetic survival into the next generation. We only really help kin and in precise proportion as they share our genes. "Scratch an altruist," said Michael Ghiselin, "and watch a hypocrite bleed."[9]

The core of Neo-Darwinism was the belief

> that evolution proceeded by mere chance, random genetic mutation, which produced the variety on which natural selection could work. Stephen J. Gould drew the conclusion that if the tape of evolution were to be replayed there would be no certainty that *Homo sapiens* would emerge. So not only were human beings not made by an act of special divine creation, their very existence was pure accident. So we are nothing, our planet is insignificant, our existence a mere caesura in time. Our noblest thoughts conceal base intentions. There is no freedom, just necessity. There is no truth, just hegemonic narrative. There is no moral beauty, just a sordid struggle to survive.[10]

As a result, the advances of Western culture were "taken by social Darwinists as evidence that he [Westerners]—and it was *he*—was especially fit to dominate other races," including the so-called Black, Yellow and Brown racial groups.[11] The slaughter that this belief supported, even encouraged, is well documented. The persons killed due to communism and Nazism alone equalled an estimated 167 million. Millions more died from disease and famine, and later from injuries caused by the communist and Nazi movements.

Darwinism was a critical factor in causing this Holocaust and was a major factor in causing the extent of the Second World War, if not,

---

9  Sacks, *Great Partnership*, 116–117.
10  Sacks, *Great Partnership*, 116–117.
11  Maybury-Lewis, *Millennium*, 51.

to some extent, the First World War as well.[12] World War I was seven times greater than all 605 recorded wars in history put together, and World War II was four times greater than World War I. Thus, World War II was twenty-eight times greater than all known wars in history put together.

As is often said, evil exists not so much due to evil persons, but more to the masses of good people who do nothing. One study, the most comprehensive survey ever completed, found that fifty-four percent of those surveyed in 102 countries and territories have never even heard of the Holocaust.[13] One cannot expect people to do anything about evil if they are ignorant of its existence. This book covers one major negative effect of Darwinism, its adverse effect on sexual morals including promiscuity, abortion and even psychotherapy and its contribution to anti-Christianity. The fact is, "Darwinian beliefs have been used to justify anarchy, fascism, liberal capitalism, and almost anything in between."[14] This volume looks at only one of these areas, namely the entire field of morality.

The following chapters were written to stand independently, allowing a reader to read the chapters of most interest first. As a result, some minor repetition exists.

---

12 Jerry Bergman, *Hitler and the Nazi Darwinian Worldview: How the Nazi Eugenic Crusade for a Superior Race Caused the Greatest Holocaust in World History* (Kitchener: Joshua Press, 2012); Bergman, *Darwin Effect*.

13 Elwood McQuaid, "New survey shows extent of worldwide anti-Semitism," *Israel My Glory* 72, No. 4 (2014): 25.

14 Brown, *Darwin Wars*.

## Charles Darwin (1809-1882)

Darwin's *On the Origin of Species* influenced many in the late nineteenth and early twentieth century, and its influence continues to this day.

# 01

# Darwin and morality

||||||||||||||||||||||||||||||||||||||||||||||||||||||||||||||||||||||||||||||||||||||||||||||||||||||||||||||||||||||||||||||||

D arwin dramatically changed our world, especially the view of our place in it, more than almost any other man in history except Jesus Christ, whose effect was far different than Darwin's. The problem is that when Darwinian evolution displaced religion with secularism and secular institutions such as psychology, it

> left many situations vacant. Science has nowadays the prestige that theology once had as a source of authoritative answers to such questions as "Who are we?", "Why are we here?" and others whose answers are not strictly factual or even numerical.[1]

The moral harm that this theory has caused was recognized almost as soon as Darwin's book on evolution was published. Darwin's former biology professor, Adam Sedgwick, wrote to him shortly after his evolution book was published in 1859, stating that "I have read your book [*On the Origin of Species*] with more pain than pleasure."[2] Sedgwick

---

1 Brown, *Darwin Wars*, ix.
2 Adam Sedgwick, November 24, 1859, in *The Correspondence of Charles Darwin*

added that he was angry about certain parts of the book because he "felt that Charles had ignored morality," and that "the argument of creation by natural selection would 'sink the human race into a lower grade of degradation than any into which it has fallen since its written records tell us of its history.' He begged Charles to accept God's revelation" on creation.[3] He concluded that

> Lastly then, I greatly dislike the concluding chapter—not as a summary—for in that light it appears good—but I dislike it from the tone of triumphant confidence in which you appeal to the rising generation (in a tone I condemned in the author of the Vestiges).

The world into which Darwin led us was further detailed on the centennial of the publication of *On the Origin of Species* by the leading paleontologist of the last century. Eminent biologist George Gaylord Simpson, the "co-architect of the Modern Synthesis of evolutionary theory" wrote an essay for the journal *Science* titled "The world into which Darwin led us." The essay examined "how the Darwinian revolution changed, completely and forever, long-cherished concepts of ourselves."[4] The fact is, in the twentieth century the prestige of science, specifically Darwinism, has been used to justify almost everything, especially various forms of totalitarianism.[5]

Darwin was the chief initiator of this moral revolution.[6] The Darwinian revolution delivered three major blows to our previous perceptions of our place and purpose in the universe:

1. It asserted that the world and the universe are, in general,

---

(Cambridge: Cambridge University Press, 1991), vol. 7, 397). Darwin Correspondence Project; https://www.darwinproject.ac.uk/letter/?docId=letters/DCP-LETT-2548.xml ;query=sedgwick;brand=default; accessed August 15, 2016.

3   Sedgwick, *Correspondence of Charles Darwin.*

4   Sean B. Carroll, *Remarkable Creatures: Epic Adventures in the Search for the Origins of Species* (Boston: Houghton Mifflin Harcourt, 2009), 278.

5   Brown, *Darwin Wars*, ix.

6   George Gaylord Simpson, "The world into which Darwin led us," *Science* 131, No. 3405 (1960): 966–974.

hostile places, and not peaceful and orderly as perceived by Darwin's predecessors.

2. Furthermore, Darwin's new view of our evolutionary "ancestry meant that humans have no special status" other than a distinct animal species. To Simpson, our kinship with amoeba, tapeworms, fleas, and monkeys represented "togetherness and brotherhood with a vengeance, beyond the wildest dreams of copy writers or of theologians."

3. "The struggle for life made it extremely improbable that anything in the world exists specifically for our benefit or ill.... 'It is no more true that fruits, for instance, evolved for the delectation of men than that men evolved for the delectation of tigers.'"[7]

The revolution that Darwin began did not end with his death.[8] Although the major elements of this philosophical revolution were clear to Simpson a half-century ago, the "ensuing decades have even shaken Simpson's sober view of the world." One example is the evolutionary conclusion that the universe was even "more hostile and uncaring than he [Simpson] knew."

For example, Simpson interpreted both the "geological and fossil record as documenting steady, gradual, orderly change."[9] Further research found evidence "that the face of the earth has been remodeled and the planet's inhabitants extinguished by cataclysmic events.... Catastrophic scenarios were long disdained by geologists as unmodern and unscientific, until Chicxulub" where an asteroid or comet that struck Mexico is theorized to cause the extinction of the dinosaurs.[10]

This fact was interpreted by many Darwinists as supporting the evolutionary "view that life does not evolve toward a goal. Regarding the contradiction between the notion of life evolving progressively and

---

7  Paraphrased from Carroll, *Remarkable Creatures*, 277–278.

8  An example of the continuing debate in this area is in the special issue of the journal *Zygon*. See Johan De Tavernier, "Morality and nature: Evolutionary challenges to Christian ethics," *Zygon* 49, No. 1 (March 2014): 171–189.

9  Carroll, *Remarkable Creatures*, 278.

10  Carroll, *Remarkable Creatures*, 278–279.

the pervasiveness of extinction, Simpson noted, 'If that is a foreordained plan, it is an oddly ineffective one.'"[11] Simpson stressed in his paper that Darwin changed the world to the degree that today Darwinism colours "the whole of our attitude toward life and toward ourselves, and hence our whole perceptual world" which includes our morals.[12]

Simpson concluded that "it is a characteristic of this world to which Darwin opened the door that …the future of mankind is dim, indeed— if there is any future."[13] If most people enter the door that Darwin opened, as this book documents, the future of humanity may well be dim. Fortunately, many people conclude the future of humankind will brighten if we reject Darwinism and, especially, its implications.

It is Simpson's worldview that motivates censorship and social pressure to conform to the moral world that is documented in the later chapters of this book. As Simpson concluded, the "influence of Darwin, or more broadly of the concept of evolution, has…literally led us to a different world," namely monism, the view that the material world is all that exists and all that has ever existed.[14] Well-known philosopher Harry A. Overstreet wrote that this materialism had "its roots in the science of the late nineteenth century," and specifically it

> began with the publication of Darwin's *Origin of Species*. Materialism, or the belief that matter…is the sole type of existence in the universe…was backed by all the contemporary science of the late nineteenth century. Its main support was, however, derived from the inductive investigations on biology and psychology.[15]

He opined that, in order to explain the evolutionary process,

> that has led from the amoeba to man, including also the development of intelligence in man, they found it necessary to invoke

---

11  Carroll, *Remarkable Creatures*, 278–279.

12  Simpson, "World into which Darwin led us," 969.

13  Simpson, "World into which Darwin led us," 974.

14  Simpson, "World into which Darwin led us," 966.

15  Harry Overstreet, "The philosophy of materialism," in *The Popular Educator Library*, Vol. 5 (New York: National Educational Alliance Incorporated, 1940), 2375.

neither mind nor purpose, neither creative force nor divine agency; they relied solely upon the operation of natural forces. Darwin ascribed the development to chance variations of which the fittest survived.[16]

The moral revolution was expressed eloquently by professor of evolutionary psychology at Swansea University, Steve Stewart-Williams, who writes that

> human beings are unique among the animals in being able to comprehend the ultimate meaninglessness of existence. The philosopher Herman Tennesen [wrote that human existence] "may yield the most horrifying, vertiginously pernicious, unendurable insights into the fatuous futility and monstrous absurdity of...human existence."[17]

The human problem is that theists

> want to think that there is some ultimate purpose or meaning behind their lives.... Like the search for God, the search for the meaning of life is a wild goose chase. Darwin showed us that there is no reason to think that there is a teleological explanation for life. We are here because we evolved, and evolution occurred for no particular reason. Thus, on a Darwinian view, not only is our species not as special as we had once thought, but our lives are ultimately without purpose or meaning. Life just winds on aimlessly, a pointless, meandering sequence of events. Sometimes it's pleasant, sometimes not, but it lacks any overall purpose or goal or destination.[18]

---

16 Overstreet, "Philosophy of materialism," 2375.

17 Steve Stewart-Williams, *Darwin, God and the Meaning of Life: How Evolutionary Theory Undermines Everything You Thought You Knew* (New York: Cambridge University Press, 2010), 197.

18 Stewart-Williams, *Darwin, God and the Meaning of Life*, 197.

## EVOLUTION AND MORALS

Retired Johns Hopkins department of pediatric neurosurgery chair, Ben Carson, wrote that the Darwinian opposition

> to traditional morality is another form of religion, although its believers would never admit it. This religious belief is the theory of evolution. In this belief system, only the strong survive and there are no moral implications associated with the actions necessary to survive and thrive. As I have stated and written publicly, it might be more difficult for evolutionists to describe the basis of morality than it would be for a creationist.[19]

The moral effects of Darwinism have been most thoroughly explored especially in relation to the Holocaust, yet even this event has been irresponsibly challenged by several leading diehard Darwinists. One of the most controversial sections of the film *Expelled: No Intelligence Allowed*, starring Ben Stein,[20] was the part that explained the contribution of Darwinism to the Holocaust. Ironically, this part of the film was one of the most carefully documented historical events in the entire movie.

I am not denying the adverse influence of other factors, such as the media and poverty on morality, but this book focuses only on the influence of Darwin. The de-mystification of the natural world and the notion of secular positivistic science have roots much older than Darwin's writings: Lucretius, Francis Bacon, Thomas Hobbes, John Locke, David Hume, Adam Smith, the natural philosophers of the English Royal Society, the French encyclopedists, Jeremy Bentham, James and John Stuart Mill, Thomas Paine, the medieval nominalist philosophers, Maimonides, Baruch Spinoza, Immanuel Kant and G.W.F. Hegel. Darwin wrote at the same time that Robert Chambers (1802–1871) published his *Vestiges of the Natural History of Creation* (1844). Jean-Baptiste Lamarck (1744–1829) and Alfred Russel Wallace

---

19  Ben Carson, *One Nation: What We Can All Do To Save America's Future* (New York: Sentinel, 2014), 195–196.

20  *Expelled: No Intelligence Allowed*, 97 min., directed by Nathan Frankowski. Premise Media Corporation/Rampant Films, 2008.

(1823–1913) were searching for the same solution. Darwin's achievement was substantially summative and as popularizer, rather than some unique new breakthrough in thought. It was Darwin's writings and his followers that inspired the events reviewed in this book, not Lamarck, Wallace or Chambers.

## DARWIN AND MURDER

It is well documented that German evolutionary biologists, scientists, physicians, public health officials and academics played a critical role in supporting and implementing the Nazis' program of racial eugenics that culminated in the Holocaust. Eugenics is the use of various means of producing what the powers that be judge to be a superior race. An example of the extreme form is to murder those judged to be inferior and encourage those judged to be superior to have large families. A problem always is who does the judging and on what basis do they judge a group as superior.

Viktor Frankl, the famed founder of the school of psychology termed logotherapy, was in four Nazi concentration camps between 1942 and 1945, a horrendous experience. His family died, he suffered horribly, and he spent years watching those around him suffering and dying. Dr. Frankl astutely evaluated the influence of modern scientists and academics in helping to prepare the way for the Nazi atrocities by concluding that the

> gas chambers of Auschwitz were the ultimate consequence of the theory that man is nothing but the product of heredity and environment—or, as the Nazis liked to say, of "Blood and Soil." I am absolutely convinced that the gas chambers of Auschwitz, Treblinka, and Maidanek were ultimately prepared not in some Ministry...in Berlin, but rather at the desks and in the lecture halls of nihilistic scientists and philosophers.[21]

Dr. Frankl accurately summarized the case against academia and the scientists in Germany.

---

21 Victor Frankl, *The Doctor and the Soul: From Psychotherapy to Logotherapy*, 3rd ed. (New York: Vintage Books, 1986), xxxii.

An exhibition titled "Deadly Medicine" that ran from April 22, 2004, to October 16, 2005, at the U.S. Holocaust Memorial Museum in Washington, D.C., eloquently documented this fact. Since then, the exhibit has been travelling to museums throughout the world, including at the National World War II Museum in New Orleans, Louisiana.

A compilation based on the exhibition includes well-written essays by many internationally recognized authorities on Nazism which document that the scientific establishment was crucial in planning and carrying out the Holocaust. This beautifully reproduced and lavishly illustrated compilation with many never-before-published photographs provides a compelling visual documentation of the Darwinian eugenic origins of the Holocaust.

From 1933 to 1945, the Nazi regime attempted to realize its goal of a biologically "healthy" and ethnically homogeneous population through social Darwinistic programs designed to cleanse German society of those persons whom the eugenic scientists perceived to be threatening to the German people's eugenic health.

The myth that Darwinian eugenics was not central to the Holocaust serves to protect the deeply held, but erroneous, conviction that Darwinism did not have a deleterious influence on Nazi Germany or morals as a whole. In fact, although both German eugenics and its British counterpart developed independently,

> both were heavily influenced by Charles Darwin's principles of evolution. In Germany, the zoologist Ernst Haeckel popularized social Darwinism—the extension of Darwin's theory of survival of the fittest (natural selection) to competition in human society. Haeckel's writings substantiated the fears of a falling birthrate among the "better" (or "productive") elements of society and pointed ominously to an increasing hereditary 'degeneration' — the transmission of physically and mentally unhealthy traits—of the human species.[22]

---

22 Dieter Kuntz and Susan Bachrach, ed., *Deadly Medicine: Creating the Master Race* (Chapel Hill: University of North Carolina Press, 2006), 17.

In addition,

German biologist August Weisman lent additional scientific support to the conclusion that natural selection no longer operated effectively in contemporary society because modern medicine and social welfare enabled the unfit to survive and reproduce their own "genetically defective" kind.[23]

Haeckel's and Weisman's ideas both clearly echo those of Darwin in his 1871 book *The Descent of Man* that argued for the evolution of humankind from lower forms of life. In this book, Darwin made the implications of evolution to eugenics crystal clear. Darwin noted that civilization does its

utmost to check the process of elimination; we build asylums for the imbecile, the maimed, and the sick; we institute poor-laws; and our medical men exert their utmost skill to save the life of every one to the last moment. There is reason to believe that vaccination has preserved thousands, who from a weak constitution would formerly have succumbed to small-pox. Thus the weak members of civilized societies propagate their kind. No one who has attended to the breeding of domestic animals will doubt that this must be highly injurious to the race of man. It is surprising how soon a want of care, or care wrongly directed, leads to the degeneration of a domestic race; but excepting in the case of man himself, hardly any one is so ignorant as to allow his worst animals to breed.[24]

The Nazi solution, in harmony with Darwin's admonition, was to sterilize, then murder, those persons the eugenics experts, mostly academics, judged as evolutionarily less fit. The fact is, "Darwin's work sparked great interest in biological determinism and the application

---

23 Kuntz and Bachrach, ed., *Deadly Medicine*, 17.
24 Charles Darwin, *The Descent of Man, and Selection in Relation to Sex* (London: John Murray, 1871), 168.

of the principle of natural selection to human society."[25] Darwin's cousin, Francis Galton, the man who coined the word "eugenics" and a founder of the eugenics movement, was "inspired by Darwin's assertion that various animals increased in number in a state of nature."[26] Four of Darwin's sons and one of his granddaughters were leaders in the eugenic movement.

Another myth about eugenics in the Third Reich is the belief that only marginal physicians in extreme situations participated in crimes against humanity and that German mainstream medicine was not corrupted by the surrounding maelstrom. Professors Robert Lifton, Robert N. Proctor, Michael H. Kater and Henry Friedlander, among others, have done much scholarly work to document the falsehood of these myths.

Yet, another claim used to distance establishment science from its eugenic past is the claim that the eugenic movement was not science but, instead, pseudoscience. Professor Müller-Hill debunked this myth as follows:

> Can science save face by claiming that what was practiced in Nazi Germany was not real science, that it was only pseudoscience? …science [is]…what the majority of scientists working in the field call science at the time it is being done. Referees decide what can be published and what is to be funded—therefore, what is published in scientific journals and funded by grant agencies must be considered science. Under this definition, scientists— specifically, German human or medical geneticists…were, during the 1930s and 1940s, deeply involved in the crimes of the Nazi government."[27]

Nazi propaganda, medical documents, scientific instruments, transport lists and photographs of sites, perpetrators and victims all document this. Most vivid, and most important, are the photos of the victims and documentary material, including artwork, personal letters

---

25 Kuntz and Bachrach, ed., *Deadly Medicine*, 44.
26 Kuntz and Bachrach, ed., *Deadly Medicine*, 44.
27 Kuntz and Bachrach, ed., *Deadly Medicine*, 185.

and artifacts that render the horrors the victims suffered in the name of Darwinian eugenics horrifyingly real. This documentation is essential to understanding the relationship between Nazi Darwinian political philosophy and medical science.

This book asserts that Darwinism was at the core of Nazi social thought, and explanations "based on genes and evolution have spread to cover almost every area of science and popular culture in the last thirty years"[28] including morality, as will be documented in this volume. The Nazi's goal was to produce, by the application of evolutionary principles such as natural selection, a racially pure, cohesive society that would reverse what the Nazi scientists saw as racial degeneration.

Heredity was assigned a central role in improving German society, taking the biology-is-destiny philosophy to its logical extreme. The belief in the innate inequality of individuals and, by extension, of racial groups, became dogma. So Nazi "scientists" used Darwinism to assess their victims on the basis of their physical, cultural and genetic traits. These scientists focused on the value or lack thereof, as interpreted by the Nazi movement, of persons to the collective German society.

A logical extension of the assignment of unequal values to individuals was their unequal rights and lack of worth as humans. As do Darwinists today, the Nazis strongly opposed the Christian teaching that we are all created "in the image of God." Both Nazi and modern political philosophy derived its origin from evolution and turned to biology, both for an explanation of social ills, and for solutions to their goal of population improvement through the application of Darwinist principles.

A major conclusion of this work is that the Nazi horrors and the moral problems covered in the following chapters were a result of "a long chain of experts, all physicians by training, who promoted a biological or scientific racism that helped make the Holocaust possible."[29] A major role for scientists then was to search for the means of achieving racial diagnosis:

---

28 Brown, *Darwin Wars*, ix–xx.
29 Kuntz and Bachrach, ed., *Deadly Medicine*, 122.

Much scientific research in racial science, human genetics, and serology during the Third Reich dealt with discovering diagnostic techniques to determine a person's race. The search focused on...numerous physical and racial characteristics, from the shape of nostrils to the structure of the iris of the eye.[30]

Biologists and anthropologists

led in research in racial genetics.... As scientists were particularly keen to find blood markers for Jews and Gypsies, serological tests were conducted on these groups in concentration camps.... The third area of research, racial genetics, studied such morphological characteristics as the skeleton, muscular system, and shape of the head and face, including skin, hair, eye color. The inheritance of every bodily detail was investigated—eyelids, eyebrows, ears, nostril shape, hair color, spinal column, and so on.[31]

The leading German biological scientists believed that sterilization and involuntary euthanasia should be applied on a wholesale basis. They argued that it was the central mechanism required to reverse genetic degeneration caused by ignoring evolution and counterselection. They believed this was happening in Germany. And of course, a major culprit was supposedly Aryan Germans marrying non-Aryans and then having large families.

The physicians and other biological experts with the requisite training and authority to influence, formulate and implement Nazi policy were essential to the success of this applied eugenics program. The Nazis used extensive propaganda to convince the public that eugenic programs were necessary to maintain their nation's health. Likewise, the same is true of the effects of evolution on morality detailed in this book.[32]

A major problem the Nazi had was determining who was a Jew, Gypsy or other "inferior" race. Some Nazis argued that a person with

---

30 Kuntz and Bachrach, ed., *Deadly Medicine*, 122–123.

31 Kuntz and Bachrach, ed., *Deadly Medicine*, 122–123.

32 For example, Kuntz and Bachrach, ed., *Deadly Medicine*, 62–69.

three Jewish grandparents was officially Jewish. Other experts concluded that persons with only one such grandparent were Jewish.
When the scientists appealed to Hitler to decide, he deferred, telling
them that was for the scientists to figure out. Finally a compromise
was reached.

## THE FINAL SOLUTION TO THE JEWISH AND LIVES-NOT-WORTH-LIVING PROBLEM

What resulted in the end was a medicalization of mass murder, facilitated by technological innovations first made in German health care
institutions and directed at what scientists regarded as the serious
genetic threat posed by the so-called unproductive and unfit members
of German society. The Holocaust demonstrated the willingness of
these professionals, especially the scientists and medical doctors, to
participate in the Final Solution to the Jewish problem, which was
extermination in the death camps of all Jews in Europe. As Benno
Müller-Hill writes, the

> involvement of science, or, specifically, genetics, in the abhorrent
> crimes of Nazi Germany is one of the most disturbing events for
> scientists, and the public alike, to contemplate. Science is about
> knowledge and truth. So, we must ask ourselves, how could
> German scientists support anti-Semitism and the racial measures
> of the Nazis?[33]

The facts disprove many common myths about medicine, science,
evolution and academia. The road to the Holocaust began with killing
grossly deformed children in 1939. This rapidly progressed to murdering fully healthy putative "inferior" races, including not only Jews, but
also Negroes, Slavics and Gypsies (Roma and Sinti), all with the solid
backing of the leading German scientists.

Aside from Charles Darwin, other scientists influential in the development of Nazi Germany's eugenic program included Darwin's cousin
Francis Galton. Galton was honoured in Nazi Germany not only for

---

33 Benno Müller-Hill, "Reflections of a German Scientist," Kuntz and Bachrach,
ed., *Deadly Medicine*, 185.

his writings, but also for the tools he developed to measure racial traits, such as skull size.[34] Early on, German eugenicists also worked closely with scientists from America and also many European countries.[35]

Kuntz concluded Nazism began with Charles Darwin and ended in 1945 with the victory of the Allies. The result was over 55 million dead, directly and indirectly, from the war.[36] Only 23 German physicians, scientists and administrators were prosecuted for war crimes in the trial. Why not more? Because the Allies recognized that prosecuting all of those involved in this tragic decade of history would have deprived Germany of most of its leading medical and health science practitioners.

## THE KENYA NATIVES AND DARWINISM

Darwinian Nazi racism is the most well known example, but by far not the only example. Even the British Isles was infected with Darwinian racism. One example is in Kenya in the 1800s where the natives were seen as inferior by their white British rulers. The result was a sense of entitlement on the part of the British that resulted from their

perception of profound racial superiority that infused every rung of the colony's white socioeconomic ladder. By virtue of their skin color, whites of all classes were the master race and therefore deserving of privilege. To the settlers there was nothing noble about the African "savage." Many believed the African to be biologically inferior, with smaller brain sizes, a limited capacity to feel pain or emotion, and even different nutritional needs, requiring only a bowl of maize meal, or *posho*, to maintain their health.[37]

The British also believed that

---

34 Kuntz and Bachrach, ed., *Deadly Medicine*, 42–43.

35 Kuntz and Bachrach, ed., *Deadly Medicine*, 55–59.

36 Kuntz and Bachrach, ed., *Deadly Medicine*, 200–204.

37 Caroline Elkins, *Imperial Reckoning: The Untold Story of Britain's Gulag in Kenya* (New York: Henry Holt, 2005), 12.

African men had to be controlled; they were unpredictable and sexually aggressive, threatening both white women and the maintenance of their idealized chastity as well as the racial purity of the colony's European community. Virulent racist ideology grew more intense over time as the so-called native was moved along the racist spectrum from stupid, inferior, lazy, and childlike to savage, barbaric, atavistic, and animal-like.[38]

The end result was a holocaust involving 1.5 million people that lived in hunger, fear and death for eight years in villages surrounded by barbed-wire.

## THE DARWIN WARS

The fact is, disputes in science commonly are

acrimonious. Scientists are not generally kinder or less arrogant than the general run of humanity. But the Darwin wars—the disputes over the scope and importance of evolutionary explanations in the world—have been nastier than most.[39]

Nonetheless, in spite of the controversy over evolution among Darwinists today, evolution is being pushed on students as never before in history; yet many scientists recognize that the Darwinian worldview is seriously problematic.[40] One example of the dogmatic Darwinists is Professor Richard Rorty, who is judged by his peers as "one of the most original and important philosophers writing today," and also one of the most influential philosophers outside of the confines of professional academic philosophy. His views that

have made him famous as a public intellectual arise out of his specifically philosophical reflections on topics that remain central to the Anglo-American tradition of analytic philosophy: the

---

38 Elkins, *Imperial Reckoning*, 12.

39 Brown, *Darwin Wars*, ix.

40 Michael Clough, "Diminish students' resistance to biological evolution," *The American Biology Teacher* 56, No. 7 (1994): 409–415.

nature and significance of objective reality and truth, and of our knowledge of them.[41]

Richard Rorty is an example of an unfettered Darwinist ideologue who embodies the zealots teaching at "public universities, criminalizing religious freedom, and institutionalizing secular religion" which reflects the driving conviction of influential postmodern scholars.[42] Specifically, Professor Rorty wrote that he, like most professors who

teach humanities or social science in colleges and universities... try to arrange things so that students who enter as bigoted, homophobic, religious fundamentalists will leave college with views more like our own.... The fundamentalist parents of our fundamentalist students think that the entire "American liberal establishment" is engaged in a conspiracy. The parents have a point... We are going to go right on trying to discredit you in the eyes of your children, trying to strip your fundamentalist religious community of dignity, trying to make your views seem silly rather than discussable. We are not so exclusivist as to tolerate intolerance such as yours.... I think those students are lucky to find themselves under...people like me, and to have escaped the grip of their frightening, vicious, dangerous parents. When it comes to reshaping values, liberal universities know precisely what they're doing. And the reality is that about four out of five students walk away from their Christian faith by the time they are in their twenties.[43]

On the other side, ironically, the most well-known atheist today, Richard Dawkins, has realized that the war on Christians by him and many academics may in the end be an enormous mistake because

There are no Christians, as far as I know, blowing up buildings. I am not aware of any Christian suicide bombers. I am not aware

41  Robert B. Brandon, ed., *Rorty and His Critics* (Oxford: Blackwell, 2000), ix.

42  Richard Rorty, "Universality and Truth," Brandon, ed., *Rorty and His Critics*, 21–22.

43  Rorty, "Universality and Truth," 21–22.

of any major Christian denomination that believes the penalty for apostasy is death. I have mixed feelings about the decline of Christianity, in so far as Christianity might be a bulwark against something worse.[44]

In harmony with the above conclusions, Dawkins made the following statement in 2000 during an Australian Broadcasting Corporation interview:

There have in the past been attempts to base a morality on evolution. I don't want to have anything to do with that. The kind of world that a Darwinian, going back to survival of the fittest now, and nature red in tooth and claw, I think nature really is red in tooth and claw. I think if you look out at the way wild nature is, out there in the bush, in the prairie, it is extremely ruthless, extremely unpleasant, it's exactly the kind of world that I would not wish to live in. And so any kind of politics that is based upon Darwinism for me would be bad politics, it would be immoral. Putting it another way, I'm a passionate Darwinian when it comes to science, when it comes to explaining the world, but I'm a passionate anti-Darwinian when it comes to morality and politics.[45]

## FROM LAW BASED ON CHRISTIANITY TO LAW BASED ON SECULAR HUMANISM

A ten-year study of 15,000 political documents produced by the 55 authors of the United States Constitution was completed by University of Houston political science professor Donald Lutz and Dr. Charles Hyneman.[46] English jurist William Blackstone was third on the list of

---

44 Ruth Gledhill, "Scandal and schism leave Christians praying for a 'new Reformation,'" *The Times* (UK) (April 2, 2010).

45 Richard Dawkins, "The Descent of Man (Episode 1: The Moral Animal)." A series of radio shows broadcast in January and February 2000 by the Australian Broadcasting Corporation, produced by Tom Morton; http://www.abc.net.au/science/descent/trans1.htm; accessed August 16, 2016.

46 Donald Lutz and Charles Hyneman, "Toward a theory of constitutional amendment," *American Political Science Review* 88 (1994): 355–370.

most quoted sources. Only the Bible (34% of cited sources) and political philosopher Charles de Montesquieu (8.3%) outranked him. Of the possible sources from which the founders drew their ideas, perspectives, values and notions about liberty and responsibility, the one that dominates was the Bible.

The fact is, the original four-volume 1773 edition of Sir William Blackstone's classic masterpiece *Commentaries on the Laws of England* "formed the core of American jurisprudence both before and after ratification of the U.S. Constitution."[47] The introduction to the newest reprint concluded: "Sir William Blackstone's *Commentaries on the Laws of England, 1765–69*, is the most important legal treatise ever written in the English language."[48] A central factor in how this foundation of American law was overturned was the rejection of Blackstone and the acceptance of Darwinism. After the Civil War, several leading "influential individuals embraced a new idea: Darwinian evolution. *The Origin of Species*, published by Charles Darwin in 1859, had a huge impact on the movers and shakers who saw no room in American jurisprudence for Blackstone's God based view of nature."[49]

Thus, the rejection of Blackstone's work began with Darwin's writing completed 150 years ago. In short, Blackstone's work was rejected because his

> ideas were rooted in a Judeo-Christian view of the world. God designed the world to express certain ideas and to operate under certain laws—and this theory is called "Natural Law." The influence of Blackstone and other thinkers of a similar vein led to familiar founding sentiments such as the mention of "the Laws of Nature and Nature's God" in the Declaration of Independence.[50]

---

47  Ed Vitagliano, "Sir William Blackstone and the long war against law," *afa Journal* (January 2015); http://www.afajournal.org/past-issues/2015/january/sir-william-blackstone-and-the-long-war-against-law/; accessed August 16, 2016.

48  William Blackstone, *Commentaries on the Laws of England: A Facsimile of the First Edition of 1765–1769* (Chicago: The University of Chicago Press, 2002).

49  Vitagliano, "Sir William Blackstone": 15.

50  Vitagliano, "Sir William Blackstone": 14.

The basis of law was, as stated by Alabama Supreme Court Justice Tom Parker, when God "created man and imbued him with free will to conduct himself in all parts of life, He laid down certain immutable laws of human nature."[51] And

> in creating mankind, God "gave him also the faculty of reason to discover the purpose, or the purport, of those laws." Human laws are therefore to be the product of people comprehending God's purposes and fashioning their own regulations of human conduct to reflect the Divine will.[52]

After Darwin, this legal position radically changed. One factor involved Harvard University's president, Charles Eliot, working to "introduce evolution into the teaching of law" by hiring Christopher Langdell to be the new dean of Harvard Law School. Dean Langdell served from 1870 to 1895 and during this time changed the curriculum foundation from Blackstone's *Commentaries* to the so-called case law approach, meaning basing court decisions on the writings of other judges. Thus began the revolution in American jurisprudence, a process that eventually succeeded, as Judge Parker notes, in changing "the focus from the God who gave immutable principles…to the judge—the man— who was writing the law."[53]

By studying past case decisions, judges were able to evolve the law from Christian-centred to man-centred. In addition, "Further advance of the Darwinian impulse in law came with the influence of the late U.S. Supreme Court Justice Oliver Wendell Holmes," who served on the court for 30 years, from 1902 until 1932. This long term enabled Holmes to have a major impact on American law, moving it from a Judeo-Christian base to a secular humanistic base.

Holmes is best known today for a *Harvard Law Review* article published in 1897. In that article, Holmes opined that "every word of moral significance" should be "banished" from law, and other ideas should be adopted that "convey legal ideas uncolored by anything outside the

---

51  Vitagliano, "Sir William Blackstone": 14.
52  Vitagliano, "Sir William Blackstone": 15.
53  Tom Parker, quoted in Vitagliano, "Sir William Blackstone": 15.

law" such as theology, especially Christian morality.[54] The result of Holmes's efforts achieved "a complete break from Blackstone and the past" and instituted a radically new source of legal authority, secular humanism.[55] As a result, "Morality was separated from jurisprudence; human expertise and reason were divorced from...'Nature's God;' absolute truth was denied; and the responsibility for determining truth was placed firmly in the hands of judges."[56]

What could change this problem, Judge Parker opined, is the large number of lawsuits fought today in defense of religious liberty. A factor that works against this, maintains Judge Parker, "While many Christians have come to see the need for a return to founding principles in law, there remains a large percentage of the Christian community that eschews involvement in politics and culture."[57]

Unfortunately, as Judge Parker noted, he and many others are very frustrated by those Christians

> who attempt to bury their heads in the sand and not see their role in contending or striving for truth.... Because absent their involvement, these [secularist] trends will take down their children, even as we see the signs of them taking down our society right now.[58]

---

54 Oliver Wendell Holmes, Jr., "The path of the law," *Harvard Law Review* 10 (1897): 457.

55 Vitagliano, "Sir William Blackstone": 15.

56 Parker, quoted in Vitagliano, "Sir William Blackstone": 15.

57 Vitagliano, "Sir William Blackstone": 15.

58 Parker, quoted in Vitagliano, "Sir William Blackstone": 15.

# Havelock Ellis: eugenic and sexual revolutionary

||||||||||||||||||||||||||||||||||||||||||||||||||||||||||||||||||||||||||||||||||||||||||||||||||||||||||||||||||||||||||

**H**avelock Ellis (February 2, 1859–July 8, 1939) was a British physician, a prolific writer, a social reformer and a major force behind the so-called new sexual morality.[1] His biographer wrote, "Havelock Ellis was a revolutionary, one of the seminal figures responsible for the creation of a modern sensibility; although, like most revolutionaries, he would not have been happy with the world he helped to create."[2]

Ellis was, foremost, a leader in the sexual revolution and co-author of the first textbook in English on homosexuality titled *Sexual Inversion*. The book was co-authored with John Addington Symonds and originally published in German in 1896.[3] Ellis also published on a wide variety of sexual practices, both normal and abnormal, including transgender psychology. Ellis scholar, George Grant, even called Ellis the iconoclastic grandfather of the

---

1 Ivan Crozier, "Havelock Ellis, eugenicist," *Studies in History and Philosophy of Biological and Biomedical Sciences* 39, No.2 (2008): 187–194.

2 Phyllis Grosskurth, *Havelock Ellis: A Biography* (New York: Knopf, 1980), xi.

3 Havelock Ellis and John Addington Symonds, *Das konträre Geschlechtsgefühl (Sexual Inversion)* (Leipzig: George H. Wigand's, 1896).

sexual revolution. The author of nearly fifty books on every aspect of concupiscence from sexual inversion to auto-eroticism, from the revolution of obscenity to the mechanism of detumescence, from sexual periodicity to pornographic eonism, he had provided the free love movement with much of its intellectual apologia.[4]

His goal was to normalize and make socially acceptable a wide variety of sexual practices, including some that still are illegal today and some that are regarded as abhorrent. Ellis spent his entire life working toward this goal. He is credited with introducing the notions of narcissism and autoeroticism, concepts later adopted by psychoanalysis. In 1891, when he was 32,

Ellis married the English writer, and women's rights proponent, Edith Lees. From the beginning, their marriage was unconventional for several reasons, including the fact that Edith Lees was a practicing lesbian, and this fact may have stimulated Ellis's interest in homosexuality. At the end of the honeymoon, Ellis went back to his bachelor rooms in Paddington, and his wife lived at Fellowship House. Their open marriage was a central subject in Ellis's autobiography, *My Life*. They did enjoy reading and discussing books together, and both plumbed "the pages of Darwin."[5]

In the end, Ellis concluded that Darwin "is one of the most brilliant and versatile heroes of science."[6] Ellis's adulation was such that he even wrote that the date that Darwin's *On the Origin of Species* was published is "one of the greatest dates in the whole history of science." Ellis then closely followed his new heroes of evolution including, Darwin, Spencer and Frazer.[7] As a result of accepting evolution, "Ellis adapted the

---

4   George Grant, *Killer Angel: A Biography of Planned Parenthood's Margaret Sanger* (Franklin: Standfast, 2014), 43–44.

5   Isaac Goldberg, *Havelock Ellis: A Biographical and Critical Survey* (London: Constable and Company, 1926), 52.

6   Goldberg, *Havelock Ellis*, 342.

7   Grosskurth, *Havelock Ellis*, 217.

## Havelock Ellis (1859-1939)

An influential sexologist, Ellis was one of the most successful revolutionaries to overthrow traditional Judeo-Christian morality and replace it with the so-called "new morality."

creeds of both radical secularism and scientific naturalism. He no longer believed in institutionalized or dogmatic religion; he believed in the 'facts' of science."[8]

According to Ellis, in his autobiography *My Life*, his friends were much amused at his being considered an expert on sex for the reason that he suffered from impotence until the age of 60. He then discovered that he could become aroused by the sight of a woman urinating. Ellis named this condition "undinism." After his wife, Edith Lees, died, Ellis formed a relationship with a French woman named Françoise Lafitte. Grant explains that because Ellis was sexually impotent,

> he spent his life in pursuit of new and ever more exotic sensual pleasures. He staged elaborate orgies for his Malthusian and Eugenicist friends; he enticed his wife into innumerable lesbian affairs while he luridly observed in a nearby closet; he experimented with mescaline and various other psychotropic and psychedelic drugs; and he established an underground network for both homosexual and heterosexual extemporaneous encounters.[9]

## HE BECOMES AN ANTI-CHRISTIAN

As a youth, Ellis was "a devout Christian," but this drastically changed due to "reading in various fields including evolution and eugenics," which eventually caused him to abandon his Christianity.[10] Ellis writes that he realized that after this he "no longer possessed any religious faith. All the Christian dogmas I had been brought up to accept unquestioned had slipped away, and they had dragged with them what I had experienced of religion."

This ensued when he became convinced that science had proven the universe was like a

> factory filled by an inextricable web of wheels and looms and flying shuttles, in a deafening din, ...as the most competent sci-

---

8  Crozier, "Havelock Ellis, eugenicist," 188.

9  Grant, *Killer Angel*, 44.

10  Crozier, "Havelock Ellis, eugenicist," 188.

entific authorities declared it to be made. It was a world I was prepared to accept.... [T]here were other visions of the universe a little less disheartening, such as that presented by Herbert Spencer's *First Principles*. But the dominant feeling always was that the scientific outlook, by which I mainly meant the outlook of Darwin and Huxley, commended itself to me as presenting a sound view of the world.[11]

Both his education and friends caused Ellis's Christian faith to slowly erode to the degree that he objected to using "the terminology of orthodox Christianity."[12] In his life goal of freeing society from the Judeo-Christian morality, Ellis saw Christianity as responsible "for the obscurantist attitudes toward sex prevailing in the Western world" in his day.[13] His life goal was to free humankind from these restraints to allow free love and promiscuity to flourish.

He also openly advocated sexual practices, such as bestiality even for children, that were then, and often today, considered sexual perversions, or at least deviant sexual behaviour.[14] He also attempted to argue that these practices should not be termed perversions, but rather for children he preferred the term "pre-genital," and for adults he preferred more neutral terms to avoid the stigma of the term perversion. He was both tactful and careful, but made his point, even if one had at times to read between the lines. To Margaret Sanger,

Ellis was a modern-day saint. She adored him at once, both for his radical ideas and for his unusual bedroom behavior. Their antics are beyond the pale of decent discussion and somehow manage to transcend the descriptive capacities of pedestrian prose. They are best left unexamined.[15]

---

11  Ellis, quoted in Goldberg, *Havelock Ellis*, 55, 57.

12  Grosskurth, *Havelock Ellis*, 18, 100.

13  Grosskurth, *Havelock Ellis*, 229.

14  Havelock Ellis, *Psychology of Sex: A Manual for Students* (New York: Emerson Books, 1938), 152–217.

15  Grant, *Killer Angel*, 44.

## HIS EUGENIC ACTIVITIES

Like many intellectuals of his era, Ellis energenically supported eugenics and was an active member of the eugenics society from 1907 until his death in 1939.[16] He also served as president of the Galton Institute and was elected a fellow and vice president of the Eugenics Education Society. His many writings on the subject of eugenics include *The Task of Social Hygiene*, where he wrote, "Eventually, it seems evident, a general system, whether private or public, whereby all personal facts, biological and mental, normal and morbid, are duly and systematically registered, must become inevitable if we are to have a real guide as to those persons who are most fit, or most unfit to carry on the race."[17] In fact, eugenics was rarely

far from the surface of the writings of sexologist Havelock Ellis. Often explicit, and regularly skirting around the edges of the debates concerning "the race" and its future in those writings which were not directly concerned with the topic, it is clear that eugenics represented for Ellis the most significant interface between individual sexual expression, the species and the state.[18]

His books, *Sexual Selection in Man* and *The Problem of Race-Regeneration* and even his book *The Psychology of Sex* cover in some detail his evolutionary eugenics beliefs.[19]

His major contribution to eugenics was in the area of the "sterilization of the unfit."[20] He argued that sterilization should be done either by vasectomy or tying the fallopian tubes, stressing that it "must always be remembered that the sterilization of the unfit, if it is to be a practical and humane measure commanding general approval, must be

---

16 Crozier, "Havelock Ellis, eugenicist," 187.

17 Havelock Ellis, *The Task of Social Hygiene* (Boston: Houghton Mifflin, 1912), 48.

18 Crozier, "Havelock Ellis, eugenicist," 187.

19 Ellis, *Psychology of Sex*; Havelock Ellis, *Die Gattenwahl beim Menschen: mit Rücksicht auf Sinnesphysiologie und allgemeine Biologie* [The Mate Selection in Humans: with Regard to Sensory Physiology and General Biology] (Würzburg: Stuber Verlag, 1906); Havelock Ellis, *Sexual Selection in Man and The Problem of Race-Regeneration* (London: Moffat Yard, 1911).

20 Crozier, "Havelock Ellis, eugenicist," 191.

voluntary on the part of the person undergoing it, and never compulsory."[21] Ellis developed this view further in his 1911 book titled *The Problem of Race-Regeneration*,

> in which he argued that it would be best to "persuade" the "unfit" to "volunteer" for sterilization by withdrawing Poor Relief from those who refused such "persuasion." Education was therefore necessary to convince the "tainted" of their "unfitness," but possibilities for coercion were also recognized in order to achieve these social ends.[22]

Ellis concluded that war "destroyed the 'best stocks' of all nations" and, to offset this problem, he argued that the solution was to encourage the fitter stock to produce more offspring,

> together with improved economic conditions, care, education, and, if necessary, pressure to bear on the people of the other class to enable them to limit their families…to decrease the number of the unfit, and in some degree to destroy at the source the stream of feeble mindedness which is so disastrous in its effects alike on society and the race.[23]

According to Ellis, World War I only exaggerated this problem.[24] Specifically, the war caused a reduction "of possible husbands together with the elimination of many of the men most desirable as husbands which was a great hardship inflicted on the girls who are to-day growing up to be women."[25] He wrote that one effect of this "disparity between the number of women and men was illegitimacy. As this was a topic held in particular social opprobrium, Ellis advocated revision of its social status."[26] His reason for revising morality was due to his

---

21  Grosskurth, *Havelock Ellis*, 217.

22  Crozier, "Havelock Ellis, eugenicist," 191.

23  Havelock Ellis, "Eugenics in relation to war," in *The Philosophy of Conflict and Other Essays in War-Time* (London: Constable, 1919), 121–122.

24  Crozier, "Havelock Ellis, eugenicist," 192.

25  Ellis, "Eugenics in relation to war," 124–125.

26  Crozier, "Havelock Ellis, eugenicist," 192.

goal of eugenics, and in particular,

> it was the social attitude towards single motherhood...that raised
> a potential eugenics problem in Ellis's eyes. He noted that "many
> a girl is now willing to accept the attentions and even the mar-
> riage offers of a feeble-minded man whom she would not have
> looked at before the war...thus the sexual hardships imposed
> upon the young women of to-day serve to exasperate the evils
> caused directly by the war on the future of the race by increasing
> the proportion of feeble-minded among the population." ...The
> solution to this problem was, for Ellis, to change outdated social
> and moral attitudes.[27]

To do this, he believed that eugenics was the answer to unhappiness
and the other many problems humankind faced and that real progress
in solving these problems could occur only

> through the instrumentality of science: that is, that man had it
> in his control to create a better race. Nowadays—with the hor-
> rors of mass exterminations behind us—such racial views are
> very much in discredit. But in 1906 it seemed to him a matter of
> social duty to support Francis Galton's notion that those [per-
> sons] desiring them should be supplied with "eugenics certifi-
> cates" of fitness, especially before marriage.[28]

Ellis wrote that never before in history has it been so urgent

> to do all in our power to prevent the breeding of the unfit and to
> limit the less fit members of society, so that even the most hard-
> ened opponent of birth control can scarcely remain longer deaf
> to the appeal of humanity and the future race.... Never before
> has it been so urgent to enlarge and re-quicken our sexual moral-
> ity and social customs in such a way that women may be enabled

---

27 Crozier, "Havelock Ellis, eugenicist," 192.
28 Grosskurth, *Havelock Ellis*, 410.

to allow free play to their best impulses and ideals in the purification and fortification of the race of the future.[29]

In short, for Ellis the acceptance and application of eugenics was the logical outcome of education, specifically sexual

> education, and equal education of both sexes, was the means by which superstition would be overcome, that society would be reformed, and that social problems would be obviated. Ellis was committed to the view that this should happen at the individual level; social reform began through access to knowledge. His own self-education—reading figures such as Drysdale, [John Stuart] Mill, Darwin, and Malthus, as well as anti-religious writers such as Renan and Strauss—exemplifies this development perfectly.[30]

Ellis even once advocated force to insure that his eugenic goals were achieved, writing that the steps to "eugenic progress are clear. There will be a time to invoke compulsion and the law...when we are quite sure that those who refuse to act in accordance with sound knowledge refuse deliberately or because they are congenitally incapable of doing anything else."[31] These persons are

> a real anti-social danger and a focus of racial poisons.... It is on this nucleus that we not only may, but must, apply such degree of pressure as may be necessary, alike in the interests of the community of to-day and the race of to-morrow. This pressure may in the mildest degree consist of...social inducements...proceeding to sterilization when these inducements fail, and in the ultimate and extreme degree to complete segregation. It is along such lines as these...that we may reasonably expect eugenic progress.[32]

---

29 Ellis, "Eugenics in relation to war," 127.

30 Crozier, "Havelock Ellis, eugenicist," 194.

31 Havelock Ellis, "Birth-control and eugenics," *The Eugenics Review* 9, No. 1 (1917): 41.

32 Ellis, "Birth-control and eugenics": 41.

Ellis no doubt was influenced by the avid eugenicist and leading statistician Karl Pearson, whose work he always had greatly admired.[33] His mentor, Karl "Pearson, was a Social Darwinist who developed into an imperialist, a nationalist, and a racist" who believed

> that war was a necessary means of eliminating inferior stock. In the midst of the Boer War he upheld the validity of the conflict in an extraordinary speech. A nation, he said was "an organized whole," which was "kept up to a high pitch of external efficiency by contest, chiefly by way of war with inferior races, and with equal races by the struggle for trade-routes and for the sources of raw material and of food supply."[34]

Professor Pearson also was highly critical of Virchow, "the leader of the German opposition to Darwinism, and Pearson, an avowed Darwinist, had been a student in Germany during the bitter Darwin controversy."[35] It must be acknowledged that the "theory of evolution as proposed by Darwin" also influenced Francis Galton, who established an "anthropometric laboratory" set up to investigate the intellectual differences of men and women. The "major conclusion to come from Galton's research was that women tend in all their capacities to be inferior to men."[36] In contrast, Ellis concluded that males are more likely found at both the lower and higher IQ levels.

Ellis also concluded that the "time for vain discussion is over. The day for action [to deal with the problem of inferior races and humans] has arrived which will never dawn again."[37] His attitude toward "inferior races" was illustrated when "Norman Haire repeatedly told him of the suicides and tragedies of Jews in Germany he showed absolutely no interest. It is true that he seldom read a newspaper, but he cannot be excused for cutting himself off from reality to this extent."[38]

---

33 Grosskurth, *Havelock Ellis*, 172.

34 Grosskurth, *Havelock Ellis*, 411.

35 Grosskurth, *Havelock Ellis*, 177.

36 Stephanie A. Shields, "Functionalism, Darwinism, and the psychology of women: A study in social myth," *American Psychologist* 30, No.7 (July 1975): 743.

37 Ellis, "Birth-control and eugenics," 41.

38 Grosskurth, *Havelock Ellis*, 415.

## SUMMARY

Havelock Ellis was one of the most influential sexologists in history. Inspired by Darwin and eugenicists, he was one of the most successful revolutionaries to overthrow traditional Judeo-Christian morality and replace it with the so-called new morality that is prevalent today.

# Darwin, Kinsey and the sexual revolution

||||||||||||||||||||||||||||||||||||||||||||||||||||||||||||||||||||||||||||||||||||||||||||||||||||||||||||||||||||||||||||||

**A**lfred Kinsey is considered the father of the modern Western sexual revolution. A review of his life and work reveals the fact that Darwinism was critically important in his lifelong crusade to overturn traditional sexual morality. The means he used to achieve this goal was to convince both the public and the scientific world that what was widely then regarded as deviant behaviour, including adultery, fornication, homosexuality, sadomasochism, bestiality and pedophilia, were all widely practiced and, therefore, "normal" and, consequently, acceptable. Kinsey's research now has been shown by extensive empirical studies to be lethally flawed and worse than useless. Kinsey's sexual revolution has contributed to major social problems, an epidemic of disease and the breakdown of the family.

## KINSEY'S INFLUENCE

Few men have had a more profound deleterious influence on modern society than Alfred Kinsey (June 23, 1894—August 26, 1956). Kinsey, "more than any other human being" brought on both the sexual and the gay liberation movements.[1] Called the father of the sexual revolu-

---

1  Daniel J. Flynn, *Intellectual Morons: How Ideology Makes Smart People Fall for Stupid Ideas* (New York: Crown Forum, 2004), 34.

tion, Kinsey is lionized by some and condemned by others. He is especially condemned in view of the increasing evidence that the modern sexual revolution has exacerbated many social problems and has caused an enormous amount of sickness, misery and death. Many condemn Kinsey because, like both Freud and Darwin, Kinsey's work has adversely affected sexual morality. The thousands of reviews of Kinsey's work indicate that many writers fully, or largely, supported his goal of highly sexualized, uninhibited open marriage and freedom to indulge in sexual behaviour of any kind, which he openly and aggressively advocated for most of his life.

His critics note that Kinsey ignored many of the factors that most people consider very important in relationships: enduring love and companionship. Although many once applauded Kinsey as one of the most important researchers since Darwin, most now realize that his fraudulent research has caused an enormous amount of harm across America and throughout the world.

Although Freud cracked the door open to a society largely free of sexual prohibitions, Kinsey opened it wide, ending what many of his supporters call our historical, sexual Puritanism.[2] In fact, with the notable exceptions of Christian, Muslim and Jewish societies, unrestrained sexual freedom has been common in history. Both Licht and Kiefer document that the sexually free society Kinsey envisioned once existed in both ancient Greece and ancient Rome.[3] Betty Friedan, Margaret Sanger and *Cosmopolitan* magazine's Helen Gurley Brown all furthered Kinsey's revolution, even glamorizing the "newly liberated single women who had come to symbolize the sexual revolution… and encouraged single women to flaunt their sexual prowess and to have intercourse freely."[4]

The debate over Kinsey has recently intensified, partly because several new incriminating biographies have been published that make

2   Andrea Tone, *Devices and Desires: A History of Contraceptives in America* (New York: Hill and Wang, 2002).

3   Hans Licht, *Sexual Life in Ancient Greece* (London: Abbey Library, 1971); Otto Kiefer, *Sexual Life in Ancient Rome* (London: Abbey Library, 1971).

4   Andrea Tone, "Historical Influences on Women's Sexual and Reproductive Health," in *Handbook of Women's Sexual and Reproductive Health*, ed. Gina M. Wingood and Ralph J. DiClemente (New York: Kluwer Academic/Plenum, 2002), 15.

## Alfred Kinsey (1894-1956)

Considered the father of the sexual revolution, Kinsey took the Darwinian and Freudian theories to their logical expression: promoting open, unrestricted sexual behaviour of any kind. Note his trademark conservative dress, including his ever present bow tie. In order to appeal to the masses and present himself as an objective scientist, Kinsey deliberately dressed this way to avoid presenting an image of a radical.

ample use of the extensive and revealing Kinsey Institute archives. Kinsey has also been in the news because of the rash of publicity about pedophilia—such as the allegations against Catholic priests and the claim that Kinsey's work resulted in the encouragement of a wide variety of intergenerational sex. Judging by the sale of what is called soft child pornography, studies indicate that pedophiliacs consist of as much as ten percent of the population. Soft child pornography slips under the law against child pornography by using photographs of children who appear to be thirteen, but are actually at least eighteen. Interestingly, Kinsey's goal in college was to work with young boys in such institutions as the YMCA.[5]

Yet another reason for the resurgence in the discussions of Kinsey is that homosexual behaviour played a key role in his research and was an important component in Kinsey's own life. Hugh Hefner, who led the pornographic revolution, labelled himself Kinsey's "pamphleteer."[6] Kinsey's work has greatly strengthened the burgeoning homosexuality movement and served as a critical basis for the legalization of both hardcore pornography and homosexual marriage.

### KINSEY'S PERSONAL LIFE

Kinsey's teenage years were deeply troubled. James H. Jones concludes in his biography of Kinsey that by adolescence "Kinsey's behavior was clearly pathological, satisfying every criterion of sexual perversion." He was so obsessed with masochism, Jones claims, that he could not satisfy his sexual urges without first experiencing physical and emotional pain.[7]

Accounts of his masochism reveal involvement in behaviour that is now considered, not only gruesome, but openly dangerous. His sexual behaviour at times landed him in a hospital for the reason that, as drug users need more drugs to achieve a high because the mind adapts, masochism requires increased pain levels to achieve the same sexual

---

5   Tom Bethell, "Kinsey as pervert," *The American Spectator* 38, No. 3 (April 2005): 42–44.

6   Flynn, *Intellectual Morons*, 35.

7   For example, see James H. Jones, *Alfred Kinsey: A Private Life* (New York: Norton, 1997), 82, 533.

effect.[8] His involvement in a variety of abnormal sexual practices was accompanied by a lack of normal sexual relationships.[9] When he met his future wife in 1920, he had never been on a date with a woman; and when he married her, he didn't consummate the marriage until months later.[10]

Some commentators blame Kinsey's sexual problems on his strict upbringing. This is a questionable conclusion because children in different cultures, such as the Amish, many Muslim cultures, as well as many Christian homes in America, experience a strict upbringing, but very few become sadomasochists. Kinsey's rebellion did not involve keeping his private life private, as most people do, but in openly flaunting part of his private life to the world, as few people do.

## FROM THEIST TO DARWINIST AND ATHEIST

Kinsey—a tall, blond, handsome youth—was an Eagle Scout, a Sunday school teacher and apparently religiously devout.[11] A major, if not a critical, influence that demolished his devoutness was his embracing of Darwinism and, later, eugenics.[12] Kinsey's school newspaper informed the class of 1914 that they would have to work hard because the students will be entering a world where, in the language of social Darwinism, "only the fittest survive."[13] His class also predicted that Kinsey would become "a second Darwin."[14]

Critical in his life was the influence of a high school biology teacher, Natalie Roeth, who both inspired Kinsey and set him on the road to study biology and eventually become a fervent evolutionist. Roeth also influenced him to eventually not only reject Christianity, but become a militant campaigner against all forms of theistic religion.

---

8   Jones, *Alfred Kinsey*, 610.

9   Flynn, *Intellectual Morons*, 38.

10   Flynn, *Intellectual Morons*, 37.

11   Jack Cashill, *Hoodwinked: How Intellectual Hucksters Have Hijacked American Culture* (Nashville: Nelson Current, 2005), 239; Cornelia Christenson, *Kinsey: A Biography* (Bloomington: Indiana University Press, 1971), 19–20, 30.

12   Judith Reisman, *Kinsey: Crimes and Consequences* (Arlington: The Institute for Media Education, 1998), 6.

13   Jones, *Alfred Kinsey*, 101.

14   Jones, *Alfred Kinsey*, 87.

Fellow sex researcher, Wardell Pomeroy, wrote that "Kinsey began to lose his [religious] beliefs as a college student, when his study of science disclosed to him what he saw as a basic incongruity between it and religion."[15]

Drawn by a love of nature, he felt his career choice allowed him to combine biology and the outdoors. Always a good student—he was high-school valedictorian—Kinsey excelled in college and finished his doctorate at Harvard, where he became a committed atheist. Kinsey concluded that science held the key to uplifting humanity, an idea that both inspired and dominated his human sexuality work. His acceptance of eugenics also permeated his work, although this was not always obvious.

His militant atheism was allegedly partly a result of "vigorously" rebelling against the strict religion of his father. His father was a Methodist, today considered one of the more liberal Protestant denominations in America. Rather than rebelling against his strict upbringing, some argue that Kinsey indulged in deviant sexual behaviour from a very early age; and his strict upbringing may, in part, have been his father's attempt to deal with his misbehaviour.

Kinsey not only became an atheist, but actively fought against both Judaism and Catholicism.[16] He repeatedly attacked what he termed the "self-appointed rule" of religious institutions in regulating sexual conduct, causing the "sexual dysfunction then presumed rampant" in America. He continued to attack all churches until his death.[17]

Kinsey's early fascination with Darwinism was related to his first love, biology. He became an international expert on an insect called the gull-wasp and wrote some of the most authoritative works ever published in this obscure field. Once he began his new career liberating the Western world from sexual restrictions—actually demolishing restrictions—he pursued this goal with the same gusto that he once pursued his gull-wasp research. However, in his new role, because he was far more of an advocate than a scientist, many critics have con-

---

15  Wardell B. Pomeroy, *Dr. Kinsey and the Institute for Sex Research* (New York: Harper and Row, 1972), 29.

16  Jones, *Alfred Kinsey*, 611.

17  Cashill, *Hoodwinked*, 242.

cluded that Kinsey's work was unscientific, even fraudulent, if not criminal, because of openly condoning pedophilia activities.

## KINSEY AS A BIOLOGY TEXTBOOK AUTHOR

Kinsey was also the author of several leading biology textbooks, all of which were "unapologetically pro-evolution."[18] His *An Introduction to Biology*, published by J.B. Lippincott in 1926, was a leading high school biology textbook that went through many editions and sold almost half-a-million copies.[19] The large amount of money his textbooks earned allowed Kinsey to do research that he would normally not have been able to afford. In his biology texts, Kinsey strongly advocated Darwinism—the Scopes Trial was held only one year before his first textbook was published. Almost forty pages were devoted to this topic alone. Cashill opined that to

> keep parents at bay, he pioneered the kind of bait-and-switch pseudo-science that dominates high school texts to this day. The formula was simple: merely define evolution as "the scientific word for change" and ridicule those who challenged evolution as denying the small changes obvious to anyone who had bred anything in a still largely rural America. In the accompanying teacher's manual, he counseled teachers on how to handle those parents who saw through or around the deception.[20]

For example, Kinsey actually defined *evolution* as merely "the scientific word for change"[21] but, in his writings, often implied molecules-to-man evolution. Furthermore, his textbook index did not contain either the name Darwin or the term evolution. Chapter 19 of Kinsey's biology text titled *New Kinds of Organisms* covers not only breeding, but also the importance of mutations in producing new organisms,

---

18 Cashill, *Hoodwinked*, 241.
19 E.J. Daniels, *I Accuse Kinsey* (Orlando: Christ for the World Publishers, 1954), 130.
20 Cashill, *Hoodwinked*, 241.
21 Alfred C. Kinsey, *An Introduction to Biology* (Philadelphia: J.B. Lippincott, 1926), 196.

concluding that "new kinds of plants and animals are continually coming into existence by slight variations from their ancestors."[22] Kinsey even used the now discredited Ancon sheep argument to prove Darwinism, noting that

> larger variations are often called mutations or sports, but they are not fundamentally different from smaller variations. We have historic records that even such larger mutations have occurred in single generations. In the year 1791 a New England farmer found a lamb in his flock which had short and crooked legs. With the eye of a thrifty Yankee, he saw what an advantage it would be to have a breed of sheep which could not jump fences, so he carefully took care of the freak lamb, bred from it, and got other animals with short and crooked legs. It was thus that the breed Ancon sheep came into existence.[23]

This lethal mutation is now recognized as a form of a disease called achondroplasia.[24] The other examples of mutations he discussed are likewise very questionable. His only example of mutations producing a new animal breed was the Ancon sheep—all other examples were plants, although Kinsey does note that "at least 400 mutations have been observed" in fruit flies, but admitted that most changes were no greater than minor colour alterations, yet mused "think what the result might be in a thousand or a million years in any one line of descent!"[25]

However, the examples of "reversion" that Kinsey discussed do not support evolution, but rather de-evolution. Nonetheless, there is no doubt that this book converted many readers. Breeding successes of plants and animals also are given as proof of evolution. Kinsey then implied that small changes could accumulate to produce molecules-

---

22 Kinsey, *Introduction to Biology*, 189.

23 Kinsey, *Introduction to Biology*, 189–190; Alfred C. Kinsey, *New Introduction to Biology* (Philadelphia: J.B. Lippincott, 1933), 414.

24 Jerry Bergman, "Ancon sheep: A now disproven example of microevolution," *Rivista di Biologia/ Biology Forum* 98, No. 3 (Sep.–Dec. 2005): 435–448.

25 Kinsey, *Introduction to Biology*, 192.

to-human evolution. He concluded that mammals and reptiles "probably originated directly from long-extinct, reptile-like ancestors.... Few, if any, of the ancestral forms are still in existence."[26]

The other evidences for evolution that he cites include homology, vestigial organs—"small and useless structures which are always to be found in species"—embryology and the geographical distribution of life.[27] He wrote that a modern fly has only one pair of wings, but behind the pair are what he incorrectly called two vestigial wings, which was to him "proof positive that the insects had four-wing ancestors."[28] This example is—if it were true—proof of de-evolution. These vestigial wings are not wings but halteres that are incredibly well designed, efficient organs long known for their function as flight stabilizers, like airplane gyroscopes that prevent excessive roll, pitch or yaw by beating in antiphase to the actual wings.

After discussing Lamarck, Kinsey covered the survival-of-the-fittest law, which he states is "also spoken of at times as Darwinism."[29] The chapter on fossils includes a picture of a modern-looking gull-wasp (Kinsey's primary research area until he moved on to human sexual reproduction), caught in an allegedly twenty-five-million-year-old section of amber.[30] He added that "we may determine the age of a fossil from the age of a rock in which it is preserved."[31] He then reviewed the geological ages, concluding that "the more highly developed plants and animals appear only among the fossils of later times, noting that this parallels modern classification systems, which is "striking evidence of the order of evolution."[32] The "intermediate" fossils discussed include *Archaeopteryx*.[33]

Kinsey concluded that, although numerous biologists before Darwin believed that species change, it was Darwin who produced

---

26 Kinsey, *Introduction to Biology*, 199.
27 Kinsey, *Introduction to Biology*, 200–201.
28 Kinsey, *Introduction to Biology*, 201.
29 Kinsey, *Introduction to Biology*, 205.
30 Kinsey, *Introduction to Biology*, 210.
31 Kinsey, *Introduction to Biology*, 217.
32 Kinsey, *Introduction to Biology*, 217.
33 Kinsey, *Introduction to Biology*, 218–219.

such abundant proof that the whole scientific world was convinced of the truth of the idea. Since then modern biology has kept evolutionary notions to the fore. It has reclassified the plants and animals and arranged them to show their origins from common ancestors.[34]

Had Kinsey lived to study genetic sequence comparisons, he would not have been able to make this claim today. In an excellent chapter on the scientific method, Kinsey concluded that "a scientist doesn't believe things unless he has good proofs for them," and then he discusses the criteria for proofs, which he largely ignored in his presentation of evolution.

Stressing that every part of biology has been affected by evolution, Kinsey claimed "there are no biologists who are not agreed that evolution has occurred."[35] The 1943 revised edition included a few changes, such as the index now containing the terms Darwin and evolution, but still including most of the erroneous information about evolution, such as the Ancon sheep claims. Kinsey even argued that an adequate presentation of biological principles cannot be made without reference to evolutionary concepts.[36] He concludes that, if one is discreet, evolution can effectively be taught in school, even if the community is opposed to its instruction. Kinsey's agenda—to indoctrinate the young in Darwinism—was effective, but Kinsey could not openly advance his own atheistic Darwinistic agenda; but rather to be effective,

"He had to appear disinterested. . . his pronouncements value-free." Kinsey, however, knew how to mold young minds. He would marshal his evidence so precisely and present it so matter-of-factly that students were drawn to one inevitable conclusion: his own.[37]

---

34 Kinsey, *Introduction to Biology*, 522–523.

35 Alfred C. Kinsey, *Methods in Biology* (Chicago: J.B. Lippincott, 1937), 224.

36 Kinsey, *Methods in Biology*, 224.

37 Cashill, *Hoodwinked*, 243. This was the same strategy taken by the Comte de Buffon to get his materialistic cosmology accepted in the eighteenth century.

## KINSEY'S GULL-WASP RESEARCH

Kinsey's gull-wasp research actually was an ambitious effort to prove Darwinism. The two areas he focused on, natural selection and the origin of species, were obvious in his *The Gull-Wasps Cynips: A Study in the Origin of Species* monograph. His work, although positively received by the handful of fellow entomologists who specialized in wasps, barely made a ripple in society. Kinsey collected a phenomenal 17,000 gull-wasps, all of which he cataloged and evaluated. He concluded that no two individual wasps were identical, thus convincing himself of the veracity of natural selection.

Actually, it only documented the enormous variety in the natural world, not evolution. Kinsey's second major work on gull-wasps, The *Origin of Higher Categories in Cynips*, published in 1935, also failed to convince the world of the truth of Darwinism and, conversely, the falsity of religion. This was the last monograph he would publish on gull-wasps. With missionary zeal, he then plunged into his human sexuality work.

## KINSEY ACTIVELY SUPPORTED EUGENICS

Kinsey actively supported eugenics in his writing and lecturing. In his 1937 text designed to train biology teachers, Kinsey predicted that eugenics should have a

> permanent place, both in high school and college teaching. Events in the last decade have made the younger generation wonder how eugenic factors account for the dependence of a third of the population on the other two thirds, even in times of prosperity. It is one of the most hopeful signs for the future that young people are becoming interested in problems of human breeding.[38]

He concluded that it was a big mistake not to apply information about human heredity to social problems. He even advocated that "eugenics ideas should be given to boys and girls as early as their first interest in companions of the opposite sex."[39]

---

38 Kinsey, *Methods in Biology*, 222.
39 Kinsey, *Methods in Biology*, 222–223.

After noting the problems of applying eugenics to people, such as determining which people are "undesirable," Kinsey stressed that "there would be little difficulty in selecting the ten percent which is the greatest drain on the advancement of our social institutions." He added that limiting the reproduction of "this ten percent might be necessary before we can expect any decrease in the number of helpless dependents."[40] He concluded that people who were "hereditarily sound and environmentally privileged may contribute to society by planning to have as many or more children than the average" family.[41]

Kinsey's list of eugenic references is especially telling—he recommended Dugdale's now infamous *The Jukes*,[42] Goddard's *The Kallikak Family*,[43] Davenport's *Heredity in Relation to Eugenics*[44] and Castle's *Genetics and Eugenics*.[45] Both the Jukes and Kallikak accounts have been completely refuted by modern research.[46]

### KINSEY'S DRIFT INTO SEX RESEARCH

After he graduated from college, Kinsey was hired by Indiana University to teach introduction to biology, entomology and insect taxonomy. He preferred fieldwork to teaching and soon was spending a great deal of his time working with students on projects, especially topics dealing with human sexuality. Soon he began dispensing sexual advice to students. Kinsey's first sexual case histories came from "counselling" sessions with students, launching his sexologist career. This led to Kinsey teaching a course in marriage, which, in turn, led to research that cumulated in his two volumes on human sexuality.

---

40  Kinsey, *Methods in Biology*, 224.

41  Kinsey, *Methods in Biology*, 224.

42  Richard Dugdale, *The Jukes: A Study in Crime, Pauperism, Disease and Heredity* (New York: Putnam, 1910).

43  Henry Goddard, *The Kallikak Family: A Study in the Heredity of Feeble-mindedness* (New York: MacMillan, 1912).

44  Charles Davenport, *Heredity in Relation to Eugenics: A Textbook for Students of Biology and a Reference Book for Animal and Plant Breeders* (New York: Henry Holt, 1916).

45  William E. Castle, *Genetics and Eugenics* (Cambridge: Harvard University Press, 1930).

46  J. David Smith, *Minds Made Feeble: The Myth and Legacy of the Kallikaks* (Rockville: Aspen, 1985).

Although all his training was in biology, not psychology, sociology, marriage, family or even anthropology, he plunged ahead. Kinsey discussed in his course the most intimate details of sexual behaviour without either embarrassment or euphemisms.[47] He also showed graphic slides depicting sexual intercourse and a variety of sexual behaviours, including sadomasochism. According to Reisman, although cloaked in the mantel of science, the course content was not objective, but openly advocated not only sexual freedom, but also Darwinism, and was against religion.[48]

## KINSEY BECOMES A FULL TIME SEX "RESEARCHER"

Kinsey at first agreed that the course would be open only to married seniors and that he would not exploit outside publicity. He soon violated these rules, opening the course up to anybody, and also sought outside publicity for his work and ideas. Kinsey's students often remarked that no matter what they were talking about, he would twist the conversations to sex, commonly asking them about their personal sex lives. Many persons were offended by the marriage course's content and the salacious class discussions. Appropriately charged with exploiting students, his peers petitioned the university president to remove Kinsey from the marriage course. President Herman B. Wells gave Kinsey a choice: he could keep his "research" or his marriage class, but not both. The class ended and Kinsey devoted most of his time to his "research" while remaining a paid university professor.

As his work in human sexuality increased, he invested less and less time in his family, which soon created much friction in his marriage. Eventually, and evidently to keep his marriage together, his wife Clara agreed to participate in both his professional life and his sexual research. They had what is now referred to as an open marriage, where each spouse freely took on lovers, although Alfred Kinsey seemed to take on more male than female lovers.

Kinsey dominated his researchers in numerous ways. In the name of research, he openly encouraged sexual relationships among his staff, behaviour that he called "interstaff sex," but stressed that they need to

47  Christenson, *Kinsey: A Biography.*
48  Jones, *Alfred Kinsey*, 190, 192, 340–349.

be discreet about their sexual involvements due to the negative publicity that public awareness could produce.[49] Kinsey also regularly seduced his subordinates, including graduate students and staff members, males included, whether they were married or single.[50] Several carried on love affairs with him for years, all evidently approved by his wife, who carried on her own affairs. Not unexpectedly, these affairs resulted in some tragic consequences, such as Kinsey's health problems.[51]

One of his earliest researchers who earned his doctorate under Kinsey in 1928 was Ralph Boris. Letters that survive reveal that they discussed intimate details of their respective marriages, and soon Kinsey fell in love with the "handsome young zoologist," but his desires were frustrated by society's then general condemnation of homosexuality. Boris was happily married to his college sweetheart and, much to the consternation of Kinsey, did not care to continue the affair. Thus, it ended. This experience is evidently what triggered Kinsey's interest in homosexuality, an interest that continued until he died.

His second researcher, Clyde Martin, entered Indiana University in the fall of 1937. Although Martin was more heterosexual than homosexual, Kinsey was attracted to Martin and used his authority as a professor to seduce the younger man. Eventually, Martin had an affair with Kinsey's wife—with Kinsey's blessing. Later, Martin married and ended these sexual liaisons.

Another important researcher, Wardell Pomeroy, was recruited by Kinsey when he was still working as a prison psychologist for the state of Indiana. Pomeroy's help was critical to obtain case histories from convicted sexual offenders, especially pedophiles. Kinsey also had an affair with Pomeroy, even though Pomeroy was married at the time. This scenario repeated itself with many, if not most, of Kinsey's co-researchers, even those who were his students. Much of this information became public, partly because people trained to help others talk about their sexual relationships tend to talk freely about their own.

Kinsey later moved into filming sex involving his staff, students and others, producing not only heterosexual, but also homosexual and

49 Jones, *Alfred Kinsey*, 499.
50 Pomeroy, *Dr. Kinsey*.
51 Jones, *Alfred Kinsey*, 500.

even sadomasochism pornography—all in the name of science.[52] The films and photographs of his subjects and staff having sex with each other were placed in a large library of erotica that Kinsey was collecting. This large collection eventually attracted the attention of the U.S. Customs Office, resulting in a lawsuit that remained unsettled when Kinsey died in 1956.

Kinsey's work was motivated largely by his own personal crusade against virtually all taboos and most laws against most forms of sexual behaviour. He, like Darwin, opened the floodgates. Soon Masters and Johnson followed, going even further, filming the sexual behaviour of more than 700 subjects.

Kinsey was also a crusader for prisoners—especially those jailed for sex crimes, offenses for which he believed they never should have been imprisoned in the first place. He rationalized that they were just doing what many other people do, and everyone's sin is no one's sin—by definition commonality makes a behaviour non-deviant, thus normal. Kinsey did not seem to have many compunctions about any type of sexual behaviour, except possibly only that which is violently forced on another person and causes physical injury.

Kinsey's views, especially his involvement in communism, eventually resulted in a House of Representatives investigation of him and his work. One outcome was that his funding was terminated, which soon ended most of his research. Kinsey spent the next couple of years unsuccessfully trying to secure new sources of funding. His health at this time also began to decline, partly as a result of his promiscuous sexual behaviour. While working in his garden, he bruised his leg, causing a fatal embolism, and died on August 25, 1956, at age sixty-nine.

## RESEARCHER OR PROSELYTIZER?

Kinsey, although he presented himself as a scientist, is viewed by many biographers as an activist whose goal was to change the world through science, especially by changing the norms circumscribing human sexual behaviour.[53] The goal of his research was clear: he wanted to

---

52 Jones, *Alfred Kinsey*, 611.
53 Flynn, *Intellectual Morons*, 39.

show that abnormal sexual behaviour was common, and therefore normal, and, consequently, acceptable. Behaviour that was common could not be abnormal, wrong or condemned, and laws now exist to "protect" criticism of behaviour once considered abnormal. The classic "If everybody else is doing it, why can't we?" approach was very successful—he began the process that eventually completely eviscerated Western morals.

Other Darwinists have used similar techniques to achieve the same end. For example, Bruce Bagemihl documented in a massive study that "homosexual, bisexual, and transgender wildlife" and even intergenerational sexuality are common, thus normal, in the animal kingdom.[54] Therefore, since such behaviour is normal, thus acceptable for animals, it is also normal for humans since, in contrast to the biblical view that humans were created in God's image, humans are no different than animals.

Some of Kinsey's conclusions seem unrealistic on their face. An example is the claim that from 67 to 98 percent of all men, depending on their social class, have premarital sex. Kinsey claimed, based on his limited sample, that half of all men and 26 percent of all women had extra-marital affairs, and 37 percent of all men have had at least one homosexual experience. Kinsey also concluded that about ten percent of the population is exclusively homosexual.[55] In contrast to his flawed studies, numerous recent scientific studies have consistently found only about two percent of the male population are exclusively homosexual. The implication of these irresponsible claims was clear: premarital sex, adultery, sado-masochism and homosexuality are all "normal" and, furthermore, traditional sexual morality—Judeo-Christian sexual morality in particular—is "unnatural." He often confused the fallacy of what is with what ought to be.

The implication that average is normal is disproved by the fact that average is clearly often not desirable. The average American's eating

54  Bruce Bagemihl, *Biological Exuberance: Animal Homosexuality and Natural Diversity* (New York: St. Martin's Press, 1999).

55  William Mosher, Anjani Chandra and Jo Jones, "Sexual behavior and selected health measures: Men and women 15–44 years of age, United States, 2002," *Advanced Data from Vital and Health Statistics* 362 (September 15, 2005); http://www.cdc.gov/nchs/data/ad/ad362.pdf; accessed August 17, 2016.

habits, excess body weight and driving speed are certainly not desirable. The average American dies of heart disease, cancer or diabetes, hardly desirable conditions. Few persons advocating promiscuity discussed this critical concern.

## THE ACCURACY OF HIS DATA

Since the period in which Kinsey was most actively collecting his data is often thought of as repressive and conservative, one may question the apparent ease at which Kinsey was able to gather the thousands of detailed intimate personal sex histories that he used as raw data for his research. Using volunteers is a serious error when questioning people about their sex life, something many people then, and many people today, are unwilling to talk about very freely, especially to strangers.

The lack of sample representation is another major concern—volunteers were utilized for both of his studies, and a highly disproportionate number were upper-class college students, drifters, male prostitutes, homosexuals found in gay bars, hardened criminals and prison inmates convicted of sexual offenses.[56] The elderly, blacks, Southerners and those with strong religious views were almost entirely omitted. About eighty percent of his sample was non-religious, or at least religiously inactive, at a time when over half of the population was religiously active.[57] This sampling bias alone would have skewed his results enormously.

His sample of women was disproportionately from the upper-classes, and numerous studies have found adultery and promiscuity more common in the upper-class compared to the middle class. For his female sexual behaviour study, Kinsey included 5,940 women. Fully 75 percent of them had attended college, and 19.4 percent were in graduate school or had completed graduate school. When the survey was completed, only 7.5 percent of American white women had attended college.[58] The occupations of those who contributed to the

---

56 Edward O. Laumann, et al., *The Social Organization of Sexuality: Sexual Practices in the United States* (Chicago: The University of Chicago Press, 1994), 44–46.

57 Flynn, *Intellectual Morons*, 40.

58 Daniels, *I Accuse Kinsey*, 24.

case histories included a significant number of prostitutes and women who worked in burlesque and other sex trade occupations.[59]

Another problem is that a disproportionately small number of Kinsey's sample of women was influenced by religious values. These factors would all highly inflate the mean (arithmetic average) that Kinsey reported. Kinsey's arguments for spousal unfaithfulness relied on case histories that showed this behaviour produced positive results.[60] In contrast to the published research, Kinsey implied that Judeo-Christian morality is to blame for problems that range from frigidity to sexual deviance.

A major problem with Kinsey's research is the difficulty of relying on memory when relating past behaviour to the interviewer. When asked about sexual activities, subjects may be able to accurately assess events that occurred in the past week or two, but most could not produce accurate information about the past decade. Furthermore, it is difficult for most people to remember many of the minute details Kinsey's questionnaire asked. When memory is inadequate, we tend to embellish, exaggerate, forget or distort, as has been verified by numerous memory studies.[61] Especially problematic were questions asked about early sexual behaviour, such as the age one first became aware of distinct sexual feelings. As has been said, it is easy to forget, but easier to disremember.

Another problem is that both Kinsey's questions and how they were worded likely influenced the answers they obtained. The interviewers were, according to their writings, committed to a certain worldview and tended to see this worldview in the answers they obtained. A statistical problem is that Kinsey used the mean for most of his charts, a statistical method that is highly influenced by a few extreme num-

59 Daniels, *I Accuse Kinsey*, 39.

60 Jonathan Gathorne-Hardy, *Sex the Measure of All Things: A Life of Alfred C. Kinsey* (Bloomington: Indiana University Press, 1998).

61 Elizabeth F. Loftus, "Creating false memories," *Scientific American* 277, No. 3 (1997): 70–75; Elizabeth F. Loftus, Maryanne Garry and Julie Feldman, "Forgetting sexual trauma: What does it mean when 38% forget?" *Journal of Consulting and Clinical Psychology* 62, No. 6 (1994): 1177–1181; Elizabeth F. Loftus and Hunter G. Hoffman, "Misinformation and memory: The creation of new memories," *Journal of Experimental Psychology* 118, No. 1 (1989): 100–104.

bers. If a few people indulge in certain behaviours at a very high level, even though most people rarely indulged in that behaviour, the average number of occurrences of that behaviour per individual will be inflated. For this reason, the median (the middle number when the numbers are ranked) is often used for income and many other statistics.[62] To more thoroughly convey the findings, Kinsey should also have provided the median and perhaps even the mode (the most common number).

Although Kinsey claimed to be "dispassionately objective," his methods for presenting the data were indicative of his bias, and it is clear that he was on a crusade. It is also obvious from his writing that his acceptance of Darwinism was a critical step. For example, in his report on women, Kinsey condemns what he calls the inconsistency of religious and legal codes.[63] He also makes many questionable judgements regarding sexual behaviours, such as claiming that promiscuity helps girls select more suitable marriage mates, when the research shows the opposite.[64] In addition, he claimed that most men approve of premarital and extra-marital sexual relationships on the path to this crusade.[65]

An evaluation of Kinsey's work was completed by a well-known Kinsey contemporary, William Kroger, professor of obstetrics and gynecology at Chicago Medical School. Dr. Kroger concluded that, from his experience, it is difficult to conclude that a normal, healthy female will bare her innermost secrets about sex, especially several hundred questions worth, to strangers or their professors.[66] He concluded that "women won't tell you the truth about their sex life, even when they are paying you to find out what is wrong with them."[67]

Another concern is that lack of experience, or a feeling of rejection, may cause some interviewees to use the interviews to inflate their egos

---

62 Jerry Bergman, *Understanding Educational Measurement and Evaluation* (Boston: Houghton Mifflin, 1981).

63 Alfred C. Kinsey, *Sexual Behavior in the Human Male* (Philadelphia: Saunders, 1948), 258.

64 Kinsey, *Sexual Behavior*, 360.

65 Kinsey, *Sexual Behavior*, 559.

66 Edmund Bergler and William Kroger, *Kinsey's Myth of Female Sexuality: The Medical Facts* (New York: Grune and Stratton, 1954).

67 Bergler and Kroger, *Kinsey's Myth*.

by exaggerating their sexual activities. Another common response is to confess, and even exaggerate, one's shortcomings in an effort to elicit sympathy or atone for guilt. These are only some of the many reasons why objective research has consistently failed, even today, to verify most of Kinsey's major contentions.

Critics concluded that Kinsey should have been more open and honest about his sample population and its limits when applying his data to the general population. At best, it applies to the sexual behaviour of specific, limited groups, in contrast to Kinsey's claim that it applied to normal human males and females in general. The fact is, Kinsey's estimates were known to be flawed from the outset because of his irresponsible sampling procedures.[68] Reisman argued that Kinsey's work was openly fraudulent and that his research was specifically designed to put Kinsey's own sexual proclivities on a scientific basis in order to justify them.[69]

A very disturbing aspect of his study is that his "researchers," or those they interviewed, or both, claimed that children as young as two months old actively engaged in adult sexual behaviour. Table 34, titled "Preadolescent males," listed their ages (from five months up), the number of adult sexual responses and the time involved to respond. This research, Kinsey concluded, substantiated the Freudian view that sexuality is a component present in humans from their earliest infancy.[70] It was this claim that motivated Dr. Judith Reisman to review Kinsey's work and to become an active critic of Kinsey.

It is not surprising that a public outcry against the Kinsey survey conclusions soon resulted. All of these sampling problems are well documented—even his editor, Lloyd Potter, recognized this problem.[71] Unfortunately, many in the media did not, some even claiming that his sample of 12,000 men was a "cross section" of Americans.[72]

---

68 Edward O. Laumann and Robert T. Michael, *Sex, Love and Health in America: Private Choices and Public Policies* (Chicago: The University of Chicago Press, 2001), 14.

69 Reisman, *Kinsey: Crimes.*

70 Kinsey, *Sexual Behavior*, 180.

71 Cashill, *Hoodwinked*, 247.

72 Cashill, *Hoodwinked*, 247.

By far the most damaging critique of his work was comparisons of his results to that of similar studies. A replication study by University of Chicago sociologist Edward Laumann found that Kinsey's results were higher—sometimes almost eight times higher—for virtually every piece of data that Laumann researched. The only category that did not follow this pattern was oral sexual behaviour, which was slightly lower. This may be due to changes in actual behaviour in the time between the studies.[73]

For example, Kinsey concluded 37 percent of the population had overt homosexual experiences, while Laumann et al. found only 4.9 percent.[74] Kinsey also started the myth that ten percent of the population is homosexual, a statistic that is still commonly cited today.[75] Studies consistently have found only one to, at most, three percent of the population are self-defined homosexuals.[76] Another example is Kinsey's report that 74 percent of all men patronized prostitutes, Laumann found only 15 percent. Likely too, many of these behaviours were actually higher when Laumann did his research in the 1990s, indicating Kinsey's results were probably not even close to the actual 1948 rate.

## KINSEY AND HOMOSEXUALITY

One area where Kinsey may have been correct was his conclusion that homosexuality actually falls on a continuum from one to seven (one was exclusively heterosexual and seven exclusively homosexual). The vast majority of the population, Kinsey concluded, fall somewhere between two and six, and very few people were exclusively homosexual or heterosexual.

Ironically, this conclusion is widely rejected in popular culture today. The common assumption is that almost all adults are either exclusively heterosexual or homosexual, which goes contrary to not only Kinsey's research, but also numerous other studies on the sexual

---

73 Laumann's study was published in 1994; Kinsey's in 1948, almost forty years earlier.

74 Laumann, et al., *Social Organization*, 294.

75 Laumann, et al., *Social Organization*, 287.

76 Laumann, et al., *Social Organization*, 311.

behaviour of Americans. Furthermore, it commonly is assumed that involvement in homosexual behaviour "proves" one is gay regardless of one's past heterosexual experiences.

On the other hand, a category called bisexuality is commonly used now, presumably where one has proclivities for both behaviours, although this view does not tend to be prominent in the popular literature. The term homosexual is often ignored in the scientific literature because the medical community recognizes that this term falsely implies that the behaviour is genetic, or at least generally unchangeable. For this reason, the expression "men who have sex with men" is often used instead.

Kinsey's frequent trips to gay bars likely influenced his conclusions; after taking sexual histories, he allegedly had sex with no small number of men in this pre-AIDS age. One of Kinsey's goals was public tolerance for what he tried to convince the world was the enormous variety of sexual behaviour, especially sodomy, in which normal persons were involved. The importance of his influence is indicated by the 2003 U.S. Supreme Court decision that ruled all sodomy laws in America were unconstitutional,[77] in spite of the obvious enormous adverse health consequences that result from this behaviour, as is now well-documented in the medical literature.

Kinsey's work was also critically important in society's increasing acceptance of homosexual behaviour. He planned to do an entire book on homosexuality but died before it could be completed. Normalization of homosexuality has had profound implications for society. For example, a generation ago child molestation largely involved female victims; it now increasingly involves male victims. Furthermore, according to the U.S. Center for Disease Control (CDC) data, the homosexually orientated are over thirty times more likely to be involved in pedophilia than heterosexuals. Another effect is the issue that is now splitting some religious denominations. The most well-known example is the Episcopal Church, but the Methodist Church and many other denominations are affected as well.

---

77 *Lawrence v. Texas*, 593 U.S. 588 (2003); https://supreme.justia.com/cases/federal/us/539/558/case.html; accessed August 22, 2016.

## MEDIA SUPPORT FOR HIS WORK

When Kinsey released his findings, the reaction by the media was overwhelmingly positive.[78] Despite the plethora of studies that have disproved most of Kinsey's major results, the liberal media often still tout them as valid.[79] All too often, media reaction to valid criticism of the study is similar to a *London Times* article that stated, when the Kinsey report was published, "impact on American society was likened to that of Darwin's theory of evolution. And there are still plenty of people who don't want to believe that, either."[80] On the other side, in 2005 the magazine *Human Events* rated the Kinsey Report the third most harmful book published in the last century.

## THE EFFECTS OF THE KINSEY REVOLUTION ON SOCIETY

It is well documented that Kinsey's work was a critical factor in bringing about the so-called sexual revolution. Around the turn of the century, illegitimacy in America was around one percent. Now it averages close to sixty percent in some populations, and in African Americans it is over seventy percent. The divorce rate in 1920 was below 17 percent; it now is about 50 percent.[81] Close to half of all American children are now reared by one biological parent, most often the mother.

A fractured family (family is defined as a mother and father and one or more children) is the single most important factor that drives almost all major social problems, including delinquency, poor school performance, drinking, teen pregnancy, drug use, social deviancy, promiscuity, poverty, truancy and school misbehaviour.[82] Children born to unwed mothers are over ten times more likely to live in poverty than children with fathers in the home. Children reared in fatherless homes account for 63 percent of all teen suicides, 71 percent

---

78 Flynn, *Intellectual Morons*, 49.

79 David Hackett, "Indiana University shuns Kinsey biographer," *The Journal Gazette* (March 11, 2003): 2C.

80 "Alfred Kinsey: The swinging detective—he opened their eyes to sex," *London Sunday Times*, April 7, 2005.

81 Roderick Phillips, *Putting Asunder: A History of Divorce in Western Society* (New York: Cambridge University Press, 1988); Kevin White, *Sexual Liberation or Sexual License? The American Revolt against Victorianism* (Chicago: Ivan Dee, 2000).

82 William Gairdner, *The War against the Family* (Toronto: Stoddard, 1992).

of high school dropouts, 75 percent of the children in chemical-abuse centres, 80 percent of rapists, 85 percent of youths in prison, 85 percent of children who exhibit behavioural disorders and 90 percent of the homeless and runaway children.[83]

These problems tend to continue into the next generation. Children from intact homes are more likely to have successful marriages and less likely to divorce and less likely to experience all of the problems noted above.[84] Critically important is the fact that the majority of persons living in poverty consist of single mothers and their children. The importance of a father in the normal growth and development of both boys and girls has been well documented.[85] As documented by William Gairdner, no single factor influences how a child turns out as much as an intact family.[86] The "children of divorce and never-married mothers are less successful in life by almost every measure" than even the children of widowed mothers.[87]

The harm caused by the Kinsey report has also been documented in other areas. For example, the testimony of some women who claim that after learning about the Kinsey report, they began to suspect their husband of unfaithfulness, even though before this they had no reason to be suspicious, nor did they have any evidence.[88] This distrust can be very damaging to a relationship.

Kinsey rarely discussed the relationship between sexual experiences and happiness, or even sexual experience level and satisfaction levels obtained from these experiences. Some sexual behaviour, especially promiscuity, often translates into unhappiness and lack of sexual satisfaction.

---

83 For a summary see Cynthia R. Daniels, *Lost Fathers: The Politics of Fatherlessness in America* (New York: St. Martin's Press, 1998).

84 Barbara Dafoe Whitehead, *The Divorce Culture* (New York: Alfred A. Knopf, 1997).

85 Christina Hoff Sommers, *The War against Boys* (New York: Simon and Schuster, 2000); Daniels, *Lost Fathers*.

86 Gairdner, *War against the Family*.

87 Daniels, *Lost Fathers*, 34.

88 Sue Ellin Browder, "Kinsey's secret: The phony science of the sexual revolution," *Crisis* 22, No. 5 (May 2004): 12–17.

## THE STATUS OF KINSEY'S WORK TODAY

Reading about Kinsey's life strains the credibility of many people today. Part of the reason is the recent reversion back to what Kinsey's supporters called puritanical attitudes as a result of AIDS, the extreme elements of the women's movement and multi-million dollar pedophilia lawsuits.[89] Many women today interpret the behaviour that Kinsey advocated as exploitative, such as supervisors in an academic setting coercing students to have sex with them. Although Kinsey hid this behaviour at first, it was later openly flaunted with the support of some high-level officials at Indiana University, including its president.[90] If a professor in an American, Canadian or European university today regularly seduced students or subordinates, this would be grounds for, and likely result in, immediate termination. The fact is, many scholars now recognize the enormous harm that Kinsey caused society.

---

89 "Alfred Kinsey: The swinging detective."

90 Jones, *Alfred Kinsey*, 348. It is likely that Kinsey was deemed ideologically useful and was protected. A priest or pastor caught in the same acts would have been exposed and ruthlessly pilloried.

## Margaret Sanger (1879-1966)

Considered the leader of the birth-control and abortion movement, Sanger was a radical eugenicist who advocated sterilization of the "feeble-minded" and promoted a racist agenda in her clinics. She also was a strong proponent of the "free love" movement and encouraged women to embrace freedom from the constraints of marriage and children.

# 04

# Abortion leader Margaret Sanger: Darwinist, racist and eugenicist

||||||||||||||||||||||||||||||||||||||||||||||||||||||||||||||||||||||||||||||||||||||||||||||||||||||||||||||||||||||

**P**lanned Parenthood, the leading organization advocating abortion in the United States today, was founded by Margaret Sanger. It is well documented that Darwinism had a profound influence on her thinking, including her conversion to and active support of eugenics. Sanger was specifically concerned with reducing the population of the "less fit," including "inferior races" such as "Negroes." She also openly advocated sexual license, often now called "free love" or "hooking up." One major result of her lifelong work was to support the sexual revolution that has radically changed Western society.

## MARGARET SANGER

Margaret (Maggie) Sanger (September 14, 1879–September 6, 1966) was the most prominent leader of the modern birth control and free love movements.[1] Sanger's mother was a devout Irish Catholic, and her father, Michael Higgins, was an unstable man unable to adequately provide for his large family. Although a skilled stonemason and tomb-

---

1    Ruth Clifford Engs, *The Eugenics Movement: An Encyclopedia* (Westport: Greenwood Press, 2005), 198.

stone carver, his radical leftist politics alienated many of his custom-ers.[2] When he had the money, he drank heavily while his eleven children suffered bitterly from cold, privation and even hunger.[3] He was also bitterly anti-religious. When Maggie was baptized on March 23, 1893, at St. Mary's Catholic Church, the event "had to be kept secret because her father would have been furious" if he had found out.[4]

Sanger left her unhappy home as a teen, returning only briefly to study nursing at a co-educational boarding school called Claverack College.[5] She was reportedly a poor student, skipped classes and neglected her part-time job. Sanger dropped out of school and, after a brief stay at home to help care for her dying mother, moved in with her older sister and worked as a first-grade teacher of immigrant chil-dren. She left this position after only two terms. This unhappy experi-ence may have contributed to her later enthusiastic embrace of Darwinian eugenics.

As a child, Maggie "used to sneak off to church on Sundays;" but when an adult, she became a skeptic and a radical like her father,[6] actively involved in Marxist secular humanism and Darwinian eugen-ics. Her lifelong "archenemy" became the Catholic Church.[7]

About this time she met architect and painter, William Sanger, at a party. He pursued her with gusto. They married in 1902 and soon had three children. She turned out to be a very difficult woman to live with. William tried everything within his power to please his wife. Grant writes that, not long after her initiation into radical causes such as anarchism, Margaret informed

---

2  Donald DeMarco and Benjamin D. Wiker, *Architects of the Culture of Death* (San Francisco: Ignatius Press, 2004), 287.

3  George Grant, *Killer Angel: A Short Biography of Planned Parenthood's Founder, Margaret Sanger* (Franklin: Stand Fast Books, 2001), 30.

4  Madeline Gray, *Margaret Sanger: A Biography of the Champion of Birth Control* (New York: Richard Marek Publishers, 1979), 17.

5  Emily Taft Douglas, *Margaret Sanger: Pioneer of the Future* (Garrett Park: Garrett Park Press, 1975).

6  Gray, *Margaret Sanger*, 16.

7  Vickie Cox, *Margaret Sanger: Rebel for Women's Rights* (Philadelphia: Chelsea House, 2005), 89.

her bewildered husband that she needed emancipation from every taint of Christianized capitalism—including the strict bonds of the marriage bed. She even suggested to him that they seriously consider experimenting with various trysts, infidelities, fornications, and adulteries. Because of her careful tutoring in socialist dogma, she had undergone a sexual liberation—at least intellectually—and she was now ready to test its authenticity physically.[8]

Margaret was also a very distracted mother who did not like caring for children, including her own.[9] She detested domestic life and grossly neglected her children to the point that at times her neighbours were forced to step in to care for them.[10]

The letters her children wrote to their mother vividly reveal this neglect. When Sanger was formally introduced to Marxism, anarchism, secular humanism, free love and Darwinism, she found her passion in life. Sanger married twice and had no qualms about using her husbands' wealth to support her work. Her good friend, Mabel Dodge Luhan, wrote that Sanger introduced her social circle to her liberal ideas about sex. Mrs. Luhan added, Sanger was the

first person I ever knew who was openly an ardent propagandist for the joys of the flesh. This, in those days, was radical indeed when the sense of sin was still so indubitably mixed with the sense of pleasure.... Margaret Sanger...personally...set out to rehabilitate it.... [S]he was one of its first conscious promulgators. Margaret Sanger was an advocate of the flesh.[11]

In an attempt to deal with his wife's promiscuity, William Sanger took the family to Paris in an attempt to reinvigorate their marriage. The attempt failed to convince Margaret to live a monogamous life,

---

8 Grant, *Killer Angel*, 22.
9 Gray, *Margaret Sanger*, 36, 40, 47.
10 Cox, *Margaret Sanger*, 18.
11 Mabel Dodge Luhan, *Movers and Shakers: Volume Three of Intimate Memories* (New York: Harcourt, Brace, 1936), 69–70.

and they eventually divorced. Reading Havelock Ellis's "[m]assive, seven-volume *Studies in the Psychology of Sex*...stirred in her a new lust for lust."[12] She soon had public affairs with some of the most famous men of her day, including H.G. Wells, George Bernard Shaw, and her hero, Havelock Ellis. This last affair so distressed Mr. Ellis's wife, Edith, that she twice attempted suicide.[13] Nor did Sanger confine her sexual exploits to males, but females as well.[14]

Margaret Sanger's second husband, oil magnate and founder of the 3-in-1 Oil Company, James Noah H. Slee, was also very wealthy—one stock deal alone netted him four million dollars.[15] He, too, pursued Margaret with gusto, giving her expensive gifts and sending her roses almost every day. Sanger wrote to her secretary about Slee: "I don't want to marry anyone, particularly a stodgy churchgoer.... Yet...how often am I going to meet a man with nine million dollars?"[16]

Before she would consent to marry Mr. Slee, she convinced him to sign an agreement giving her total sexual freedom, even living separately. Slee was not allowed to ever question where she was or whom she was with.[17] Ms. Sanger also never took Slee's last name. In the first issue of her journal titled *The Woman Rebel*, she wrote that marriage is "a degenerate institution" and that modesty is an "obscene prudery." She also wrote "it is as foolish to promise to love forever as to promise to live forever."[18] This conclusion may have been influenced by her involvement in the so-called "free love" movement.[19] Her sexualizing became part of her work. Luhan wrote that Sanger

taught us the way to a heightening of pleasure and of prolonging it, and...sexualizing of the whole body until it should become

---

12 Grant, *Killer Angel*, 22.

13 DeMarco and Wiker, *Architects*, 293; Gray, *Margaret Sanger*, 227–228.

14 Ellen Chesler, *Woman of Valor: Margaret Sanger and the Birth Control Movement in America* (New York: Simon and Schuster, 1992), 186.

15 Gray, *Margaret Sanger*, 253.

16 Gray, *Margaret Sanger*, 167.

17 Cox, *Margaret Sanger*, 78.

18 Margaret Sanger, *Margaret Sanger: An Autobiography* (New York: Norton, 1938), 355.

19 DeMarco and Wiker, *Architects*, 290.

sensitive and alive throughout, and complete. She made love into a serious undertaking—with the body so illumined and conscious that it would be able to interpret and express in all its parts the language of the spirit's pleasure.[20]

In the end, her sexual promiscuity resulted in behaviour that neither of her two husbands could cope with. She once gave the following moral advice to her sixteen-year-old granddaughter: "Kissing, petting and even intercourse are alright as long as they are sincere. I have never given a kiss in my life that wasn't sincere. As for intercourse, I'd say three times a day was about right."[21]

## SANGER CONVERTS TO EUGENICS

Early in her career, Sanger left America for Europe to avoid a jail term. In Europe she became a follower of Thomas Malthus, the same man that inspired Charles Darwin. Malthus's disciples—then called Malthusians or neo-Malthusians—taught that "if Western civilization were to survive, the physically unfit, the materially poor, the spiritually diseased, the racially inferior, and the mentally incompetent had to somehow be suppressed and isolated—or perhaps even eliminated."[22]

As Sanger stressed in a talk given at the Fifth International Neo-Malthusian and Birth Control Conference, the end goal of her movement was to produce a superior race: "To-day the average reliance of civilization is based upon iron and steel, bricks and mortar, and we must change this to the...evolution of humanity itself."[23]

To achieve this eugenic goal, she advocated euthanasia, segregation in work camps, sterilization and abortion.[24] She was very successful in achieving this goal—more than half of the American states launched programs that sterilized their "unfit...with Virginia, California, and

20 Luhan, *Movers and Shakers*, 71.

21 Gray, *Margaret Sanger*, 227–228.

22 Grant, *Killer Angel*, 67.

23 Margaret Sanger, "Individual and family aspects of birth control," in *Report of the Fifth International Neo-Malthusian and Birth Control Conference, Given on July 11–14, 1922 at Kingsway Hall, London.* ed., Raymond Pierpoint (London: Heinemann, 1922), 31.

24 Flynn, *Intellectual Morons*, 150.

Kansas leading the way."[25] Sanger was also very influenced by sociologist and sexologist Havelock Ellis, who "always considered himself both a eugenicist and a socialist." Ellis frequently published articles in *Birth Control Review*, and Ellis shaped Sanger's "ideas in significant ways." To Margaret Sanger, "Ellis was a modern-day saint."[26] Furthermore,

> Ellis made his most important contribution to the eugenics doctrine...when he assigned women to act as its chief enforcers. Women are critical agents of civilizations progress...because... they alone have the power to produce and nurture...fitter babies. ...Increased sex expression and wider use of birth control were thus significant tools in the eugenic program, and accordingly, he condemned eugenicists who refused to endorse birth control.[27]

Not only Ellis, but several of Sanger's closest associates, including Dorothy Brush, Robert Latou Dickinson, H.C.P. Blacker, Frederick Osborn and Clarence Gamble of the Procter and Gamble Corporation, were all eugenicists.[28] Sanger wrote her concern was not just the fact that feeble-mindedness "leads to immorality and criminality" but

> because both are burdens and dangers to the intelligence of the community...there is sufficient evidence to lead us to believe that the so-called "borderline cases" are a greater menace than the out-and-out "defective delinquents" who can be supervised, controlled and prevented from procreating their kind...psychological tests indicate that the mental defective who is glib and plausible, bright looking and attractive, but with a mental vision of seven, eight, or nine years, may not merely lower the whole level of intelligence in a school or in a society, but may be encouraged by church and state to increase and multiply until he dominates...an entire community. The presence in the public schools of the mentally defective children of men and women who

---

25 Flynn, *Intellectual Morons*, 150.

26 Grant, *Killer Angel*, 44.

27 Chesler, *Woman of Valor*, 123.

28 Angela Franks, *Margaret Sanger's Eugenic Legacy* (Jefferson: McFarland, 2005), 125.

should never have been parents is a problem that is becoming more and more difficult.[29]

As early as 1917, Sanger was openly giving "public support to the eugenics movement" and to so-called "race betterment" programs.[30] The eugenicists on her board believed that use of "birth control would eliminate disease and deformity as well as empty the jails and orphanages."[31] Sanger "supported sterilization for the incarcerated and considered birth control a necessary component of racial improvement."[32] Sanger's end goal was the same as Hitler's: to "create a race of [human] thoroughbreds," a pure and superior race and her journal even "eerily" foretold the "horrors of the Nazi 'final solution.'"[33] Her eugenics crusade, although toned down later in her life, was to consume her until her death in 1966.[34]

## SANGER'S WRITINGS

Sanger wrote extensively, leaving ample documentation of her beliefs and goals. She founded *Birth Control Review*, published from 1917 until the early 1940s, and was either an editor or contributor to this publication during most of its existence. Sanger's close relationships with eugenicists were clearly documented in the pages of *Birth Control Review* from its inception. Eugenics also "soon became a constant, even a dominant, theme at birth-control conferences."[35] Hundreds of the movement's speeches and articles emphasized the important role of birth control in eugenics programs. In the 1920s

---

29 Margaret H. Sanger, *The Pivot of Civilization* (Amherst: Humanity Books, 2003), 115.

30 Engs, *Eugenics Movement*, 199–200.

31 Gray, *Margaret Sanger*, 253.

32 Tone, *Devices and Desires*, 145.

33 Claire M. Roche, "Reproducing the Working Class: Tillie Olsen, Margaret Sanger, and American Eugenics," in *Evolution and Eugenics in American Literature and Culture, 1880-1940: Essays on Ideological Conflict and Complicity*, eds. Lois A. Cuddy and Claire M. Roche (Danvers: Rosemont Publishing, 2003), 265.

34 Douglas, *Margaret Sanger*.

35 Linda Gordon, *Woman's Body, Woman's Right: A Social History of Birth Control in America* (New York: Grossman Publishers, 1976), 282.

eugenics became a popular craze in this country—promoted in newspapers and magazines as a kind of secular religion. A national advocacy organization, the American Eugenics Society, was founded in 1923 to foster broader public understanding of eugenic principles through such public relations gimmickry as sermon contests in churches and synagogues and "fitter family" contests at state fairs.[36]

The sweeping claims published in *Birth Control Review* make it clear that the influence of eugenics was foundational to her birth control movement: "The Eugenic touch-stone is the final and infallible test of all ethics and all politics."[37] Integral to this was the 1920s eugenics platform, and the belief that sterilization was a

> method that could be legislated and enforced on whole groups of the population to include those deemed "feebleminded." Despite the significant ethical and moral implications of sterilization programs, Sanger continued to associate her movement with that of the eugenicists, in part to defend against attacks from religious institutions, especially the Catholic Church.[38]

Sanger believed that her movement was "working in accord with the universal law of evolution."[39] Her magazine even argued for "state-sponsored sterilization programs," forcibly sterilizing the "less capable."[40] Sanger's Darwinian views were also expressed in her writing. For example, she maintained that the brains of Australian Aborigines were evolutionarily only one step above chimpanzees, and just under the blacks, Jews and Italians.[41] When arguing for eugenics, Sanger quoted Darwin as an authority on the importance of "natural checks" of the population, such as war, which helped to reduce the popula-

36 Chesler, *Woman of Valor*, 215.

37 David Kennedy, *Birth Control in America: The Career of Margaret Sanger* (New Haven: Yale University Press, 1970), 17.

38 Roche, "Reproducing the Working Class," 263.

39 Douglas, *Margaret Sanger*, 130.

40 Roche, "Reproducing the Working Class," 264.

41 Flynn, *Intellectual Morons*, 153.

tion.[42] The many academics and scientists that she won to her cause, included Harvard University sociologist E.M. East, University of Michigan president Clarence C. Little and Johns Hopkins psychiatrist Alfred Meyer.[43]

Sanger also made her eugenic views clear in the books she authored, such as *The Pivot of Civilization* and *Woman Rebel*, stressing that birth control was not only "important with respect to controlling the numbers of unfit in the population," but was the "only viable means to improve the human race."[44] She boldly proclaimed that birth control was the only viable way to improve the human race.[45] Writing that: "Birth control itself...is nothing more or less than the facilitation of the process of weeding out the unfit, of preventing the birth of defectives or of those who will become defectives."[46]

While in her later years, Sanger redefined what she meant by the class of people who were "unfit." She increasingly saw "feeblemindedness, the bogey of all hereditarians, as antecedent to poverty and social organization in the genesis of social problems."[47] She also opposed charity because it allowed the less fit to survive and propagate even more unfit.[48] The influence of Darwin on Sanger's racism ideas is obvious from her writings. For example, she wrote that a

fish as large as a man has a brain no larger than the kernel of an almond. In all fish and reptiles where there is no great brain development, there is also no conscious sexual control. The lower down in the scale of human development we go the less sexual control we find. It is said the aboriginal Australian, the lowest known species of the human family, just a step higher than the chimpanzee in brain development, has so little sexual control that police authority alone prevents him from obtaining sexual

---

42 Margaret H. Sanger, *Women and the New Race* (New York: Blue Ribbon Books, 1920), 159.

43 Chesler, *Woman of Valor*, 217.

44 Roche, "Reproducing the Working Class," 263.

45 Peter Engelman, "Foreword" to Sanger, *Pivot of Civilization*, 9.

46 Sanger, *Women and the New Race*, 229.

47 Kennedy, *Birth Control in America*, 115.

48 Sanger, *Pivot of Civilization*, chapter 5.

satisfaction on the streets. According to one writer, the rapist has just enough brain development to raise him above the animal, but like the animal, when in heat, knows no law except nature, which impels him to procreate, whatever the result.[49]

The influence of German biologist Ernst Haeckel is also obvious, such as where Sanger wrote that, from the first few weeks of the ovum's existence, the human embryo must pass through its evolutionary history (worm, fish, reptile, mammal and primate stages) "step by step within the uterus in a very short period" of time.[50]

## WAS SANGER A MEDICAL QUACK?

Margaret Sanger had no formal medical or scientific training aside from, at best, what is equivalent to practical nurse training required for an LPN, a program she never finished. Nonetheless, she wrote extensively on medical matters. Some of her advice was very naïve, such as recommending a laxative to induce an abortion. Those who followed her advice sometimes received a rude awakening—and wrote angry letters to Sanger in response to the pain that it caused them. [51] Her writings also reveal that she sometimes advocated dangerous quack remedies, such as taking high levels of quinine to cause an abortion.[52] She also "frequently consulted psychics, mediums, and other clairvoyants" for medical and other advice.[53] We will never know how much suffering, or how many lives were ruined by her advice.

## RACISM AND BIRTH CONTROL CLINICS

Margaret Sanger opened her first birth control clinic in 1916 in the impoverished Brownsville section of Brooklyn to help control what she called the "over breeding" problem. The two-room storefront clinic was a great contrast to Margaret's plush Greenwich Village

---

49 Margaret H. Sanger, *What Every Girl Should Know* (New York: Belvedere Publishers, 1980), 40.

50 Sanger, *What Every Girl Should Know*, 45.

51 Flynn, *Intellectual Morons*.

52 Flynn, *Intellectual Morons*, 149.

53 Flynn, *Intellectual Morons*, 157.

home, but "since the clientele she wished to attract—'immigrant Southern Europeans, Slavs, Latins, and Jews'—could only be found 'in the coarser neighborhoods and tenements,' she was forced to venture out of her comfortable confines."[54]

Sanger turned her attention to Negroes by opening a new clinic in Harlem in 1930. As her organization grew, Sanger organized more clinics in other communities, "in alliance with eugenicists, and through initiatives such as the Negro Project...exploited black stereotypes in order to reduce the fertility of African Americans"[55] and other "dysgenic races" besides Blacks such as Hispanics. The all-white staff and the sign identifying the clinic as a "research bureau" raised the suspicions of the black community. They feared that the clinic's actual goal was to "experiment on and sterilize black people."[56] Their fears were not unfounded: she once addressed the women's branch of the Ku Klux Klan in Silver Lake, New Jersey, and received a "dozen invitations to speak to similar groups."[57] She was also on good terms with other racist organizations.[58]

Sanger believed the "Negro district" was the "headquarters for the criminal element" and concluded that, as the title of a book by a member of her board proclaimed, *The Rising Tide of Color Against White World Supremacy*, was a rise that had to be stemmed.[59] To deal with the problem of resistance among the black population, Sanger recruited black doctors, nurses, ministers and social workers "to gain black patients' trust" in order "to limit or even erase the black presence in America."[60]

## SANGER AND THE NAZIS

The Nazis relied on American expertise in developing their own eugenic programs that resulted in as many as 3.5 million persons coer-

---

54 George Grant, *Grand Illusions: The Legacy of Planned Parenthood* (Brentwood: Wolgemuth and Hyatt, 1988), 92.

55 Harriet Washington, *Medical Apartheid: The Dark History of Medical Experimentation on Black Americans from Colonial Times to the Present* (New York: Doubleday, 2006), 196.

56 Tone, *Devices and Desires*, 147.

57 Sanger, *Margaret Sanger*, 366–367.

58 Flynn, *Intellectual Morons*, 153.

59 Washington, *Medical Apartheid*, 196.

60 Washington, *Medical Apartheid*, 197–198.

cively sterilized.[61] The Nazi template was the model law developed by Harry Laughlin, a frequent contributor to Sanger's *Birth Control Review*.[62] Laughlin was also a great admirer of the German eugenics program and was proud of his contribution to it. The American eugenic contribution to Nazi eugenic programs was recognized by the University of Heidelberg by awarding Laughlin an honorary doctorate.[63]

To insure that her eugenic goals were implemented, her Birth Control League board was "made up almost exclusively of sociologists and eugenicists," as were the Nazis.[64] Margaret and the Malthusian eugenicists she worked with did not narrowly discriminate, but targeted every "non-Aryan" ethnic group, whether red, black, yellow or white by setting up clinics wherever they judged a sufficient population of minorities lived. In addition, she included the "feeble-minded, syphilitic, irresponsible, and defective" and persons "bred unhindered" in her program to reduce their numbers.[65] Since Margaret and her cohorts estimated as many as seventy percent of the population fell into these "undesirable" categories, they realized that they had their work cut out for them. Much of the early grass-roots work in her movement was done by various "radicals," mostly socialists and communists.[66] Sanger quoted fellow birth control worker, Mrs. Besant, who told a court that she has

> no doubt that if natural checks were allowed to operate right through the human as they do in the animal world, a better result would follow. Among the brutes, the weaker are driven to the wall, the diseased fall out in the race of life. The old brutes, when feeble or sickly, are killed. If men insisted that those who were sickly should be allowed to die without help of medicine or science, if those who are weak were put upon one side and crushed, if those who were old and useless were killed, if those

61 Franks, *Margaret Sanger's Eugenic Legacy*, 181.

62 Franks, *Margaret Sanger's Eugenic Legacy*, 182.

63 Franks, *Margaret Sanger's Eugenic Legacy*, 182. See also André Pichot, *The Pure Society: From Darwin to Hitler* (New York: Verso, 2009).

64 Gray, *Margaret Sanger*, 240, 287.

65 Grant, *Grand Illusions*, 92.

66 Gordon, *Woman's Body*, 228.

who were not capable of providing food for themselves were allowed to starve, if all this were done, the struggle for existence among men would be as real as it is among brutes and would doubtless result in the production of a higher race of men.[67]

## SANGER'S WAR AGAINST THE CHURCH

Many churches opposed Sanger because she championed eugenics, abortion and concentration camps for the unfit but also "sex without consequences," all practices that Christianity has historically opposed.[68] She stressed that she was especially opposed to the Catholic Church because they were against "science," by which Sanger meant evolution, eugenics and other programs attempting to achieve "race improvement."[69] Sanger "sought out allegiances with eugenicists" to help blunt the opposition from the religious community.[70]

The church's view that the handicapped, diseased and deformed were all equals in the eyes of God, "struck Sanger as anathema to the dictates of the Brave New World" that she wanted to create.[71] She even argued that persons "whose religious scruples prevent their exercising control over their numbers" were "irresponsible and reckless," and that the "procreation of this group should be stopped."[72]

Sanger attributed "everything from child labor to world war," and even insanity, epilepsy, criminality, prostitution, pauperism and mental defectiveness, to "unchecked breeding."[73] The church taught these were all sins that could be overcome and had collected many success stories to support their claim and followed up on these successes with activities such as Catholic charities.

Sanger eventually recognized that her solution to the problems of crime, poverty and other social problems would never work, at least

---

67 Sanger, *Women and the New Race*, 160.

68 Flynn, *Intellectual Morons*, 6, 154.

69 Robert Marshall and Charles Donovan, *Blessed Are the Barren: The Social Policy of Planned Parenthood* (San Francisco: Ignatius, 1991).

70 Nancy Ordover, *American Eugenics* (Minneapolis: University of Minnesota Press, 2003), 138.

71 Flynn, *Intellectual Morons*, 155.

72 Marshall and Dovovan, *Blessed Are the Barren*, 1.

73 Ordover, *American Eugenics*, 140.

not in America. She then proposed what she thought was a realistic solution that would help to prevent bringing the "weak, the helpless, and the unwanted children into the world," to help solve the problem of overcrowded families, cities and nations.[74]

The solution she proposed was so-called "positive eugenics," which involved encouraging selective population control, and a means of achieving this more realistic goal was birth control. It was for this reason Sanger did little to support positive eugenics until much later in her career. An example of positive eugenics include encouraging the fit to have large families, a goal then often supported by the churches. Previously, she had advocated negative eugenics, the prevention of procreation through the unfit by law and various forms of coercion.[75]

### EXPORTING EUGENICS AND STERILIZATION

Sanger worked hard to spread her eugenic ideas about "human weeds" not only in America but to the rest of the world. Eugenics, sterilization and birth control projects on a large scale became an Anglo-American export.[76] Sanger's birth control movement was the largest in the world, and in England its head offices were based at the London Eugenics Society. Sanger's movement became a "truly international organization with the bulk of its multi-million annual budget coming from the United States."[77] Most of the financial support came from state taxes, and the rest was donated by large corporations, such as General Motors.

Sanger's movement had an impact in many nations, including India, Singapore, Japan, China, Korea and much of Europe. Her programs involving sterilization of the unfit were adopted by Sweden, Norway, Finland, Denmark and, most infamously, by Nazi Germany.[78]

---

74  Sanger, *Women and the New Race*, 161.

75  Jean Baker, *Margaret Sanger: A Life of Passion* (New York: Hill and Wang, 2012).

76  Stephen Trombley, *The Right To Reproduce: A History of Coercive Sterilization* (London: Weidenfeld and Nicolson, 1988), 214.

77  Trombley, *Right To Reproduce*, 215.

78  Flynn, *Intellectual Morons*, 151.

## REASONS FOR HER ENORMOUS SUCCESS

Sanger "was the most famous American popularizer of eugenics, and much of her support came from eugenicists.[79] A major reason for her success, though, was because she met a genuine need of the poor, many of whom had large families that they could not adequately support. America at that time was changing from an agricultural to an industrial society. Large families that lived on farms needed the low-cost labour provided by many children, but large families often could not be properly supported by factory work. This motivated a drive to limit family size, a need that Sanger exploited to further her eugenic goals. The problem is, "Sanger's zeal blinded her to the reality that her actions occasionally worked against her desired purposes."[80]

It was only after World War II and the horrors of the Holocaust that Sanger abandoned her dream of producing a socialist, perfected eugenic society. She then played down her eugenic and socialist ideals, and increasingly stressed the goals now advocated by Planned Parenthood. In Trombley's words, "after the Nazi atrocities," she clothed her movement in the words that Planned Parenthood advocates use today because the "Nazi's eugenics became a word to strike fear in the hearts of ordinary people. Thus, eugenics reemerged from the doldrums of the post-Nazi period to exert an influence on a much larger scale than had ever been previously imagined."[81]

Partly because of her past association with known racists and a history of several decades of racist and eugenic rhetoric, the American Birth Control League name was changed to Planned Parenthood in 1942.[82] Unfortunately, despite the name change, the racism of her movement has lingered on to this day.[83]

## REWRITING HISTORY

Although Sanger's involvement in eugenics and radical politics is well documented, many people today are attempting to whitewash her past

---

79 Washington, *Medical Apartheid*, 194.
80 Flynn, *Intellectual Morons*, 149.
81 Trombley, *Right To Reproduce*, 215–216.
82 Gordon, *Woman's Body*, 340.
83 Marshall and Donovan, *Blessed Are the Barren*, 288–289.

eugenics involvement. Her "hagiographers, and her most devoted followers in the abortion rights movement, deny and gloss over the eugenicist nature of her program."[84] Angela Franks, in her extensively documented history of Sanger's eugenic involvement, wrote that, in spite of "academic silence...the historical record is quite clear that Sanger's involvement with eugenics included constant collaboration with professional eugenicists," including many of the leading eugenicists in both England and America.[85]

Reasons for rewriting (or ignoring) history include the fear that "exposing birth control's political history to hostile lawmakers and anti-choice lobbyists" could affect their political goals.[86] Other persons hid her past because they were concerned about tarnishing her "perceived labors on behalf of gender equity, self-determination, and redress of economic and personal privation."[87] Even many reprints of Sanger's writings select sections that give a very distorted picture of her beliefs and goals.[88]

Today, Planned Parenthood stresses "family planning," but the fact is, "Sanger sold birth control as the crypto-eugenicist Marie Stopes had, as offering 'freedom from fear'...which in aggregate would contribute to the wider social good. The reasoning was straightforwardly eugenic."[89] To the end of her life, Sanger supported eugenics. In one of her last speeches she "attacked welfare programs for not eliminating the 'feeble minded and unfit' and proposed 'incentive sterilization,'" which was actually a program to bribe the "unfit" to be sterilized.[90]

---

84 Flynn, *Intellectual Morons*, 151.

85 Franks, *Margaret Sanger's Eugenic Legacy*, 126.

86 Ordover, *American Eugenics*, 137.

87 Ordover, *American Eugenics*, 137.

88 For examples, see Pat Andrews, "Margaret Sanger: Women and the New Race," in *Voices of Diversity: Perspectives on American Political Ideals and Institutions* (Guilford: Dushkin Publishing Group, 1995), 100–102, and Diane Ravitch, ed., "Margaret Sanger: The Right to One's Body," in *The American Reader: Words that Moved a Nation* (New York: Harper Collins Publishers, 1990), 249–252.

89 Trombley, *Right to Reproduce*, 215.

90 Cox, *Margaret Sanger*, 101.

## SANGER'S MODERN STATUS AS AN ICON

Surprisingly, Margaret Sanger still is widely admired for her work in the birth control movement. *Time-Life* listed her as one of the most influential persons of the twentieth century.[91] Planned Parenthood today is active throughout the world, and boasts three-quarters of a billion dollars in annual revenue, most of which is paid for by taxpayers.[92] Gloria Steinem wrote a laudatory chapter on Sanger in a *Time* volume that listed the 100 most important Americans. Steinem falsely implied that Sanger opposed eugenics and what it stood for, and lionized her as a heroine of the women's movement.[93] Sanger also was given many honours during her lifetime, including an honorary doctorate of law by Smith College.[94] Ehrlich and Ehrlich wrote that

America's heroine in the family planning movement was Margaret Sanger, a nurse.... Sanger and others who joined her rapidly growing birth control movement (then known as the Birth Control League) led the fight for...legal changes and for support from medical, educational, health and religious organizations. In time, clinics were established throughout the United States, and their activities were expanded.... These additional services are still a part of most family-planning programs, even in underdeveloped countries.[95]

## SUMMARY

Sanger was openly influenced by Darwinists and various social radicals in her highly successful campaign in support of eugenics and against Judeo-Christian morality. She worked hard to produce a socialist state based on eugenics, and her movement thrived partly because it

---

91 Kelly Knauer, *Great People of the 20th Century* (New York: Time Books, 1996), 72–73.

92 Flynn, *Intellectual Morons*, 162.

93 Gloria Steinem, "Margaret Sanger: Her crusade to legalize birth control spurred the movement toward women's liberation," in *Time 100. Leaders & Revolutionaries/ Artists and Entertainers* (New York: Time Books, 1998), 14–15.

94 Cox, *Margaret Sanger*, 100.

95 Paul R. Ehrlich and Anne H. Ehrlich, *Population Resources Environment: Issues in Human Ecology* (San Francisco: W.H. Freeman, 1970), 234.

fulfilled a real need in the early 1900s.[96] Her movement also played a major role in loosening sexual morality, especially among women, contributing to the current high rate of illegitimacy and sexual immorality.

Her goals for society may not have worked in her own life: Flynn claims Sanger died an alcoholic addicted to painkillers, a bitter woman feeling both abandoned and alone, a victim of her youthful, selfish hedonism.[97] She lived and died by her credo published in the *Woman Rebel*, namely "The Right to be Lazy. The Right to be an Unmarried Mother. The Right to Destroy...and the Right to Love."[98]

---

96 Peter Bagge, *Woman Rebel: The Margaret Sanger Story* (New York: Drawn and Quarterly, 2013).

97 Flynn, *Intellectual Morons*, 161.

98 Gray, *Margaret Sanger*, 72.

# 05

# Evolution exploited to justify abortion

||||||||||||||||||||||||||||||||||||||||||||||||||||||||||||||||||||||||||||||||||||||||||||||||||||||||||||||||||||||||||

**T**he importance of Darwinism in justifying abortion originally focused on the "ontogeny recapitulates phylogeny" evolutionary argument. This theory teaches that all human embryos pass through the early stages of our human evolutionary ancestors, from a simple single cell to our putative ape ancestors. This argumentation concludes that abortion is not murder because the human embryo is not human when abortions are usually performed, but rather a fish. Consequently, because the embryo is in the fish stage at this time, abortion does not destroy *human* life, thus is morally justified. This ontogeny argument, although now refuted, still is used by some to support human abortion today.

According to U.S. Centers for Disease Control and Prevention statistics, over 50 million abortions were performed in the United States alone since 1973.[1] Worldwide, the number is estimated at 45.6 million

---

1 Dan Joseph, "Nearly 50 million abortions have been performed in U.S. since *Roe v. Wade* decision legalized abortion," January 25, 2011; http://cnsnews.com/news/article/nearly-50-million-abortions-have-been-performed-us-roe-v-wade-decision-legalized; accessed September 2, 2016.

abortions in 1995, 41.6 million in 2003 and 43.8 million in 2008.[2] Abortion is a major means of birth control in many nations, and about one in five pregnancies ended in abortion in 2008.[3]

The Jewish and Christian teaching against abortion is summarized in Exodus 21:22–23 which says, "if a man hits a pregnant woman and she gives birth prematurely but there is no serious injury, the offender must be fined. But if a serious injury resulting in death occurs, you are to take life for life."[4] For comparison, the 1599 edition of the Geneva Bible[5] says, if a man strikes "a woman with child, so that her child depart from her and death follow not, he shall be surely punished...as the Judges determine. But if death follows, then thou shalt pay life for life."

One of the strongest arguments for abortion is that ontogeny is stated to recapitulate phylogeny, the theory that Darwin saw as one of the most powerful arguments for his evolution theory. British embryologist, Lewis Wolpert, noted that the recapitulation theory is most commonly associated with the German evolutionist, Ernst Haeckel, who is best known by historians for influencing Hitler's eugenics program.[6]

Ontogeny recapitulates phylogeny, often called the biogenetic law, literally means that the stages of human development in the womb recapitulates (repeats) the phylogeny (the physical appearance) of lower animals. Thus, as the embryo develops, it goes through the past adult stages of the entire evolution of life, from the primitive ancient first cell to a modern human. Thus, as humans developed, the adult forms of vertebrates in the evolutionary tree appear in the embryonic forms. Although fully debunked, this belief is still found in some modern biology textbooks.[7]

---

2    Gilda Sedgh, et al., "Induced abortion: Incidence and trends worldwide from 1995 to 2008," *The Lancet* 379 (2012): 625–632.

3    Sedgh, et al., "Induced abortion."

4    Paraphrase by the author (Bergman).

5    A historically very significant translation of the Bible into English, printed in England, which preceded the King James translation by fifty-one years. It was one of the most popular and widely accepted English translations of the Bible.

6    Lewis Wolpert, *The Triumph of the Embryo* (Oxford: Oxford University Press, 1992), 185.

7    E. Ward Kischer and Dianne N. Irving, *The Human Development Hoax: Time to Tell the Truth* (Clinton Township: Gold Leaf Press, 1997), 106; Jerry Bergman, "The

According to evolution, human life began as a single cell that evolved into an amoeba-like creature, then a fish, next an amphibian, then a reptile, a primate and, eventually, after many millions of years, a human being. Consequently, at a certain stage during pregnancy, the human embryo passes through a "fish" stage and even develops "gill-slits" at this stage.

German biologist Ernst Haeckel also argued that the pinnacle of evolution, *Homo sapiens*, "passed through the adult stages of its ancestors, and thus a study of embryonic development could reveal how animals evolved. He coined the phrase 'ontogeny recapitulates phylogeny' to summarize his famous, or rather now infamous, law."[8] The "law" has now been scientifically refuted.[9]

## USE OF "ONTOGENY RECAPITULATES PHYLOGENY" AS JUSTIFICATION FOR ABORTION

The recapitulation theory argument for abortion has a long pedigree—even Ernst Haeckel used it to justify abortion in the late 1800s. Haeckel's views also "became a major cultural force in shaping the militant nationalism in Germany" that led to the Holocaust, which resulted in the loss of over eleven million lives.[10] The recapitulation theory also has been used as an argument to justify abortion even in the late stages of embryo development, because the embryo at this stage is not yet human, but is now at the amphibian stage.[11]

Another factor influencing the acceptance of abortion was Darwin's theory that viewed humans as mere animals. The "intellectual upheaval sparked by the publication of the theory of evolution" resulted in a

---

rise and fall of Haeckel's biogenetic law," *Creation Research Society Quarterly* 37, No. 2 (September 2000): 110–122; Jonathan Wells, "Haeckel's embryos & evolution," *The American Biology Teacher* 61, No. 5 (1999): 345–349.

8  Wolpert, *Triumph of the Embryo*, 185.

9  Michael Richardson, et al., "There is no highly conserved embryonic stage in the vertebrates: Implications for current theories of evolution and development," *Anatomy and Embryology* 196 (1997): 91–106.

10  Richard Milner, *The Encyclopedia of Evolution: Humanity's Search for Its Origins* (New York: Facts on File, 1990), 205.

11  Trevor Major, "Haeckel: The legacy of a lie," *Reason and Revelation* 14 (September 1, 1994): 68–70.

radical change in our view of ourselves:

> Once the weight of scientific evidence in favor of the theory became apparent, practically every earlier justification of man's supreme place in creation and his dominion over the animals had to be rejected. …Human beings now knew that they were not the special creation of God, made in the divine image and set apart from the animals; on the contrary, human beings came to realize that they were animals themselves.[12]

## ENTER PROFESSOR CYRIL CHESNUT MEANS, JR.

This change in the way that many scientists viewed humans was important in setting the stage for legalizing abortion in the United States and the rest of the world. The "most influential pro-abortion legal expert during the 1960s," Cyril Chesnut Means, Jr., "argued that babies are sub-human."[13] Means, a graduate of Harvard University, was professor of constitutional law at New York University Law School and a legal adviser for the American Church Union.

Means argued that another reason why abortion is not murder is because Jews and Christians restricted the command "be fruitful and multiply" to persons who are in the "image" and "likeness" of God, and a fetus is not a living being made in the likeness of God, but is "still at the stage known to zoologists and embryologists as that of subhuman ancestral reminiscence, which, if allowed to pass beyond that stage, will predictably become neither an image nor a likeness of God, but only a grotesque caricature of man."[14]

Means added that "the Roman pontiffs, held that an abortion performed in the early months of pregnancy was not homicide for the very reason that the fetus was not yet a human being" but rather, as argued today, a fish or reptile.[15] Furthermore, embryological research starting with "Haeckel reveals that these medieval rules were right in

---

12 Peter Singer, *Rethinking Life and Death: The Collapse of Our Traditional Ethics* (New York: Oxford University Press, 1995), 214.

13 Marvin Olasky, "Darwin matters," *World*, July 2, 2011, 96.

14 Cyril C. Means, Jr., "Eugenic abortion," *The New York Times*, April 16, 1965, 28.

15 Means, "Eugenic abortion," 28.

principle...and...[e]ugenic abortion is...a program for....preventing the birth of monsters. Now that science has...armed us with the power to detect and prevent monstrous births" this power should be utilized where appropriate.[16] He also argued that because a human fetus is a human *being* does not imply that it is a human *person*, reasoning that a

> heart donor, suffering from irreversible brain damage, is also a living human "being," but he is no longer a human "person." That is why his life may be ended by the excision of his heart for the benefit of another, the donee, who still is a human person. If there can be human "beings" who are nonpersons at one end of the life span, why not also at the other end?[17]

In 1968, Means was appointed by New York Governor Nelson Rockefeller to review New York's abortion law. Means argued that "embryological investigation, beginning with Haeckel," justified the conclusion that a fetus does not become a human being until well into a woman's pregnancy because he argued it is not wrong "to destroy a fetus, still at the stage known to zoologists and embryologists as that of subhuman ancestral reminiscence." In other words, Means implies there was nothing wrong with eliminating a fetus, deformed or otherwise, so long as it was still at a prehuman embryonic stage of evolution.[18]

## THE VALUE OF HUMAN LIFE

Evolutionists contributed in a major way, not only to abortion legalization, but also to the view that human life has no intrinsic value. Robert Williams, president of the Association of American Physicians, said in 1969 that "the fetus has not been shown to be nearer to the human being than is the unborn ape" and that much has been

> made of "quickening" of the fetus by many individuals as a time

---

16  Means, "Eugenic abortion," 28.

17  Cyril C. Means, Jr. "A fetus as person," *The New York Times*, March 17, 1972, 40. Emphasis added.

18  Means, "Eugenic abortion," 28.

when "life begins"…. In reality, quickening symbolizes a very early stage of…the recapitulation of phylogeny by ontogeny; and it takes man a relatively long time to attain the [complete] recapitulation.[19]

Dr. Milan Vuitch argued the claim that human life begins at conception was based on junk science from "one or two centuries ago" when scientists still believed the embryo was fully human. Dr. Vuitch added that scientists now know, thanks to the work of German biologist Ernst Haeckel's "law" of recapitulation, that "in the development of all Mammals [sic] each ontogeny must go through its phylogeny… the development of a single organism must go through the evolutionary pattern of development of its phylum i.e., its 'basic division of animal kingdom.'"[20]

He wrote that, in its early stages, the human embryo looks "very much like any developing zygote of any primate." Only later does it "assume more and more human features." Vuitch even claimed that Haeckel's recapitulation "law…is as valid and true now as it was at the beginning of this century."[21] Victor Eppstein added that, "If the ontogeny of the individual recapitulates the phylogeny of the race…the human fetus at various stages may be closer to a protozoan, a worm, a tadpole, a monkey, than to *Homo sapiens.*"[22]

## THE U.S. SUPREME COURT RULING

Evolutionary arguments were critical in influencing the U.S. Supreme Court to rule in 1973 that abortion was not murder, but rather was a

---

19 Rober H. Williams, "Our role in the generation, modification, and termination of life," *Archives of Internal Medicine* 124, No. 2 (August 1969): 221.

20 Milan M. Vuitch, *Letter to Senator John East dated April 22, 1981, in The Human Life Bill Appendix: Hearings Before the Subcommittee on Separation of Powers of the Committee on the Judiciary, United States Senate, Ninety-Seventh Congress, First Session, on S. 158, a Bill To Provide That Human Life Shall be Deemed to Exist from Conception, April 23, 24; May 20, 21; June 1, 10, 12, and 18. Serial No. J-97-16* (Washington: U. S. Government Printing Office, 1982), 1.

21 Vuitsch, *Letter to Senator John East*, 1–2.

22 Victor Eppstein, "When destroying life is morally justified," *The New York Times,* October 9, 1980, A34.

"constitutional right" held by all women. After the U. S. Supreme Court ruled that abortion was a constitutional right, many other nations followed using much the same logic as the U.S. Supreme Court, including Tunisia (1973), Austria (1974), France (1975), New Zealand (1977), Italy (1978), the Netherlands (1980), Belgium (1990) and, after the reunification of Germany, most abortions in that country were ruled legal up to 12 weeks.

## THE HUMAN LIFE BILL

A few months after President Ronald Reagan took office in 1981, a U.S. Senate Judiciary Committee subcommittee held hearings on the proposed "Human Life Bill" to debate the view that life begins at conception.[23] In the debates, proponents of evolution "contributed mightily" to the legalization of abortion by arguing for the theory Ernst Haeckel[24] called "'the recapitulation of phylogeny by ontogeny'—the mistaken theory that an unborn child's development mimics purported evolutionary progress."[25]

The subcommittee, chaired by Senator John East, heard eight days of testimony from an array of scientists, lawyers, ethicists, theologians and political activists on both sides of the issue. One of the pro-choice advocates, University of Michigan Medical School Department of Genetics chairman, Dr. James Neel, testified on May 20 that he found "it impossible to address...the issue of when, following conception, actual human life begins without some reference to the concepts of evolution."[26]

This testimony was significant because Neel, a National Academy of Sciences member, and then president-elect of the Sixth International

---

23 James Neel, *The Human Life Bill: Hearings Before the Subcommittee on Separation of Powers of the Committee on the Judiciary, United States Senate, Ninety-Seventh Congress, First Session, on S. 158, a Bill to Provide that Human Life Shall be Deemed to Exist from Conception, Serial No. J-97-16, May 20, 1981* (Washington, D.C.: U.S. Government Printing Office, 1982).

24 Nick Hopwood, *Haeckel's Embryos: Images, Evolution and Fraud* (Chicago: University of Chicago Press, 2015).

25 Olasky, "Darwin matters," 96.

26 Quoted by John G. West, *Darwin Day in America: How Our Politics and Culture Have Been Dehumanized in the Name of Science* (Wilmington: ISI Books, 2007), 325.

Congress of Human Genetics, represented the elite American scientific and medical establishment. Dr. Neel argued that evolutionists have proven that the early embryo passes

> through some of the stages in the evolutionary history of our species...at about 30 days after conception, the developing embryo has a series of parallel ridges and grooves in its neck... corresponding to the gill slits and gill arches of fish.... It has a caudal appendage which is quite simply labeled "tail" in many textbooks of human embryology.[27]

Professor Neel added,

> for much of their development they [humans] were equivalent to [the] earlier stages in man's evolutionary history... [Thus] it is most difficult to state, as a scientist, just when in early fetal development human personhood begins, just as I would find it impossible to say exactly when in evolution we passed over the threshold that divides us from the other living creatures.[28]

## EVOLUTIONARY ARGUMENT USED AFTER COURT RULING TO JUSTIFY ABORTION

Biology professor, Frank Zindler, an active pro-abortion advocate in the 1980s, noted that it required at least "ten days after fertilization for the conception to become anything more than a hollow ball of cells at the stage of development of certain colonial algae," and a heart begins to beat only at the fourth week, "and then it is two-chambered like that of a fish.... Hemisphere development reaches reptile-grade during the fourth month and primitive mammal-grade (opossum) during the sixth month."[29]

To justify the conclusion that abortion is similar to killing a fish, not a human, Zindler spins the following story, much of which is now

---

27 Quoted by West, *Darwin Day in America*, 325.

28 Quoted by West, *Darwin Day in America*, 325.

29 Frank R. Zindler, "An acorn is not an oak tree," *American Atheist* 27, No. 8 (1985): 28.

known to be incorrect. He writes that after the early embryo stage, a prominent yolk-sac exists in humans that is typical of a reptile and

> in the neck region we see prominent gill-clefts. The arteries carrying blood from the heart to the gills recapitulate in minute detail the aortic-arch structures of fishes. …This alleged person…has traces of pronephric kidneys, the type found in the most primitive vertebrate known to science, the hermaphroditic hagfish![30]

Zindler added,

> the brain of the three-month-old fetus is still at the reptile grade of development…. At this stage, behavior is entirely reflexive, as in earth worms. Only long after birth will the nervous system be developed sufficiently for the perception [that makes it human].[31]

In an article titled "The Question of Abortion," the late Cornell University professor, Carl Sagan, and his wife, Ann Druyan, also defended abortion based on Haeckel's "law" of recapitulation.[32] In response to the Sagan article, University of Arizona Medical School embryologist, Dr. Ward Kischer, noted that Sagan is an astrophysicist and astronomer and that Kischer could not find any indication that Sagan had formal training in human embryology. Professor Kischer wrote that in the article, Sagan and Druyan

> made several major errors concerning human development, but he also inferred that there are developmental stages in the case of the human which "resemble a worm, reptile, and a pig" [describing]…a four-week-old embryo with "something like the gill arches of a fish or an amphibian" and…a "pronounced

---

30 Zindler, "Acorn," 28.
31 Zindler, "Acorn," 28.
32 Carl Sagan and Ann Druyan, "The question of abortion: A search for answers," *Parade Magazine*, Sunday, April 22, 1990, 4–8.

tail"…in the case of human embryo, *no* gill slits ever appear. Further, the human embryo never develops a tail.[33]

Kischer added that, after the article by Sagan and Druyan appeared in *Parade*, he phoned *Parade*'s editorial office and spoke to managing editor Larry Smith to "complain about the many errors in the article and asked if *Parade* would publish a brief article of corrections. I was told they would not. Furthermore, Smith became very defensive concerning the Sagans."[34] Kischer concluded that Sagan and the editors of *Parade* were attempting to "build a consensus based on misrepresentations."[35]

Professor Kischer then carefully searched the literature for similar misrepresentations and, to his astonishment, found numerous articles written "by psychologists, philosophers, and theologians which purported to invoke embryological facts but which were, in fact, misrepresentations and outright falsehoods." He also could not find in the literature "embryologists who were answering these distorted claims."[36]

## OPPOSITION TO PRO-ABORTION ARGUMENTS

The opposition included Seton Hall University professor John Oesterreicher. He responded to the recapitulation claim by explaining that, however "superficially similar the embryos of various species may be…the human fetus does at no time pass through the stage of an amoeba, worm, fish or ape. Hence…German embryologist E. Blechschmidt names [this idea] a 'catastrophic error in the history of natural science.'"[37]

Erich Blechschmidt, a director of Göttingen University's Anatomical Institute from 1942 until 1973, was a prominent embryologist. He wrote that, until the first embryonic stages of humans were researched in detail,

---

33 Kischer and Irving, *Human Development Hoax*, 105–106.

34 Kischer and Irving, *Human Development Hoax*, 106.

35 Kischer and Irving, *Human Development Hoax*, 106.

36 Kischer and Irving, *Human Development Hoax*, 106.

37 John M. Oesterreicher, "Abortion, evolution and an untenable biogenetic law," *The New York Times*, October 24, 1980, A32.

it was believed legitimate to infer the development of man from the early development of animals...[and] that the embryos of all animals resemble each other in their early stages and therefore do not importantly differ from each other, even though it was known, for example, what differences exist between a chicken egg and a frog egg.[38]

Research completed in Professor Blechschmidt's world-class embryology lab involving analyzing thousands of human embryos and cross sections of embryo tissue now stored in the world famous Blechschmidt Human-Embryological Documentation Collection, has refuted Haeckel's biogenetic law, which Blechschmidt concluded "was one of the greatest errors in the first endeavors to give biology a scientific foundation."[39] Further,

today we know that each developmental stage of the human being is demonstrably a characteristically human one...[and a human] does not *become* a human being but rather is such from the instant of fertilization. During the entire ontogenesis, no single break can be demonstrated, either in the sense of leap from the lifeless to the live...the individual specificity of each human being remains preserved from fertilization to death.[40]

## NO FISH GILLS
Lewis Wolpert's research confirmed that the resemblance of these pharyngeal folds to fish "gill clefts" is "illusory."[41] In fact, "Human embryos merely exhibit folds in the neck area, not gill-slits." While in fish embryos pharyngeal folds do eventually "develop into gills...in a reptile, mammal, or bird they develop into other structures entirely."[42]

---

38 Erich Blechschmidt, "Human Being from the Very First," in *New Perspectives on Human Abortion*, ed. Thomas W. Hilgers, et al. (Washington: University Publications of America, 1981), 6.
39 Blechschmidt, "Human Being from the Very First," 7.
40 Blechschmidt, "Human Being from the Very First," 7. Emphasis in original.
41 Wolpert, *Triumph of the Embryo*, 185.
42 Wells, *Icons of Evolution*, 106.

Wolpert concluded that human embryos "do not pass through the adult stages of their ancestors; ontogeny does not recapitulate phylogeny."[43] Wolpert muses that it is difficult "to understand why this theory should have received such wide support. Even Freud was greatly influenced, and his ideas on the *id* and *ego* and stages in psychic development reflect Haeckel's view."[44]

Nevertheless, numerous reputable lawyers, doctors and scientists have continued to cite the recapitulation argument for abortion long after it was refuted. Recapitulation also "was invoked by some abortion-rights advocates as 'scientific' evidence that aborting a human embryo or fetus was no more immoral than destroying a fish."[45]

The problem is, in spite of this research, as Columbia University biologist Walter Bock noted,

the biogenetic law has become so deeply rooted in biological thought that it cannot be weeded out in spite of its having been demonstrated to be wrong by numerous subsequent scholars. Even today, both subtle and overt uses of the biogenetic law are frequently encountered in the general biological literature as well as in more specialized evolutionary and systematic studies.[46]

## THE RACIST ASPECTS OF ABORTION

Abortion "is a greater cause of death for African-Americans than heart disease, cancer, diabetes, AIDS, and violence combined.... [A]bout 40 to 50 percent of all African-American babies" are aborted each year.[47] Blacks account for 40.6 percent of the total number of abortions compared to 51.6 for whites and 7.8 percent for other groups, but blacks comprise only 13 percent of the population.[48]

---

43  Wolpert, *Triumph of the Embryo*, 185.

44  Wolpert, *Triumph of the Embryo*, 185.

45  West, *Darwin Day in America*, 327.

46  Walter Bock, "Evolution by orderly law," *Science* 164 (May 1969): 684.

47  Marvin Olasky, "Non-selective," *World*, December 31, 2011, 8.

48  Karen Pazol, Andreea A. Creanga and Denise J. Jamieson, "Abortion surveillance – United States, 2012: Surveillance summaries," *Centers for Disease Control and Prevention, Morbidity and Mortality Weekly Report*, November 27, 2015); http://www.cdc.gov/mmwr/preview/mmwrhtml/ss6410a1.htm; accessed November 3, 2016.

Darwinism had a profound influence on Planned Parenthood founder Margaret Sanger's thinking, including her conversion to, and active support of, eugenics.[49] Sanger was specifically concerned about reducing the population of "less fit" humans, including members of "inferior races" such as "Negroes." As Sanger stressed in a talk she presented at the Fifth International Birth Control Conference, the end goal of her movement was to produce a superior race by the "evolution of humanity itself."[50]

To produce a superior race, Sanger advocated euthanasia, segregation in work camps, sterilization and abortion of those judged by eugenicists to be inferior humans.[51] Sanger believed the "Negro district" was the "headquarters for the criminal element" of society and concluded that, as the title of a book by a member of her board proclaimed, *The Rising Tide of Color Against White World Supremacy*, was a rise that had to be stemmed.[52] To deal with the resistance problem by the black population, Sanger recruited black doctors, nurses, ministers and social workers "in order to gain black patients' trust…to limit or even erase the black presence in America."[53]

## AFTER-BIRTH ABORTIONS

The logical next step in the abortion movement is *after-birth* or *postpartum* abortions, killing a child *after* he or she is born. One study of this practice by Sara Blaffer Hrdy concluded that infanticide is part of the maternal instinct programmed into our genes by evolution.[54] Hrdy argued that if female animals perceive that they do not have the resources to rear their infants, mothers aborted, abandoned and even

---

49 Jerry Bergman, "Birth control leader Margaret Sanger: Darwinist, racist and eugenicist," *Journal of Creation* 22, No. 3 (2008): 62–67; Rebecca Messall, "The long road of eugenics: From Rockefeller to *Roe v. Wade*," *The Human Life Review* (Fall 2004): 33–96; Sanger, *Women and the New Race*.

50 Sanger, "Individual and Family Aspects," 31.

51 Franks, *Margaret Sanger's Eugenic Legacy*; Flynn, *Intellectual Morons*, 150.

52 Washington, *Medical Apartheid*, 196.

53 Washington, *Medical Apartheid*, 197–198.

54 Claudia Glenn Dowling, "Sarah Blaffer Hrdy: The scientist who destroyed our quaint concept of what a mother ought to be comes to terms with her own life," *Discover* 24, No. 3 (March 2003): 41.

killed their offspring. She then astonishingly applied this theory to *Homo sapiens*.[55]

Author Claudia Glenn Dowling maintained that a child is very costly to rear—requiring 13 million calories to attain adulthood—that "mothers since the Pleistocene have made calculated decisions about when, how, and whether to rear them."[56] Hrdy promoted this hypothesis in her 697-page tome titled *Mother Nature: Natural Selection and the Female of the Species* published in 1999. The next step was to openly apply eugenics to improve humans as had been advocated by Darwin's cousin, Francis Galton, who founded this pseudo-science in the late 1800s.

This next step was by medical ethicists affiliated with England's Oxford University. They argued, "Parents should be allowed to have their newborn babies killed because they are 'morally irrelevant,' and ending their lives is no different than abortion."[57] They also believe that "newborn babies are not 'actual persons' and have no 'moral right to life.'" For this reason, these academics from leading universities argued that "parents should be able to have their baby killed if it turns out to be disabled when it is born."[58]

These ideas were recently championed in the United States by Princeton University professor of ethics, Peter Singer, who advocates the view that newborns lack the essential characteristics of person-hood, by which he means a being that "is capable of anticipating the future, of having wants and desires for the future" and, for this reason, "Newborn human babies have no sense of their own existence over time. So killing a newborn baby is never equivalent to killing a person."[59]

If this is true then, in order to be consistent, some could add that killing one in sleep should be legal as well since in sleep one has no sense of his own awake existence. Singer also argued that if they feel

---

55  Sara Blaffer Hrdy, *Mother Nature: Natural Selection and the Female of the Species* (London: Chatto & Windus, 1999).

56  Dowling, "Sarah Blaffer Hrdy," 42.

57  Stephen Adams, "Killing babies no different from abortion, experts say," *The Telegraph*, March 1, 2012, 1.

58  Adams, "Killing babies," 1.

59  Peter Singer, "Peter Singer FAQ," http://www.petersinger.info/faq/; accessed September 4, 2016.

it does not possess the level of health that they expected or desired, a parent should be able to take a newborn back to the hospital to be euthanized within a certain period of time, such as 28 days.[60] This program has "eerie parallels between Singer's views and those of the medical establishment of the early Hitler days."[61] In fact, the Nazis allowed a three-year grace period instead of 28 days as suggested by Professor Singer.

Professor Alberto Giubilini, who studied at Cambridge University, recently presented a talk at Oxford University titled, "What is the problem with euthanasia?" He gave the exact same reasoning that Hitler and the Nazis used to justify murdering many thousands of handicapped persons, some of whom had only minor handicaps. Professor Julian Savulescu admitted that "arguments in favor of killing newborns" were "largely not new," noting that other scholars had widely defended the same practice that he and Professor Giubilini advocate.[62]

An article titled, "After-Birth Abortion: Why Should the Baby Live?" written by Giubilini and another one of Professor Savulescu's former associates, Francesca Minerva, concluded, "The moral status of an infant is equivalent to that of a fetus in the sense that both lack those properties that justify the attribution of a right to life to an individual."[63] Furthermore, they argue, as does Dr. Singer, that newborns are not "actual persons," that have "a moral right to life" but are only "potential persons."[64] The authors define "person" as "an individual who is capable of attributing to her own existence some (at least) basic value such that being deprived of this existence represents a loss to her."[65]

The authors concluded that "after-birth abortion" (killing newborns) "should be permissible in all cases where abortion is [legal],

---

60 Peter Singer and Helga Kuhse, *Should the Baby Live? The Problem of Handicapped Infants* (New York: Oxford University Press, 1986); Singer, *Rethinking Life and Death*; John Leo, "Singer's final solution," *U.S. News and World Report*, October 4, 1999, 17.

61 Leo, "Singer's final solution," 17.

62 Adams, "Killing babies," 1.

63 Alberto Giubilini and Francesca Minerva, "After-birth abortion: Why should the baby live?" *Journal of Medical Ethics* (February 2012): 2.

64 Adams, "Killing babies," 1.

65 Adams, "Killing babies," 1.

including cases where the newborn is not disabled."[66] They used the phrase "after-birth abortion" rather than "infanticide" to emphasize that "the moral status of the individual killed is comparable with that of a fetus."[67]

Citing the European statistic that only 64 percent of Down syndrome cases are diagnosed by prenatal testing, thus many Down babies are born alive; therefore, they also argued that parents should be able to have their "baby killed if it turned out to be disabled." They reason that killing Down syndrome children is ethical because to "bring up such children might be an unbearable burden on the family and on society as a whole, when the state economically provides for their care" as it does in many socialist countries.[68]

The authors have received much opposition since their article was published. Professor Savulescu responded to those making abusive and threatening comments about their postpartum abortion proposal by stating they were "fanatics opposed to the very values of a liberal society."[69]

Dr. Trevor Stammers, director of medical ethics at St Mary's University College, who is opposed to after-birth abortions, said about the proposal, that if a mother smothers her "child with a blanket, we say 'It doesn't matter, she can get another one,' …What these colleagues are spelling out is what would be the inevitable end point of a road that ethical philosophers in the States and Australia have all been treading for a long time and there is certainly nothing new [in this argument]."[70] Referring to the "after-birth abortion" expression, Dr. Stammers added: "This is just verbal manipulation," and one could just as well refer to abortions as "ante-natal infanticide."[71]

Scholars promoting this view include James Rachels in his book

66 Adams, "Killing babies," 1.

67 Giubilini and Minerva, "After-birth abortion," 2.

68 Giubilini and Minerva, "After-birth abortion," 1–2.

69 Adams, "Killing babies."

70 Quoted in John Begin, "Abortion should be legal through infancy, medical ethicists argue," Policy.mic, August 9, 2012; https://mic.com/articles/12443/abortion-should-be-legal-through-infancy-medical-ethicists-argue#.Fvrwf6EgB; accessed September 4, 2016.

71 Quoted in Adams, "Killing babies," 1.

*Created from Animals: The Moral Implications of Darwinism*. Rachels argues for the societal permissibility, not only of abortion, but also of voluntary euthanasia and infanticide for disabled babies. He concluded that evolution makes the sanctity-of-life position untenable because evolution requires the weak to perish in order to allow for the numerical increase of evolutionarily superior individuals.[72]

It is rather mind-boggling to realize that after the horrendous lesson of the Holocaust, eugenic thinking is alive and well in the West. But eugenic thinking has reappeared because evolution is still widely promoted in both the media and education as the origins of all life myth. Another reason is the elite believe they have the right to formulate their own definition of when human life begins and ends. Or, to put it more bluntly, to decide who gets to live and who dies.

## SUMMARY

The abortion issue has always been a question of how one views the embryo. Is it only a mass of protoplasm, a fish or a human person? The abortion argument is essentially "it is not human life that is sacred. It is the human person, and the early fetus is not a human person."[73] This argument was bolstered enormously by the biogenetic teaching that it is in the fish stage, or some other animal stage—a view that has now been thoroughly discredited.

And so justification for abortion was both historically, and currently, based partly on a now disproved theory, namely that ontogeny recapitulates phylogeny. This view argues that the child is not human, but in the fish stage when an abortion is normally performed; consequently, killing a child during the first three months of a pregnancy is only destroying a fish-like creature, nothing more.

It was a small step from there to legalizing abortion and to the position of some leading scholars to legalize infanticide up to a certain age, such as 28 days after birth—a position that is now being debated. The Judeo-Christian mark for the beginning of both life and person-

---

72 James Rachels, *Created from Animals: The Moral Implications of Darwinism* (New York: Oxford University Press, 1990).

73 Linda Greenhouse, "Constitutional question: Is there a right to abortion?" *The New York Times Magazine*, January 25, 1970, 90–91.

hood is at conception and stands in marked contrast to the arbitrary decisions, which have been discussed in this chapter, about when life and personhood begins.

# 06

# The failure of psychoanalysis– Freud and Darwinism

||||||||||||||||||||||||||||||||||||||||||||||||||||||||||||||||||||||||||||||||||||||||||||||||||||||||||||||||||||||||||||||||||||||||||||||||||||||

**A** review of the influence of Darwinism on psychoanalysis, specifically Freudian psychology, found that Darwin had a major influence on both its founder Sigmund Freud (1856–1939) and the development of his human behaviour theory. Freud has, in turn, profoundly influenced the psychology field. Classical Freudian psychology now has been widely discredited, and research has empirically shown much of the theory behind psychoanalysis to be erroneous. The fact is, therapy based on Classical Freudian psychology is ineffective for most patients suffering from problems of living. Today, classical Freudian thought is rarely openly used to help patients; however, much neo-Freudian thought still influences psychiatry and, to a lesser extent, psychology. The adverse influence of psychoanalysis on society and Freud's hostility against theistic religion is also reviewed.

## THE PSYCHOLOGY FIELD IS CONCERNED WITH HELPING PEOPLE

The branch of psychology that focuses on helping people, called counselling psychology, has only been in existence for little over a century and a half. Before this, most people received advice in the modern sense of counselling from trusted friends, parents, grandparents, clergy or respected persons in the community. As the medical field developed, medical doctors became a common source for help in dealing with a wide variety of psychological, marital and other personal problems. Professional psychologists, psychiatrists and counsellors eventually largely replaced both medical doctors and clergy as a major source of psychological advice.

One of the earliest branches of psychology was psychoanalysis, a theory of personality and treatment founded by the physician Sigmund Freud. Often called Freudian psychology, it has influenced the therapy world, especially psychiatry, for almost a century, but today has largely been discredited. The story of the introduction of psychoanalysis in America, as told by Os Guinness, is as follows:

> In 1909, two arrivals from Europe stood at the rail of their ship as it...entered New York harbor. The older one, a fifty-three-year-old Jew born in Moravia, poked the younger man from Switzerland.... The speaker was Sigmund Freud. His companion was his...disciple Carl Gustav Jung. And [their theory] in the form of psychoanalysis and its legacy...has had as much impact on the United States in the twentieth century as any one set of human ideas and words. ...Within six years of their arrival, their ideas had "set up a reverberation in human thought and conduct."...
>
> [In time what] were once the esoteric ideas of a small and controversial European elite have mushroomed in America into a dominant academic discipline and a vast, lucrative industry. More than five hundred brand-name therapies now jostle to compete for millions of clients in an expanding market of McFreud franchises and independent outlets that pull in more than $4 billion a year. ...The couch has become as American as the baseball diamond and the golden arches.[1]

The result was, the United States became the

---

1    Os Guinness, "America's Last Men and Their Magnificent Talking Cure," in *No God But God: Breaking With the Idols of Our Age*, ed. Os Guinness and John Steel (Chicago: Moody, 1992), 111.

## Sigmund Freud (1856–1939)

Though now largely discredited, Freud's theory of psychoanalysis was influenced significantly by Darwin's theory of evolution. Unfortunately, Freud's profound influence on the fields of psychiatry and psychotherapy has cast a long shadow. Photography by Max Halberstadt, 1921.

world capital of psychological-mindedness.... Although America had only six percent of the world's population, it boasted over a third of the world's psychiatrists and over half the world's clinical psychologists.... Eighty million...Americans have now sought help from therapists. An estimated ten million are doing so every year.[2]

## DARWINIAN ROOTS OF THE MODERN PSYCHOTHERAPY MOVEMENT

Freud's academic studies were also greatly influenced by "such world-famous scientists as...Darwin."[3] For example, "much of Freud's philosophy and general scientific attitude," including his conclusion that the human mind is "ultimately physical (or, rather, physiological), came from such great scientific theorists as Darwin."[4]

Darwin's writings, and those of his many disciples, had a major influence, not only on psychoanalysis, but also on the entire field of psychology.[5] Freud wrote "the theories of Darwin...strongly attracted me, for they held out hopes of extraordinary advance in our understanding of the world" for psychoanalysis.[6] As a result, "Freud took Darwinian biology as his foundation" to develop his psychoanalysis system.[7] One can easily access the enormous influence of Darwin on psychology as a whole, by reviewing the writings of the founders of the modern psychology field, such as Wilhelm Wundt and William James.

The most important leader of psychology at this time, Sigmund Freud, called his therapy method *psychoanalysis*, meaning to treat by analyzing the psyche or mind. His system gave birth to, or highly influenced, almost all counselling theories, including the various psychotherapies still in existence today. This includes the rational emotive approach, as well as traditional psychotherapy approaches, not only

---

2   Guinness, "America's Last Men," 111–112.

3   Paul C. Vitz, *Sigmund Freud's Christian Unconscious* (New York: The Guilford Press, 1988), 48.

4   Vitz, *Freud's Christian Unconscious*, 72.

5   Duane Schultz, *A History of Modern Psychology* (New York: Academic Press, 1972).

6   Quoted in Ernest Jones, *The Life and Work of Sigmund Freud, Volume 1: The Formative Years and The Great Discoveries 1856–1900* (New York: Basic Books, 1981), 28.

7   West, *Darwin Day in America*, 55.

Freudian, but also other psychotherapeutic therapies.[8] A major exception would be the behaviourists. Freud had little or no effect on behaviourism, but Darwin had an enormous influence, as is very apparent in Harvard's B.F. Skinner's writings.[9] Freud made it clear that "the study of evolution" was an essential part of the training required to become a psychoanalyst. Furthermore, Darwinian theory was "essential to psychoanalysis" and "has always been present in Freud's writings, albeit never explicitly."[10] Thus, those Freudian supporters who studied Freud's works were also, at least indirectly, influenced by Darwinism. It was "Darwin who pointed the way, and the excitement caused by Darwin's work was at its height in the [eighteen] seventies in every country in Europe" when psychoanalysis was developing.[11]

Freud's theory also was based on the ideas of his professional contemporaries, many of whom, such as Ivan Pavlov and Edward Titchener, also were heavily influenced by Darwin's evolutionary theory.[12] Psychologist Paul Vitz concluded that we should "never lose sight of the fact that Freud was operating in a medical environment, where... Darwinian theory" was the common model "from which one approached an understanding of the mental life."[13] Darwin had such a profound influence on Freud's psychoanalytic theories that Freud opined, in his view, Darwin's *On the Origin of Species* was one of the most significant books ever published.[14]

Freud was so involved in trying to document Darwinism in the lab that, by his third year in college, he was spending most of his time in the zoological experimental station working under Ernst Wilhelm von Brücke. By this time he had decided on a career, not in medicine as

8  C.H. Patterson, *Theories of Counseling and Psychotherapy* (New York: Harper and Row, 1966).

9  B.F. Skinner, *Beyond Freedom and Dignity* (Westminster: Random House, 1971).

10  Lucille B. Ritvo, *Darwin's Influence on Freud: A Tale of Two Sciences* (New Haven: Yale University Press, 1990), 2.

11  Jones, *Life and Work of Sigmund Freud*, 1:31.

12  E.M. Thornton, *The Freudian Fallacy* (Garden City: The Dial Press/Double Day, 1983), xv; William S. Sahakian, *History of Psychology* (Itasca: Peacock Publishers, 1968).

13  Vitz, *Freud's Christian Unconscious*, 72.

14  Vitz, *Freud's Christian Unconscious*, 115.

he originally had planned, but rather in research, specifically on the "problems of comparative anatomy posed by Darwin's evolutionary theory."[15] It took Freud eight years, instead of the usual five, to qualify as a physician because he also pursued extensive graduate work in zoology, focusing on Darwinism.[16]

In Freud's view, Darwin was not just a scientist, but rather "the great Darwin." Freud's level of enthusiasm as a follower of Darwin was such that he was called the "scientific heir to Darwin."[17] Freud earned his Ph.D. in philosophy and zoology under Franz Brentano, whom Freud considered "a Darwinist and...a genius."[18] Freud also worked with Carl Claus, one of "Darwin's most effective and prolific propagandists in the German language."[19]

In his writings, Freud referred directly to Darwin and his work more than twenty times, "always very positively."[20] Freud was especially interested in Darwin's work in the psychology field —for example, in his book *Expression of Emotions in Man and Animals*, Darwin taught the self-preservation theory, an idea that was central to his survival-of-the-fittest concept. This theory, developed by Freud and his followers from Darwinism, was based on the idea that all behaviour was the result of a few basic animal drives originally produced by natural selection to facilitate survival.

Darwin argued that all animals have a built-in innate self-preservation instinct that he called the *libido*, which included both the struggle to survive and the drive to reproduce. The animals that both survived this struggle, and left more offspring, were more likely to pass on to their progeny their "survival" genes, including those that caused a high sexual drive, compared to animals that left fewer offspring. By this means, Darwinism argued, sexual selection selected for sexual drive strength, causing sex to become the main drive in sexual animals.

---

15 Thornton, *Freudian Fallacy*, 13.

16 Thornton, *Freudian Fallacy*, 10.

17 Grace Adams, *Psychology: Science or Superstition?* (New York: Covici Frede, 1931), 118.

18 Vitz, *Freud's Christian Unconscious*, 52.

19 Peter Gay, *Freud: A Life for Our Time* (New York: W.W. Norton & Company, 1998), 31.

20 Ritvo, *Darwin's Influence on Freud*, 3.

For this reason, the sex drive became central in Freud's theory of human behaviour, and this is the reason why his system is termed *psychosexual theory*, and the application of his theory is called *psychosexual analysis* or *psychoanalysis*.[21] Freudian concepts, such as libido, id, and/or psychosexual stages, all are derived from this Darwinian conclusion.

As Darwin speculated about our evolutionary past, so too prominent psychology leaders have speculated about "which seemingly human traits might have been received intact from the dim simian past" of humans.[22] One of the Darwinian ideas that Freud accepted was the now discredited inheritance of acquired characteristics, including the inheritance of mental traits, an idea that had a profound influence on psychology up to almost the 1950s.[23]

As a youth, Freud, although very influenced by both Catholic and Judaic traditions, after he was taught Darwinism in school, totally rejected theism and became a militant atheist.[24] Nonetheless, Freud openly acknowledged that his Bible reading when a youth "had a decisive influence on his intellectual and spiritual development."[25] He rationalized that his "scientific" theory of psychoanalysis was rejected by many persons, not because of science, but rather because "powerful human feelings are hurt" by psychoanalysis theory, noting that

Darwin's theory of descent met with the same fate [as psychoanalysis], since it tore down the barrier that had been arrogantly set up between men and beasts...in an earlier paper.... I showed how the psycho-analytic view of the relation of the conscious ego to an overpowering unconscious was a severe blow to human self-love. I described this as the *psychological* blow to men's narcissism and compared it with the *biological* blow delivered by the

21 Franz G. Alexander and Sheldon T. Selesnick, *The History of Psychiatry: An Evaluation of Psychiatric Thought and Practice from Prehistoric Times to the Present* (New York: Harper & Row, 1966), 11.

22 Adams, *Psychology: Science or Superstition?*, 214.

23 Ritvo, *Darwin's Influence on Freud*, 74.

24 Jonathan Miller, ed., *Freud: The Man, His World, His Influence* (Boston: Little, Brown and Company, 1972), 7.

25 Miller, ed., *Freud: The Man*, 7.

theory of descent and the earlier *cosmological* blow aimed at it by the discovery of Copernicus.[26]

Furthermore, the evolution of life doctrine means that "no spirits, essences, or entelechies, no superior plans or ultimate purposes are at work" in the creation of humans. Thus,

> physical energies alone cause effects—somehow. Darwin had shown that there was hope of achieving in a near future some concrete insight into the "How" of evolution. The enthusiasts were convinced that Darwin had shown more than that—in fact had already told the full story. While the skeptics and the enthusiasts fought with each other, the active researchers were busy... putting together the family trees of the organisms, closing gaps, rearranging the taxonomic systems of plants and animals according to genetic relationships, discovering transformation series, finding behind the manifest diversities the homologous identities.[27]

Freud's acceptance of both Darwinism and atheism influenced his low view of humans in general. In his words,

> I have found little that is "good" about human beings on the whole. In my experience most of them are trash.... If we are to talk of ethics, I subscribe to a high ideal from which most of the human beings I have come across depart most lamentably.[28]

## THE PSYCHOANALYSIS TECHNIQUE

At the core of psychoanalysis is free-association, a technique encouraging patients to talk about whatever comes to their mind. The goal is

---

26 Sigmund Freud, *The Standard Edition of the Complete Psychological Works of Sigmund Freud: Volume XIX (1923–1925) The Ego and the Id and Other Works*, ed. James Strachey (London: The Hogarth Press and The Institute of Psycho-Analysis, 1961), 221.

27 Jones, *Life and Work of Sigmund Freud*, 1:42.

28 Ernst L. Freud and Heinrich Meng, ed., *Psychoanalysis and Faith: The Letters of Sigmund Freud & Oskar Pfister*, trans. Eric Mosbacher (New York: Basic Books, 1963), 61–62.

to uncover the "unconscious roots of human behavior in man's... ineradicable animal nature."[29] One of the therapist's major roles is to provide an accepting, supportive environment that allows the patient to shed inhibitions, open up, and mentally roam freely without direction or censorship. To help patients free-associate, they lie on a couch to encourage them to relax. The therapist then sits behind the patient when taking case notes so as to be out of his or her view in order to avoid distracting the patient. This approach is largely limited to fairly articulate patients with relatively mild symptoms: schizophrenics and most psychotic patients are rarely able to undergo psychoanalysis.

Freud taught that innate biological drives, especially sex, ultimately determine all behaviour:

> After Darwin had shaken mankind's self-esteem by proposing a theory demonstrating human kinship with other animals, Freud shattered it still further by asserting that people were far less a master in their own mental house than they had always supposed.[30]

In short, Freud taught "the ego is largely the servant of unconscious and uncontrollable forces of the mind," an idea that actually often hindered helping people with problems.[31]

## OTHER PSYCHOLOGICAL TECHNIQUES

One major problem with this approach is that it may take years to get to the root of the putative unconscious drives causing psychological problems. As a result, it is very expensive and available primarily to the wealthy, or those with sufficient insurance coverage. For this and other reasons, most psychiatrists now have abandoned traditional psychoanalysis and use a much more directive therapeutic approach, especially psychoactive drugs. An over-simplification of the common direct techniques is the client centred, nondirected Rogerian approach,

---

29 West, *Darwin Day in America*, 55.

30 Shmuel Boteach, *Moses of Oxford: A Jewish Vision of a University and Its Life*, vol. 2 (London: André Deutsch, 1994), 510.

31 Gay, *Freud: A Life for Our Time*, 449.

named after its founder, Carl Rogers. This approach involves the therapist helping you to solve your own "problems."

In contrast, in the Rational Emotive approach founded by Albert Ellis, the therapist determines your "problem" and then directs you to the best means of solving it. The Rogerian method assumes that you have the answer to your own problems and the therapist only has to help you find it. Conversely, therapists using the Rational Emotive approach believe that the therapist has the answer to your problems, and his role is to convince you of this. Many therapists today use an eclectic approach that blends these two and other theories.

Freud also taught that the Oedipus complex for males and the Electra complex for females were central to human development. The theory teaches that a universal, usually unconscious, drive exists for a child to displace in some way his or her same-sexed parent and marry his or her opposite-sexed parent. The Oedipus complex implied that sons are sexually attracted to their mothers and have a death wish against their fathers to destroy their rival for her affection.[32] This drive is believed by psychoanalysts to commonly influence behaviour.

University of Michigan Professor Richard Stuart wrote that, depending on the therapist's assumptions, a psychoanalyst might try to help a depressed patient in one of several ways. For example, a patient may be judged as suffering from "an intense lack of self-esteem associated with faulty ego development," while another therapist might judge the patient as suffering from "a severe characterological problem, with features of anger, passive-aggressive qualities," yet a third therapist might view the patient as "both pre-Oedipal and hence pre-sexual in orientation," causing the patient to retreat from adult sexual-social responsibilities.[33] These "diagnoses," all of which are very questionable, often lead to very different treatments.

An example of the application of Freud's approach to treatment is the case of a young woman called Dora who first came to Freud suffering from fainting fits, convulsions and delirium. Her symptoms

---

32 Ernst Jones, *The Life and Work of Sigmund Freud, Volume 2: Years of Maturity 1901–1919* (New York: Basic Books, 1981), 359.

33 Richard B. Stuart, *Trick or Treatment: How and When Psychotherapy Fails* (Champaign: Research Press, 1970), 5.

suggested an organic cause because Dora had grown up with a tubercular father who had contracted syphilis before her birth and both father and daughter manifested very similar asthmatic conditions. In contrast, Freud "characteristically described patients such as her as a neurotic…weak-willed woman who was repressing her subconscious wish to sleep with her father."[34] When Dora related that she had recently suffered from an appendicitis attack, Freud concluded that these attacks were not real, but rather

> a hysterical pregnancy expressing her unconscious sexual fantasies. Her coughing…Freud [concluded], was just another timid female love-song. He finally diagnosed her painful asthmatic symptoms as a reaction to hearing her father wheeze while copulating. Reading the whole case history of Dora without prejudice, it is hard to avoid the conclusion that once Freud had made up his mind…he would not take no for an answer, using all his ingenuity and his considerable powers of persuasion to compel his patient to admit that he was right.[35]

Although, this entire line of reasoning is recognized as grossly irresponsible today, Freud's ideas still have considerable influence on modern practitioners, not only of psychoanalysis, but also, to a lesser degree, on psychology.

## FREUD AND RELIGION
Highly influenced by Darwin who "had undertaken to place man firmly in the animal kingdom," Freud declared himself to be an atheist in 1874, while still a medical student.[36] One reason Freud actively opposed religion was because he concluded that it suppressed and inhibited freedom, especially sexual freedom.[37] Freud postulated that

---

34  Boteach, *Moses of Oxford*, 515.

35  Boteach, *Moses of Oxford*, 515.

36  Gay, *Freud: A Life for Our Time*, 29, 35.

37  Robert R. Holt, "Freud's Impact on Modern Morality and Our World View," in *Darwin, Marx and Freud: Their Influence on Moral Theory*, ed. Arthur L. Caplan and Bruce Jennings (New York: Plenum, 1984), 149.

basic drives, such as sex, were all programmed in humans by evolution. For this reason, Freud opposed certain "suppressive, inhibitory rules of conventional morality, especially antagonism to sexual pleasure, which he believed were contributory causes of neurosis."[38] His therapy involved eradicating self-destructive guilt by helping patients alter their ethical standards to reduce the burden of their sin.

Freud hoped to achieve this by helping his patients be "more assertive of their own desires and more willing to express their impulses and enjoy a full sexual life."[39] Critics argue that this teaching was, in part, responsible for the modern "new morality," which actually is closer to no morality—including open marriage and the sexual promiscuity now common in today's world.

Freud taught that religion, like every other aspect of mind, including instinct, had evolved from animals. For this reason, Freud believed the human mind "could be accounted for without the necessity of invoking supernatural intervention."[40] In many ways, psychoanalysis has replaced religion: "Psychoanalysis has often been referred to as a religion because of the intensity of the disputes within the movement that so often led to rebels leaving it and setting up rival schools or splinter groups, in a manner reminiscent of religious sects."[41] Furthermore, he taught that religion is often a "harmful barrier" to good adjustment.[42] Religion is a neurotic vestige of the Oedipal complex, and Freud believed that therapy would reduce the need for religion, replacing it with more conscious and emotionally healthy ways of coping.[43]

Koenig summarized his review of therapists' view of religion as follows: "Many prominent mental health professionals of the twentieth century believe that religion has either no influence on mental

---

38  Holt, "Freud's Impact," 148–149.

39  Holt, "Freud's Impact," 179.

40  Ernest Jones, *The Life and Work of Sigmund Freud, Volume 3: The Last Phase 1919–1939* (New York: Basic Books, 1981), 304.

41  Boteach, *Moses of Oxford,* 511.

42  Cavendish Moxon, "Freud's denial of religion," *British Journal of Medical Psychology* 11 (1931): 150.

43  Harold Koenig, *Is Religion Good for Your Health?* (New York: Hayworth, 1997), 23.

health or a negative one."[44] Eli Chesen, in a widely quoted psychology work, details the case for the "harm" religion causes to mental health, especially the Christian teaching on sin and morality.[45]

Freud believed that Darwin's theory destroyed "the belief in a spiritual force working within the organism." As a result, Freud concluded that nothing now stands "in the way of the scientific method being able to explain all the mysteries of organic life and of psychology."[46] This foundation of psychology and psychiatry may explain why such a high percentage of psychology practitioners are atheists or, at the least, agnostics.

Sociologist Neil Gross of Harvard University and Solon Simmons of George Mason University surveyed 1,471 professors at both religious and secular colleges regarding politics and faith. They found that, among all professors, psychology and biology professors included the highest proportion of atheists and agnostics, about 61 percent.[47] No doubt the number of atheists at religious colleges was much lower than this, and the number at secular colleges was much higher than their data indicated.

Freud once believed that the origin of all biology was due to the "handiwork of the Creator." He rejected this view when he became convinced that evolution proved that all life was the result of a "cruel and relentless battle for existence, in which the less functional were selected out."[48] Freud wrote that the human personality, and all human traits as well, result in a conflict in which those persons with the fittest traits are more likely to survive.

Freud's ideas on religion have had a wide influence on his followers. For example, noted Yale psychologist Seymour B. Sarason in his 1992 American Psychological Association (APA) address claimed that [APA]

44 Koenig, *Is Religion Good for Your Health?*, 28.

45 Eli Chesen, *Religion May Be Hazardous to Your Health* (New York: Peter H. Wyden, 1972).

46 Alexander and Selesnick, *History of Psychiatry*, 149.

47 Neil Gross and Solon Simmons, "How religious are America's college and university professors?" Social Science Research Council web forum on "The Religious Engagements of American Undergraduates," February 6, 2007; http://religion.ssrc.org/reforum/Gross_Simmons.pdf; accessed September 6, 2016.

48 Ritvo, *Darwin's Influence on Freud*, 2.

members would usually "describe themselves as agnostic or atheistic" and the religious worldview is neither of

> personal nor professional interest to most psychologists.... Indeed, if we learn that someone is devoutly religious, or even tends in that direction, we look upon that person with puzzlement, often concluding that psychologist obviously had or has personal problems.[49]

Freud's ideas about religion influenced the field of psychology as a whole. For example, he believed that religion and theism were both illusions and attempted to support this view in his book, *The Future of an Illusion*. Freud argued religion was not only an illusion, but was a *harmful* illusion that would eventually become extinct.[50] He also believed, as did Karl Marx, that the sources of belief in God stem from fear, not evidence. When older and confident about his professional standing, as a committed Darwinist, Freud "outspokenly attacked illusions in general and religious illusions in particular."[51]

## THE ORIGIN OF ORAL AND PHALLIC STAGES

Freud's most famous and controversial idea was the Oedipus complex. In his book, *Totem and Taboo*, Freud argued that the Oedipus complex was Ernst Haeckel's "ontogenetic recapitulation of an actual occurrence in the development of civilization" at the period of Darwin's evolutionary stage that taught when humans lived as apes in small groups they often consisted of a single powerful male and several females.[52]

Psychological drives, such as the oral and phallic stages, were believed to be expressed normally only during the developmental stages that correspond to Haeckel's evolutionary developmental stages. Haeckel taught that, as we develop in the womb, we pass through the fish, reptile and mammal stages before birth. Children likewise go

---

49 Quoted in Koenig, *Is Religion Good for Your Health?*, 28.
50 George Lichtheim, "Freud and Marx," in Miller, ed., *Freud: The Man*, 6.
51 Moxon, "Freud's Denial of Religion," 150.
52 Ritvo, *Darwin's Influence on Freud*, 75.

through similar developmental stages, including the oral, anal, phallic and latent stages, until they reach adulthood.

Freud taught that these stages dominate during certain growth periods, and happiness as an adult depends on successfully meeting the needs of each developmental stage. Frustration due to failure to meet the needs of any one stage results in the development of psychological problems later in life. Psychoanalysis teaches that the full manifestation of "fixation," or failure to progress smoothly through a psychosexual stage, results in problems during puberty.

Darwin's 1876 work, *A Bibliographical Sketch of an Infant*, stimulated Freud's work in the field of psychology, especially child psychology.[53] Freud believed that Darwin had proved human bodies had evolved from animals, and it was Freud who demonstrated our minds had also evolved from the lower animals:

> The aspect of man's pride to be wounded by biological discoveries, those associated with the name of Darwin, was his belief in his unique status in the animate realm.... [M]an came not simply to assume a position of domination over other animals, but...the power of reason, the possession of an immortal soul, were his prerogatives alone. The demonstration of his essential affinity with other animals, and his descent from them, was the second great blow to man's pride.... [T]his admission had been generally made only in respect of man's body, not his mind; it was Freud's work that is gradually extending it to the latter.[54]

As a result,

> Charles Darwin, Karl Marx, and Sigmund Freud portrayed humans, not as moral spiritual beings, but as animals that inhabited a universe ruled by purely impersonal forces and whose behavior and very thoughts were dictated by the unbending forces of biology, chemistry, and environment.[55]

---

53  Alexander and Selesnick, *History of Psychiatry*, 374.
54  Jones, *Life and Work of Sigmund Freud*, 2:225.
55  Quoted in Edward Humes, *Monkey Girl* (New York: HarperCollins, 2006), 75.

This selection of traits that result from conflicts in human relations "is basic in Freud's psychoanalytic thinking, as it was in all post-Darwinian biology."[56] David Cooper concluded that since its very beginning, mainstream psychiatry has been preoccupied with the natural sciences, specifically Darwinism, which has strangled the way psychiatry views human nature, the research they do and the solutions proposed to deal with psychological problems.[57]

One psychiatrist who has exposed the fallacies of this anti-religious approach to helping clients was Karl Menninger, founder of the Menninger Clinic. In his 1974 book, *Whatever Became of Sin?* Menninger recognized as erroneous both the idea that we are ruled by our biology and that misbehaviour was a result of inappropriately met needs that became part of the human condition as a result of evolution. Menninger concluded that the biblical teaching of personal responsibility for accepting the reality of sin, and then endeavouring to properly deal with it, is central to mental health.

The psychiatric idea dominant for decades was the belief that antisocial acts, and misbehaviour in general, largely stem from defects in one's environment and education. In contrast to the view that wrongdoers are largely victims, Menninger stressed patients must come to realize that humans are not helpless victims of our circumstances, but are free moral agents able to direct our own individual future.[58] Helping clients requires aiding them to realize they have a conscience that they can use to guide their lives, necessitating personal choices. Achieving this often requires making difficult choices, but choices nonetheless.

## CRITICISM OF ORTHODOX PSYCHOANALYSIS

The antagonism of psychology as a whole to theism, and to Christianity in particular, has motivated the publishing of scores of books by both religious and nonreligious persons very critical of the entire psychology therapy field.[59] Many books and articles have been produced docu-

---

56  Ritvo, *Darwin's Influence on Freud*, 2.
57  David Cooper, *Psychiatry and Anti-Psychiatry* (London: Paladin, 1967).
58  Karl Menninger, *Whatever Became of Sin?* (New York: Hawthorn Books, 1974).
59  Martin Bobgan and Deidre Bobgan, *Psychoheresy: The Psychological Seduction of*

menting how modern psychological theories, especially Freudian theory, are antithetical to Christianity and to the Bible. Harvard graduate Thomas Kilpatrick, professor of psychology at Boston College, documents how not only Freudian psychology but also other psychology schools strike at the heart of Christian belief.[60]

Freud also faced "a flood of criticism" during his lifetime, to which Ernest Jones noted that Freud responded as did his hero, Darwin—by publishing "more evidence in support of his theories."[61] According to Jones, Freud found the "only effective reply" to his critics was the one Darwinists use, "and that is the one he consistently followed."[62] The "effective reply" was to dismiss criticism of his theories by concluding that his critics were stupid, arrogant, illogical and conscienceless.[63] A major problem with Freud's ideas was his reliance on Darwin who taught that all life was the result of "blind, clashing profane forces," an idea that produced great debate about the nature of human creatures that Darwin placed "firmly in the animal kingdom."[64]

One of the most controversial ideas of Freud was his claim that sexuality and other hidden or suppressed drives were major determinants of behaviour, and the solution to mental problems was more sexual freedom.[65] Freudian psychology was a critical factor influencing, not only the rise of atheism, but also the new morality that has led to an epidemic of sexually transmitted diseases and teenage mothers.

In a chapter titled, "What is wrong with psychoanalysis?" psychologist Hans Eysenck wrote that it is

> impossible to deny that Freudian theories have had a tremendous influence on psychiatry, on literature, and perhaps also on that

---

*Christianity* (Santa Barbara: East Gate, 1987); Martin Bobgan and Deidre Bobgan, *The Psychological Way/The Spiritual Way: Are Christianity and Psychotherapy Compatible?* (Minneapolis: Bethany House, 1979).

60 William Kirk Kilpatrick, *Psychological Seduction: The Failure of Modern Psychology* (Nashville: Thomas Nelson, 1983).

61 Jones, *Life and Work of Sigmund Freud*, 2:120–121, 426.

62 Jones, *Life and Work of Sigmund Freud*, 2:124.

63 Jones, *Life and Work of Sigmund Freud*, 2:121.

64 Gay, *Freud: A Life for Our Time*, 3–4, 35–36.

65 Leonard Gross, *God and Freud* (New York: David McKay, 1959).

whole complex of laws, folkways, and mores which we often refer to as "sexual morality." Moralists are inclined to doubt whether this influence had been essentially for the good.[66]

If psychoanalysis is true, its implications must be dealt with, but if it is a false theory, this puts the theory in a whole different light.

## FREUD'S IDEAS ALSO SEXIST

Freud's ideas have come under heavy fire for being sexist. For this reason, women are one of Freud's strongest critics, using both logical and moral critiques of his work. One major concern was that Freud's theoretical framework denied women any intrinsic identity. For example, Freudian theory taught that a young boy has a biological

> desire to lie with his mother, but feels threatened in the execution of these desires by the father, who seems to have prior rights to the mother. The boy's fear makes him give up and "repress" all these unseemly desires, which live on as the famous Oedipus complex in the subconscious, promoting all sorts of neurotic symptoms in later life. This Oedipus complex assumes the central role in Freudian speculations. Yet in Freud's female version of the Oedipus complex, a little girl's discovery of her lack of male qualities leads her to believe that she is an inferior being. She becomes disillusioned with her mother, whom she blames for her condition. This turns her towards her father as a love-object, and she desires to bear his child.[67]

Freud concluded that the result is the female child will attempt to "compensate" for her lack of male organs. Consequently, this emotional developmental stage is resolved simply by the girl's awareness that other men can enable her to have a child, therefore overcoming her continued sense of being an inferior human because she is female. As a result, women are

---

66 Hans J. Eysenck, *Uses and Abuses of Psychology* (Middlesex: Penguin Books, 1953), 221.

67 Boteach, *Moses of Oxford*, 510–511.

totally dependent on a male for fulfillment and development. Another feminist gripe is that the mother plays a secondary role in the male and female version of the Oedipus complex. In both children it is the father, either as an object of fear in the male, or as an object of desire and jealousy in the female, who plays the fundamental role in the development of the Oedipus complex.[68]

Ideas such as these are closer to Greek mythology than science and illustrate Freud's major departure from the Judeo-Christian worldview. Freud postulated that, as a result of evolution, the sex drive is a central human motivation and is, therefore, reflected in all of our behaviour, from speech to action. Consequently, Freud concluded that psychological problems were, at their core, sexual-drive problems. For example, Freud interpreted slips of the tongue, dreams and all of our daily interactions as being dominated by the sexual drive. Thus, a female dream involving water was interpreted as wanting a child, and smoking as satisfying a frustrated oral need dominated by the drive to suckle one's mother's breast.

## ORTHODOX PSYCHOANALYSIS IS NOW WIDELY DISCREDITED

Psychoanalysis now has been widely discredited by professional psychologists and others partly because the ideas it is based on have been refuted. An example is the "law of ontogenesis," the idea that we repeat our evolutionary history in the womb, transitioning through the worm, fish, reptile and mammal stages as we develop from an embryo into a fetus.[69] There is also vast literature critical of psychoanalysis published by mainline presses including that by Harvard graduate Harry K. Wells.[70] Wells documented that psychoanalysis was introduced in America only during the last century and in this short time has passed from orthodoxy, to revision, to reform, to reconstruction and, lastly, to demise.

---

68 Boteach, *Moses of Oxford*, 510–511.

69 West, *Darwin Day in America*, 55. See Chapter 5 for more on ontogenesis.

70 Harry K. Wells, *The Failure of Psychoanalysis* (New York: International Publishers, 1963).

A major problem with psychoanalysis has always been its lack of scientific support and the fact that its supporters have failed to scientifically document the efficacy of their treatment techniques.[71] Frank Kenyon concluded that "psychoanalysis is a constellation of suppositions without a trace of scientific evidence in their support."[72]

One of the most well-known scientific studies of psychotherapy by Hans Eysenck reviewed 19 studies covering over 7,000 clinical cases. Eysenck found the percentage of patients rated as cured or much improved was 44 percent for psychoanalysis, 64 percent for psychological counselling, and 72 percent for custodial or medical intervention.[73] Unfortunately, no consistent control group was included. In other studies, control groups show that those not exposed to a formal professional psychological therapy often also significantly improve. Reasons for this include the fact that time alone is a great healer, as well as help and advice from friends and clergy, plus improved life situation circumstances, and other factors. Eysenck concluded that the hypothesis that psychoanalysis is superior to other techniques in treating neurosis is simply not supported by the literature, and "Eysenck's conclusions have not been effectively refuted" since then.[74]

In a later study, Eysenck concluded that, in a wide variety of populations of both children and adults, when "untreated neurotic control groups are compared with experimental groups of neurotic patients treated by means of psychotherapy, both groups recover to approximately the same extent."[75] Conversely, patients treated by other tech-

---

71 Eysenck, *Uses and Abuses of Psychology*.

72 Frank Kenyon, *Psycho-Analysis: A Modern Delusion* (London: Secular Society/ The Pioneer Press, 1949), 141.

73 Hans J. Eysenck, "The effects of psychotherapy: A reply," *Journal of Abnormal Psychology* 50 (1955):147–148; Eysenck, *Uses and Abuses of Psychology*; Heinz Hartmann, "Comments on the Scientific Aspects of Psychoanalysis," reprinted from *The Psychoanalytic Study of the Child*, vol. 13 (New York: International Universities Press, 1958), 127–146; Lester Luborsky, "A note on Eysenck's article 'The effects of psychotherapy: An evaluation,'" *British Journal of Psychology* 45 (1954): 129–131.

74 Norman Sundberg and Leona Tyler, *Clinical Psychology* (New York: Appleton Century Crofts, 1973), 301.

75 Hans J. Eysenck, *The Effects of Psychotherapy* (New York: International Science Press, 1966), 39.

niques, such as drug or learning theory "improve significantly more quickly than do patients treated by means of psychoanalytic or eclectic psychotherapy, or not treated by psychotherapy at all."[76] Eysenck further found that research on

> military and civilian neurotics, and with both adults and children, suggests that the therapeutic effects of psychotherapy are small or non-existent, and do not in any demonstrable way add to the non-specific effects of routine medical treatment, or to such events as occur in the patients' everyday experience.[77]

More recent research has indicated that, although many patients do benefit from therapy, often the "benefits of psychotherapy are not permanent."[78] Other research finds that most of the major psychotherapies all tend to be very similar in efficacy and that the critical factor is the warmth, genuineness and other personal qualities of the therapist—all the same qualities one expects in a friend.[79] In other words, a psychotherapist is, to some degree, a paid friend.[80] Torrey, in his influential work, *The Death of Psychiatry*, argues that the vast majority of people we label "mentally ill" are not sick, but have problems of living that can be helped by teaching patients how to better deal with their problems and provide social and other supports.[81]

Among the numerous studies documenting the failure of psychotherapy is the work of University of Bridgeport in Connecticut psychology professor Dorothy Tennov.[82] After reviewing numerous studies, she concluded that although some people have been helped

---

76 Eysenck, *Effects of Psychotherapy*, 39.

77 Eysenck, *Effects of Psychotherapy*, 40.

78 Norman Sundberg, Julian Taplin and Leona Tyler, *Introduction to Clinical Psychology* (Englewood Cliffs: Prentice-Hall, 1983), 405.

79 Scott O. Lilienfeld, "Psychological treatments that cause harm," *Perspectives on Psychological Science* 2, No. 1 (2007): 53–70.

80 William Schofield, *Psychotherapy: The Purchase of Friendship* (Englewood Cliffs: Prentice-Hall, 1964).

81 E. Fuller Torrey, *The Death of Psychiatry* (Radnor: Chilton, 1974).

82 Dorothy Tennov, *Psychotherapy: The Hazardous Cure* (New York: Abelard-Schuman, 1975).

by psychotherapy, many have been harmed by it, and these cases need to be considered when evaluating the system.

Edward and Cathey Pinckney concluded that psychoanalysis, by deliberately looking for nonexistent problems, such as Oedipal and other "complexes," based on unproven theories instead of real problems, is not only a fallacious approach to helping treat mental disturbance, but also a harmful guide to life.[83] Recent research found that "several psychological treatments may produce harm in significant numbers of people," specifically from 10 to 20 percent of all patients are harmed by psychotherapy, and some are much worse off after its treatment.[84]

A major problem, as expressed by Nobel laureate neurobiologist Eric Kandel, is that psychoanalysis as a discipline was not scientific from the start, and has not yet become scientific.[85] Shmuel Boteach also writes, "Virtually everyone except for a few fundamentalist Freudians agrees that psychoanalysis is very far from being a science, since its theories are not open to refutation and cannot be used for prediction."[86]

Kandel also concluded that most problematic is the fact that scientists rarely have rigorously studied psychotherapy in depth—a problem that Kandel hopes to solve by putting psychotherapy on as "rigorous a level as psychopharmacology."[87] He added that the field of psychotherapy should take advantage of neurotechniques in treating patients, not only due to administration of drug therapy, but also the application of technology such as functional MRI (fMRI) to measure blood flow, and thus brain activity.

Under the subheading, "The End of Psychiatry," University of Chicago biological psychologist Dan Agin goes even farther than Kandel, concluding that many "people, and I am one of them, believe that the end of psychiatry will occur in this century."[88] Kandel notes that neurology

---

83 Edward R. Pinckney and Cathey Pinckney, *The Fallacy of Freud and Psychoanalysis* (Englewood Cliffs: Prentice-Hall, 1965).

84 Lilienfeld, "Psychological treatments that cause harm," 53.

85 Eric Kandel, "Does psychotherapy work?" *Discover* 27, No. 4 (April 2006): 60.

86 Boteach, *Moses of Oxford*, 511.

87 Kandel, "Does psychotherapy work?" 61.

88 Dan Agin, *Junk Science* (New York: St. Martin's Press, 2006), 151.

"treats diseases of the brain" and "psychiatry treats diseases of the mind," a dichotomy that is

> analogous to a division between diseases of the gastrointestinal tract and diseases of digestion.... Ultimately, as "biological" psychiatry becomes more and more fused with neuroscience and neurology, the faculty of departments of psychiatry will be merged into the faculties of medical neuroscience, and psychiatry will cease to exist as an independent medical discipline. ...[P]sychiatry departments will probably disappear by mid-century.[89]

He concludes that "talk therapy, particularly private-practice talk therapy," and the various forms of psychotherapy will not survive when people realize that far better ways exist to treat mental problems.

Many of the books critiquing psychoanalysis were published in the last quarter of the twentieth century, because it was during this period that new research increasingly discredited classical psychoanalysis. A forty-five-year-old *Time* magazine article, after noting that Freudian theory has "ruled the field of psychiatry in the US," concluded "many observers believe that their long domination is at an end.... [Y]ounger psychiatrists...are displaying an increasing skepticism about the doctrines and techniques of orthodox analysis."[90] Of course, Freudian ideas were far less influential in the field of psychology than in psychoanalysis.

One of the latest studies, done by Andrew Christensen of the University of California at Los Angeles, concluded that "psychotherapy doesn't work very well at all," and therapy by non-professionals "proves just as effective, or more effective, than therapy performed by psychiatrists, psychologists, social workers, and family therapists."[91]

All psychology therapy is now under fire in the media—for example, see *Newsweek*'s "Get shrunk at your own risk," which documents the harm that psychological therapy can cause.[92]

---

89 Kandel, "Does psychotherapy work?" 152.

90 "Psychoanalysis: In search of its soul," *Time* 93, No. 10 (March 7, 1969): 68.

91 Virginia Rutter, "Oops! A very embarrassing story," *Psychology Today* (March/April 1994):12.

92 Sharon Begley, "Get shrunk at your own risk," *Newsweek*, June 18, 2007, 49.

Orthodox Freudian therapy is now widely considered moribund by counselling professionals or, at the very least, far more time consuming and expensive than other equally or more effective therapies. Because of this fact, few books today are written critiquing orthodox psychoanalysis, except from an historical viewpoint.

Biting critiques have now also spread to all fields of psychology. New York University psychology professor Paul Vitz writes that psychology has become a substitute for religion, one that stresses what he calls "self worship."[93] In spite of this criticism, Darwinian ideas still have a major influence in the estimated twenty major schools of counselling psychology still practiced today.[94] Science writer and pseudoscience debunker Martin Gardner even concluded that:

> Freudian psychoanalysis died a few decades ago. To almost every psychiatrist today under the age of sixty, Freud...has become the very model of a crackpot. Whenever he said something significant, it was not original. William James, in his *Principles of Psychology*, written when Freud was a boy, discusses at length the role of the unconscious in mental illness. And where Freud was original, he spouted baloney. His book on dreams, with its elaborate and preposterous symbolism, belongs to a set [of books] called *Great Books of Bogus Science in the Western World*.[95]

In spite of the general abandonment of Freudian psychology, a dwindling core of devoted followers still cling to his theory. When at Oxford University, Rabi Boteach observed that Freud's teachings were still held to by a "devoutly loyal movement of psychoanalysts. Their uncompromising approach to his original theories and sharp emotional defenses to all attacks against Freud strongly resemble religious zealotry."[96]

---

93 Paul C. Vitz, *Psychology as Religion: The Cult of Self Worship* (Grand Rapids: Eerdmans, 1977).

94 Patterson, *Theories of Counseling and Psychotherapy*.

95 Martin Gardner, *Undiluted Hocus-Pocus: The Autobiography of Martin Gardner* (Princeton: Princeton University Press, 2013), 50.

96 Boteach, *Moses of Oxford*, 511.

## CONCLUSIONS

Both Marxism[97] and psychoanalysis[98] were based on Darwinism, and both are now widely regarded as on their last legs or worse. In 1970, psychiatry professor Joseph Wolpe concluded from a review of the research that current psychotherapeutic practices often harm the very patients that they are attempting to help.[99] Since then, new techniques have largely replaced Freudian approaches, including drug therapies.

In the end, the failure of Darwin's progeny, including psychoanalysis, is *a result of the failure of Darwinism itself* as a system that accurately explains the real world. Most of Freud's innovative ideas, such as the Oedipus complex, have been empirically discredited.[100]

Freud built his theory of the mind so completely on Darwinism that his biographer, Ernest Jones, "bestowed on Freud the title...Darwin of the mind."[101] Of note is the fact that Freud was actually a Lamarckian (i.e., he accepted the inheritance of acquired characteristics theory of Lamarck), as was Darwin. Darwin remained a Lamarckist "from the beginning to the end of his life what one must call an obstinate adherent of this discredited Lamarckism. Over and over again he implied or explicitly stated his firm belief in it."[102]

This may help explain why so many of Freud's theories are now recognized as not only wrong, but actually irresponsible or even harmful. For example, in the last book he wrote, *Moses and Monotheism*, Freud wrote that the excessive guilt that haunts Jews today

> was inherited from the unconscious memory of their forefathers having in an act of rebellion slain the father of their race, Moses. ...The guilty reactions following the numerous prehistoric acts of

97 Bergman, *Darwin Effect*.

98 Psychoanalysis as forms of materialistic religion was documented in George Steiner's *Nostalgia for the Absolute* (Toronto: House of Anansi Press, 1997).

99 Joseph Wolpe, "Introduction," in Richard B. Stuard, *Trick or Treatment: How and When Psychotherapy Fails* (Champaign: Research Press, 1970), i.

100 Robert A. Paul, "Did the primal crime take place?" *Ethos* 4, No. 3 (1976): 311–352; Seymour Fisher and Roger Greenberg, *The Scientific Evaluation of Freud's Theories and Therapy* (New York: Basic Books, 1978).

101 Jones, *Life and Work of Sigmund Freud*, 3:304.

102 Jones, *Life and Work of Sigmund Freud*, 3:311.

parricide had been inherited—they constituted in fact the "original sin" of the theologians—and they were reanimated afresh in every generation.... [T]his implies that the conscious attitudes of primitive man made such a profound impression on him as to reverberate throughout his body, producing, perhaps via Darwin's "gemmules," a corresponding impression on his seminiferous tubules so that when—perhaps years later—they produced spermatozoa each of these had been modified in such a way as to create...a child who bore within him the memory of his father's experience.[103]

Freud was driven less by science than his "liberal-individualist philosophy, itself a heritage of the Darwinian age."[104] In the end, as Nobel laureate Sir Peter Medawar concluded, "Considered in its entirety... psychoanalysis will remain forever one of the saddest and strangest of all landmarks in the history of twentieth-century thought."[105]

---

103  Jones, *Life and Work of Sigmund Freud*, 3:311–312.

104  Lichtheim, "Freud and Marx," 59.

105  Peter Medawar, "Further Comments on Psychoanalysis," in *Pluto's Republic: Incorporating The Art of the Soluble and Induction and Intuition in Scientific Thought* (New York: Oxford, 1982), 72.

# 07

# Friedrich Nietzsche:
# Anti-Christian Darwin disciple

||||||||||||||||||||||||||||||||||||||||||||||||||||||||||||||||||||||||||||||||||||||||||||||||||||||||||||||

The worldview of the influential German philosopher Friedrich Nietzsche was strongly affected by Darwinism. Nietzsche had a major impact on academia and world leaders, including Adolf Hitler. He saw Christianity as the antithesis of his philosophy and, for this reason, actively opposed Christianity. Nietzsche, as a disciple of Darwin and a supporter of eugenics, was a tragic figure. As a whole, he had a very negative influence on society.

## HIS BACKGROUND

Friedrich Nietzsche (1844–1900) is viewed by many academics as one of the most eminent philosophers of the last century[1] and the most famous philosopher of the second half of the nineteenth century.[2] Willard Wright wrote that no single

---

1   Herman Hausheer, "Superman," in *Dictionary of Philosophy*, ed. D. Runes (Totowa: Littlefield Adams, 1962), 307.

2   Jean Gayon, "Nietzsche and Darwin," in *Biology and the Foundation of Ethics*, ed. Jane Maienschein and Michael Ruse (Cambridge: Cambridge University Press, 1999), 154.

philosopher since Kant has left so undeniable an imprint on modern thought as has Friedrich Nietzsche. Even Schopenhauer, whose influence colored the greater part of Europe, made no such widespread impression. Not only in ethics and literature do we find the molding hand of Nietzsche at work, invigorating and solidifying; but in pedagogics and in art, in politics and religion, the influence of his doctrines is to be encountered.[3]

Dan Stone concluded that Nietzsche was so popular among intellectuals that his ideas actually served as a "social glue in 'progressive' intellectual circles."[4] To top this off, Antony Flew added that Nietzsche was also "one of the greatest prose stylists of modern times."[5]

Born in Röchem, Germany, in 1844, Nietzsche was the son of a Lutheran pastor.[6] Educated at the universities of Bonn and Leipzig, he was such a brilliant student that, in 1867, at the young age of 24, he was appointed professor at the University of Basel. While still a student at the University of Bonn, after studying Darwin and the then leading philosophers of his day, Nietzsche turned against religion. He spent the rest of his life actively campaigning against Christianity.[7]

## NIETZSCHE CONVERTS TO DARWINISM
Nietzsche was so devoutly religious as a youth that his friends called him the "little minister" and "a Jesus in the Temple." After studying Darwinism, he became a staunch atheist and spent the rest of his life proselytizing for his version of Darwinism.[8] He first discovered Darwin's ideas while still a student, after reading Friedrich Lange's *History of Materialism* in 1866. Lange argued that theism was ignorant

---

3   Willard Huntington Wright, "Introduction," in *The Philosophy of Nietzsche* (New York: Modern Library, 1954), vii.

4   Dan Stone, *Breeding Superman: Nietzsche, Race and Eugenics in Edwardian and Interwar Britain* (London: Liverpool University Press, 2002), 65.

5   Antony Flew, *A Dictionary of Philosophy* (New York: St. Martin's Press, 1979), 292.

6   Flew, *Dictionary of Philosophy*, 229.

7   Wright, "Introduction," vii; Flew, *Dictionary of Philosophy*, 229.

8   Will Durant, *The Story of Philosophy: The Lives and Opinions of the Greater Philosophers* (Garden City: Garden City Publishing, 1926), 437–438.

## Friedrich Nietzsche (1844-1900)

This German philospher took Darwin's teachings further and advocated for an active eugenics program hypothesizing the idea of a Superman—elites like himself, who were above the rest of humanity, and only they had the right to be **free.** Photography by F. Hartmann, Basel, circa 1875.

superstition in contrast to Darwin's *On the Origin of Species*, a work he erroneously argued was not based on faith as was Christianity. Lange taught that Christianity as a religion has

> no lawful place in science, but [Darwin] offered a comprehensive explanation for the evolution of all living beings based on observed similarities in different species. The struggle for animal existence had been going on for centuries and millennia, yet only in recent times had this basic fact begun to receive serious attention from the seekers of the truth.[9]

Shortly after he was introduced to Lange, Nietzsche accepted Lange's materialistic philosophy and abandoned God and Christianity for Darwinism. Lange also discussed in detail life's "struggle for a spot on earth" and the "extermination of other life," ideas that caused Nietzsche to support eugenics.[10] Nietzsche was also a close friend of German paleontologist, Darwin's friend Karl Ludwig Rütimeyer, who had an important role in introducing Darwinism into Germany.[11] Darwin also had a substantial influence on Arthur Schopenhauer's philosophy, and Schopenhauer had a "mighty impact" on Nietzsche.[12] It was due to the impact of Darwin that Nietzsche "subscribed to a naturalist interpretation of human behavior and genealogical modes of explanation."[13]

Darwin's theory of evolution was enthusiastically welcomed in Germany by both the scientific and academic establishments. Darwin's main disciple, and his major popularizer, both in Germany and in much of the world, was German biologist Ernst Haeckel. Although Nietzsche evidently never read Darwin's books in the original English, his writing reveals the fact that he was very influenced by German Darwinists such as Haeckel—the "most influential Darwinian biologist in Germany."[14]

---

9 Curtis Cate, *Friedrich Nietzsche* (Woodstock: Overlook Press, 2005), 74.

10 Cate, *Friedrich Nietzsche*, 74.

11 Gayon, "Nietzsche and Darwin," 159.

12 Cate, *Friedrich Nietzsche*, 66.

13 Dirk Robert Johnson, *Nietzsche's Anti-Darwinism* (New York: Cambridge University Press, 2010), 201.

14 Richard Weikart, "The Impact of Social Darwinism on Anti-Semitic Ideology in

Nietzsche is most famous for expounding his "God is dead" theory, the conclusion that God is merely another vestige of our unscientific pre-Darwinian past.[15] Nietzsche concluded that modern science, primarily Darwinism, and the increasing secularization of European society, had effectively "killed" the validity of the Judeo-Christian God. This was critical in the West because Christianity had served as the basis for both meaning and value in Western society for well over a thousand years.

His *Übermensch* idea, literally "over man," usually translated as Superman, is the view that a Superman is a "man above others...the higher type of humanity" and "the goal of evolution."[16] The connection between Nietzsche's followers and eugenicists was so close that Dan Stone concluded the difference is somewhat arbitrary.[17] Darwin's evolution theory was responsible for Nietzsche's core ethical views, and in fact

Nietzsche's philosophy could never have arisen without Darwin's *Origin of Species* and was developed in response to Darwin's discoveries. Nietzsche first became aware of Darwin's theory of evolution by natural selection as a result of reading Friedrich Albert Lange's *History of Materialism* (1866). Its impact on the young Nietzsche was...dramatic.[18]

For Nietzsche, natural selection was evolution freed from every metaphysical implication:

before Darwin's simple but fundamental discovery it had been difficult to deny that the world seemed to be following some course laid down by a directing agency; after it, the necessity for

Germany and Austria, 1860–1945," in *Jewish Tradition and the Challenge of Darwinism*, ed. Geoffrey Cantor and Marc Swetlitz (Chicago, University of Chicago Press, 2006), 97.

15 Andrew Newberg, Eugene D'Aquili and Vince Rause, *Why God Won't Go Away: Brain Science and the Biology of Belief* (New York: Ballantine Books, 2001), 128.

16 Hausheer, "Superman," 307.

17 Stone, *Breeding Superman*, 65.

18 Richard J. Hollingdale, *Nietzsche: The Man and His Philosophy* (New York: Cambridge University Press, 1999), 72–73.

such a directing agency disappeared, and what seemed to be order [in the natural world] could be explained by Darwinism. "The total nature of the world," Nietzsche wrote in *Die fröhliche Wissenschaft*, "is...to all eternity chaos" [and this idea,] which was basic to his philosophy, arose directly from his interpretation of Darwin.[19]

As a result, according to Nietzsche scholar Richard Hollingdale, Nietzsche concluded that

> God and man, as hitherto understood, no longer existed. The universe and the earth were without meaning. The sense that meaning had evaporated was what seemed to escape those who welcomed Darwin as a benefactor of mankind. "Nietzsche considered that evolution presented a correct picture of the world, but that it was a disastrous picture. His philosophy was an attempt to produce a new world-picture which took Darwinism into account but was not nullified by it."[20]

Nietzsche owed a great intellectual debt to Darwin for having demolished the last traces of natural theology, and thereby, for the first time in history, making atheism a defensible worldview. Lange's *History of Materialism* postulated that along with atheism tended to go egoism, and Nietzsche's book *Will to Power* espouses a doctrine of radical egoism.

## NIETZSCHE AND DARWIN

Nietzsche was influenced by Darwin to the point that he was called "the child of Darwin."[21] He was also, besides Herbert Spencer, the first major philosopher to stress the need to "dialogue with Darwin."[22] Nietzsche's "serious commentaries on Darwin and Darwinians began in *Human, All-Too-Human*...and developed uninterruptedly from then

---

19 Hollingdale, *Nietzsche*, 72–73.
20 Hollingdale, *Nietzsche*, 72–73.
21 Durant, *Story of Philosophy*, 301.
22 Gayon, "Nietzsche and Darwin," 155.

on."[23] Nietzsche's knowledge about Darwinism came primarily from two sources: popular books and a large network of eminent scientists and philosophers with whom Nietzsche regularly interacted.[24] As a result, Nietzsche adopted a "Darwinistic...approach to the fundamental problems of philosophy."[25]

The German Nietzsche did not always agree with the English Darwin and even openly ridiculed some of his ideas. Historian Will Durant explained this fact by concluding that Nietzsche denounced those who most influenced him, which was Nietzsche's "unconscious way of covering up his debts" to others.[26] Nietzsche did have some major reservations about Darwinism. In *Will to Power*, he expressly rejected the sufficiency of Darwinian selection to improve the species and argued that superior specimens had to be *carefully nurtured* by humans.[27] Darwin's "survival of the fittest" idea became Nietzsche's "will to power," an idea that was a cornerstone of Nietzsche's philosophy.[28] Nonetheless, the many similarities between Darwin and Nietzsche

are obvious: all [humans] rising above the merely animal is caused by struggle, war, and the brutal elimination of the less fit by the stronger. Nietzsche believed this to be the core natural truth of aristocracy—that the better should rule over, and hence should use, the lesser. "The essential characteristic of a good and healthy aristocracy" is that it "accepts with a good conscience the sacrifice of untold human beings who, *for its sake*, must be reduced and lowered to incomplete human beings, to slaves, to instruments."[29]

---

23 Gayon, "Nietzsche and Darwin," 154.

24 Gayon, "Nietzsche and Darwin," 160.

25 Cate, *Friedrich Nietzsche*, 251.

26 Durant, *Story of Philosophy*, 435.

27 Paragraphs 684–685 quoted in John S. Moore, "Nietzsche's Anti-Darwin," presented at the 11th annual conference of the Friedrich Nietzsche Society, Emmanuel College, Cambridge, September 8, 2001.

28 Janko Lavrin, *Nietzsche: A Biographical Introduction* (New York: Scribner, 1971), 27.

29 Benjamin Wiker, *10 Books that Screwed up the World* (Washington: Regnery, 2008), 107.

Furthermore, the

> "fundamental faith" of aristocracies then, is that "society" exists for them, for their sake, so that all the lesser types who serve them in society exist "only as the foundation and scaffolding on which a choice type of being is able to raise itself to its higher task and to a higher state of being." One cannot help but think of the Nazi's justification for enslaving the Slavs as "lower men."[30]

## NIETZSCHE GOES BEYOND DARWIN

Because of Nietzsche's prestige among Western intellectuals, the close relationship between Darwin and Nietzsche "has been largely ignored because of the horrifying developments that…emerged in history between 'Social Darwinism' and 'Nietzscheism.'"[31] Actually, Nietzsche often went beyond Darwin in pushing his survival-of-the-fittest ideas. Darwin attempted to give an evolutionary explanation of "moral" qualities that helped to explain the evolution of moral traits, such as sympathy for the suffering of others. Conversely, Nietzsche actually regarded

> such sympathy as destructive of evolution's forward march. That is, Nietzsche rightly sees that Darwin's praise of sympathy contradicts his own account of exactly what makes for evolutionary progress: "life itself is *essentially* appropriation, injury, overpowering of what is alien and weaker; suppression, hardness, imposition of one's own forms, incorporation and at least, at its mildest, exploitation." Since these are the very qualities that allow living things to flourish, asks Nietzsche, why are they considered evil?[32]

The movement from Nietzsche to Hitler was critical in producing Nazism and the Holocaust.[33]

---

30  Wiker, *10 Books*, 107.

31  Gayon, "Nietzsche and Darwin," 156.

32  Wiker, *10 Books*, 107. Emphasis in original.

33  Georg Lukács, *Von Nietzsche zu Hitler oder Der Irrationalismus und die Deutsche Politik* (Frankfurt am Main: Fischer Bücherei, 1966).

## NIETZSCHE'S CRITICISM OF DARWIN

Nietzsche recognized some of the serious scientific flaws in Darwin's theory. Over time, "he began to question the assumptions on which Darwin's faith in naturalism was grounded. He grew skeptical of attempts to offer a [Darwinian] metaphysical narrative account of life and nature. This position emerged from exploiting some of Darwin's insights."[34]

For example, Nietzsche had no problem with natural selection, but he had major problems with the idea that nature was the agent—noting that the "winners" were often not the most numerous individuals, but rather were a minority that were actually, in some ways the weaker humans. As evidence for this, Nietzsche noted that the less complex organisms (protists, insects, invertebrates) were far more numerous than the more complex organisms, such as humans and all primates.[35] Nietzsche's "antagonism did not emerge suddenly.... It was a product of years of serious reflection on the philosophical underpinnings of modern science, in particular Darwinism."[36]

Furthermore, Nietzsche had another problem with one aspect of Darwin's "survival-of-the-fittest" notion, noting that it raised among other problems, the question *fittest for specifically what?*[37] Nietzsche noted that it was often those who were least fit to survive "in a strictly physical sense—geniuses who died prematurely" were actually *most* fit.[38] He also noted that the weakest majority were most likely to mate and produce offspring precisely because they were the majority and, he concluded, most organisms indiscriminately mated with each other, showing little evidence of sexual selection.[39]

These factors were all the more reason why eugenics was important to Nietzsche. He believed that, in general, Darwinism was not wrong; but only certain parts of his theory were mistaken. Nevertheless, Nietzsche argued that Darwin's ideas must be applied by human intel-

---

34  Johnson, *Nietzsche's Anti-Darwinism*, 201.

35  Gayon, "Nietzsche and Darwin," 167.

36  Johnson, *Nietzsche's Anti-Darwinism*, 203.

37  Cate, *Friedrich Nietzsche*, 355.

38  Cate, *Friedrich Nietzsche*, 355.

39  Lewis Call, "Anti-Darwin, anti-Spencer: Friedrich Nietzsche's critique of Darwin and 'Darwinism,'" *History of Science* 36 (1998):1–21.

ligence to society. Robin Small even concluded that Nietzsche was "arguably more faithful to a Darwinian approach" than were many theorists, and Nietzsche in many ways was an "ultra-Darwinist" in spite of presenting valid arguments against certain aspects of Darwinism.[40] At another level, in a detailed study of Nietzsche's anti-Darwinism, Dirk Johnson concluded that

> Nietzsche's final critique of Darwin reflected a...personal opposition.... Nietzsche understood that the new evolutionary theories were decisive and were beginning to form the basis for a challenging, original, though competitive explanatory model in the realm of morality and beyond.[41]

## CHARACTERISTICS OF NIETZSCHE'S SUPERMAN

Nietzsche, in his *Thus Spake Zarathustra*, wrote that man is "not the apex of evolution, but a missing link to a higher species—an idea he clearly derived from Darwin."[42] Nietzsche's "higher species" was a small group of elite men who were above all other men, a superior human that Nietzsche explained as follows:

What is the ape to man? A laughingstock, a thing of shame. And just the same shall man be to the Superman: A laughingstock, a thing of shame. Ye have made your way from the worm to man, and much within you is still worm. Once ye were apes, and even yet man is still more of an ape than any of the apes.... The Superman is the meaning of the earth. Let your will say: The Superman *shall* be the meaning of the earth![43]

Nietzsche believed that these Supermen, creative geniuses like himself, were above the rest of humanity, and only they had the right to be free. These Supermen were not necessarily physically strong, as

---

40 Robin Small, "What Nietzsche Did During the Science Wars," in *Nietzsche and Science*, ed. Gregory Moore and Thomas H. Brobjer (Burlington: Ashgate Publishing Company, 2004), 166–167.

41 Johnson, *Nietzsche's Anti-Darwinism*, 6.

42 John P. Koster, *The Atheist Syndrome* (Brentwood: Wolgemuth & Hyatt, 1989), 82.

43 Fredrick Nietzsche, *Thus Spake Zarathustra* (New York: Modern Library, 1950), 6.

the common image of a superman implies, but, although some of them may be weak physically, they were "atypical and creative" in ways that allowed them to move humans forward socially, economically and in other ways.[44]

Nietzsche's superman is a man who is "self-contained and aloof... who evolves through ruthless competition and triumph of will."[45] Nietzsche disdained the masses, which he thought incapable of exercising true freedom. What Nietzsche contemptuously called the "herd mentality" of the masses made them fit only for submission, to be dominated by the Supermen.

## THE INFLUENCE OF LAMARCKIANISM

Another important influence on Nietzsche was Lamarckianism, the now discredited idea that physical and mental achievement can be passed on to one's offspring. The classic illustration is a giraffe that repeatedly stretched its neck to reach more of its diet of leaves at the higher levels of a tree and, the theory taught, its longer neck will consequently be passed on to its offspring. Nietzsche accepted Lamarckianism, as did Darwin, partly because Rütimeyer, Nietzsche's mentor, was a Lamarckian. In addition, "throughout his life, Nietzsche preferred to read neo-Lamarckian authors, and he adapted their ideas" to his Superman theory. This is obvious in Nietzsche's key conclusions, such as the importance of the will from within.[46] In contrast to Darwin, the "survival of the strong exceptional individual" was interpreted by Nietzsche to evolve as a result of a

> continuous effort for the maintenance and the increase of one's power in the struggle for the quality of existence. Hence Nietzsche was driven to regard the figure of the idealized warrior as being eminently suitable for the *élite* of which he dreamed. And since he waged a simultaneous war with himself, he naturally advocated hardness and Spartan ruthlessness for both battles.[47]

---

44 Gayon, "Nietzsche and Darwin," 163.
45 Milner, *Encyclopedia of Evolution*, 338.
46 Gayon, "Nietzsche and Darwin," 159.
47 Lavrin, *Nietzsche*, 27.

Nietzsche's Lamarckian ideas caused him to conclude that a person's internal "will" came from within him, and from this will one could make a person into a Superman—he called it the "will to power," a trait which could be genetically passed onto one's offspring.

The core of Nietzsche's philosophy was a blend of pagan Greek ideas, plus eugenics, modified Darwinism and Lamarckianism.[48] As noted, although Nietzsche deprecated some aspects of Darwinism, he enthusiastically accepted Darwinism's core tenets, such as the "survival-of-the-fittest" principle, which Nietzsche translated into "dominance of the fittest," that "under the new label of the 'will to power'" became "one of the cornerstones of his sociology."[49]

## NIETZSCHE'S ANTI-HUMAN PHILOSOPHY

Despite his stress on freedom for those he called the elite, Nietzsche's philosophy was, in fact, a very suppressive anti-human ideology that aimed at enslaving most humans. He taught that power ultimately decided not only who rules, but also what counts as truth. Nietzsche rejected any form of fixed truth or morality, thus undermining our very notion of human rights. He despised weakness, compassion and humanitarianism, preferring strength and domination. Nietzsche also "developed an increasing explicit justification for intentional selection in the human species (i.e., eugenics)."[50] It is this idea that had a major influence on Nazism.

## NIETZSCHE AND EUGENICS

Stone concluded that there was a "profound interconnection" between Nietzsche's philosophy and eugenics.[51] Nietzsche's writings were used by eugenic advocates in both Europe and America. Mügge writes that to

> Sir Francis Galton belongs the honour of founding the *Science* of Eugenics. To Friedrich Nietzsche belongs the honour of founding

---

48  Lavrin, *Nietzsche*, 27.
49  Lavrin, *Nietzsche*, 27.
50  Gayon, "Nietzsche and Darwin," 165.
51  Stone, *Breeding Superman*, 65.

the *Religion* of Eugenics.... Both aim at a Superman, not a Napoleonic individual, but an ideal of a race of supermen, as superior to the present mankind—many of whom, alas! have not even completed the stage of transition from animal to man—as man is superior to the worm.[52]

Nietzsche was "an ally of Galton, his Superman is a poetic dream of the latter's Eugenetics."[53] In fact, Nietzsche was more than just a supporter of Galton—he went well beyond Galton's passive eugenics and advocated a form of *active* eugenics that was both more aggressive and far more coercive, than Galton had envisioned. Furthermore, Nietzsche was in many ways more influential than Galton, especially among intellectuals and academics.

Nietzsche felt the goal of eugenics was less to produce a perfect society than it was to justify class and race prejudices.[54] Some scholars even interpreted Nietzsche's master and slave idea as roughly dividing humans into superior and inferior races, creating two separate societies. Nietzsche taught that "hybridity between the races...usually brings indubitable racial degeneracy" and "the lower races of mankind [must] give way before the evolution of the superior races" can occur.[55]

## WHY NIETZSCHE HATED CHRISTIANITY

Nietzsche was especially vehement in his rejection of Christian ethics because they cater to the poor, the weak and the downtrodden. His aristocratic morality aimed both at justifying and benefitting the strong and powerful. André Comte-Sponville noted that one of Nietzsche's more nefarious ideas was to systematically side

with force against law, with violence or cruelty against gentleness, with war against peace, who defended egoism, who placed

---

52 Maximilian Mügge, "Eugenics and the superman: A racial science, and a racial religion," *The Eugenics Review* 1, No. 3 (October 1909): 191.

53 Maximilian Mügge, *Friedrick Nietzsche: His Life and Work* (London: Fisher Unwin, 1914), 6.

54 Stone, *Breeding Superman*, 66.

55 Stone, *Breeding Superman*, 63.

instincts above reason...who claimed that there were neither moral nor immoral actions...who justified castes, eugenics, and slavery, who openly celebrated barbarity, disdain for the mass[es], the oppression of the weak, and the extermination of the sick, [and who] spoke of women and democracy in a way that was extremely unpleasant.[56]

Nietzsche condemned all religions—including Jewish, Islamic and Buddhist, but especially Christianity. He "sneered at traditional Judeo-Christian morality as tame, cowardly, and hypocritical."[57] In his *Der Antichrist*, Nietzsche released "unprecedented vehemence [and] attacks on Christian and utilitarian ethics."[58] When the young Nietzsche

had first heard of Charles Darwin and his theories, he had instinctively scoffed at the idea that human beings might be descended from apes. But that was before he had read *The Origin of Species* or had devoted any serious attention to this and other scientific subjects. Since then it had dawned on him that Darwin, with his theory of biological evolution stretched out over an enormous passage of time, had dealt to all forms of anthropomorphic religion a blow far more deadly than the one Copernicus had dealt to medieval Christianity.[59]

It was from Darwin that Nietzsche learned "the theory of evolution as the survival-of-the-fittest" as the source of evolutionary progress.[60] Nietzsche in time took Darwinism to its logical conclusion—eugenics—and a major reason why he came to hate Christianity was its teaching that all men are brothers, all descended from Adam and Eve, producing opposition to eugenics. Specifically, he believed that Christianity "imposed on Europe a servile morality—submission, gentle-

---

56 André Comte-Sponville, quoted in Gayon, "Nietzsche and Darwin, 156.

57 Koster, *Atheist Syndrome*, 83.

58 Flew, *Dictionary of Philosophy*, 229.

59 Cate, *Friedrich Nietzsche*, 354.

60 T.E. Jessop, "Friedrich Nietzsche," in *Dictionary of Christian Ethics*, ed. John Macquarrie (Philadelphia: Westminster Press, 1967), 233.

ness, and care for the weak and ungifted," which opposed the process of evolution by natural selection.[61] Nietzsche demanded an unconditional power of human will and, therefore, "there is no room for Christian...meekness and pity. He made this point...clearer than any other aspect of his teaching."[62] Furthermore, Nietzsche "preached will as the assertion of life, that is, bodily vigor and mental daring, without petty scruples. Those in whom will is strong and presses on to greatness of mind and deed are "supermen."[63]

Nietzsche concluded that it is the superior humans, the Supermen like himself, who made history, and they "alone are entitled to privilege, to dominance in every sphere, to freedom from subordination, morality as usually understood, and religion, which is false anyway and which they do not need. Other men exist for them, as tools."[64] Furthermore, those persons who are

weak in will, try to get what they want by cringing or cunning, or by combination for collective strength, democracy being simply a device of the little to hold down the big, other devices being such religious and moral pretensions as that all men are equal and that we should be kind to one another—all which is contrary to the plain intention of the evolutionary process.[65]

In short, he believed Christianity was a social system that enabled inferior humans to survive the Darwinian struggle for existence.[66] Nietzsche viewed Christianity as the religion of pity

that tends to protect the existence of degenerates.... The religion of pity carries with it the extreme, evil consequence of prolonging a number of useless lives which are really condemned by the law of selection. It preserves and increases the amount of misery

---

61 Jessop, "Friedrich Nietzsche," 233.
62 Lavrin, *Nietzsche*, 85.
63 Jessop, "Friedrich Nietzsche," 233.
64 Jessop, "Friedrich Nietzsche," 233.
65 Jessop, "Friedrich Nietzsche," 233.
66 Stone, *Breeding Superman.*

in the world and consequently makes the universe uglier…, a menace to existence and to the moral health of…humanity."[67]

The appeal to Darwin's law of survival-of-the-fittest is again brought into the service of a Nietzschean cause in Nietzsche's conclusion that Christianity's concern for the poor and the meek has "contributed to the degradation of European races and hindered the production of higher men, the evolution of humanity towards the superman."[68] His attitude toward the common men and women was expressed in his blunt words that men should be trained for war, and women "for the recreation of the warrior: all else is folly. The happiness of man is *I will*. The happiness of woman is *He will*. Thou goest to woman? Do not forget thy whip!"[69]

## NIETZSCHE INFLUENCE ON WORLD LEADERS

Nietzsche's "colossal influence in his homeland" included the leading intellectuals and government leaders.[70] In the twentieth century, many existentialist philosophers, including Martin Heidegger and Jean-Paul Sartre, embraced Nietzsche's general philosophy, denying that humans have any fixed essence, and stressing that radical free will was a right reserved only for the Supermen.

Later in the twentieth century, however, many postmodern thinkers, although heavily influenced by Nietzsche, reduced the importance of the individual agency element, thereby pushing dehumanization even further downward. The relativism that is the foundation of "postmodernism" was openly influenced by Nietzsche's teaching that there exist no absolutes, no God, no afterlife, all values that resulted from his anti-Christian philosophy.[71]

In 1917, Charles Sarolea predicted that the ideas of Nietzsche and certain other like-minded philosophers that are part of what he called

---

67 Henri Lichtenberger, *The Gospel of Superman: The Philosophy of Friedrich Nietzsche* (London: T.N. Foulis, 1910), 138–139.

68 Lichtenberger, *Gospel of Superman*, 139.

69 Nietzsche, *Thus Spake Zarathustra*, 68–70. Emphasis in original.

70 Cate, *Friedrich Nietzsche*, 569.

71 Ervin Staub, *The Roots of Evil: The Origins of Genocide and Other Group Violence* (New York: Cambridge University Press, 1992), 111–112.

the "war-triumvirate" would lead to a great war. Sarolea concluded that Nietzsche was "the spiritual father and forerunner of the Eugenicists," adding that the "Superman is not born, he must be bred" by war.[72] History has, unfortunately, proved Sarolea's prediction of a great war to come correct, namely World War II.

## NIETZSCHE INFLUENCED HITLER

Nietzsche influenced not only intellectuals and college professors, but also certain political leaders, notably Adolf Hitler.[73] Hitler's lifelong friend, August Kubizek, wrote that Nietzsche was one of Hitler's favorite authors.[74] Hitler was actually "deeply influenced by two atheist philosophers—Schopenhauer and Nietzsche."[75] Furthermore, Hitler knew that he was using social Darwinism and Nietzscheism when he wrote in *Mein Kampf* that "the State has the obligation to favor the victory of the best and of the strongest, and to impose the submission of the evil and of the weak."[76] Jean Gayon added that Nietzsche thought in this quote "that he was using language that was both scientifically 'Darwinian' and philosophically 'Nietzschean.'"[77]

Wiker added that Hitler's philosophy was an "amalgam of Machiavelli, Darwin, Schopenhauer, and Nietzsche."[78] German historian Erwin Lutzer documented that Hitler was "mesmerized" by Nietzsche's philosophy. Hitler even "considered himself the superman of Nietzsche's philosophy" and "rejoiced that the doctrine of God that always stood in the way of brutality and deceit had now been removed."[79]

Hitler admired Nietzsche to the extent that he gave special favours to Nietzsche's family.[80] Hitler visited Nietzsche's sister, a "vicious anti-

72 Charles Sarolea, *German Problems and Personalities* (London: Chatto & Windus, 1917), 92.

73 Gayon, "Nietzsche and Darwin," 155.

74 August Kubizek, *Young Hitler: The Story of Our Friendship* (London: Allan Wingate, 1954), 136.

75 Paul C. Vitz, *Faith of the Fatherless: The Psychology of Atheism* (Dallas: Spence, 1999), 106.

76 From Gayon, "Nietzsche and Darwin," 156.

77 From Gayon, "Nietzsche and Darwin," 156.

78 Wiker, *10 Books*, 152.

79 Erwin W. Lutzer, *Hitler's Cross* (Chicago: Moody Press, 1995), 28.

80 Cate, *Friedrich Nietzsche*, 575.

Semite," and posed for a photo besides Nietzsche's bust. Furthermore, the Reich Chancellery book inventory lists a first edition of Nietzsche's eight-volume collected works.[81] Staub concluded that Nietzsche was important in influencing, not only Hitler's worldview, but also the Nazi movement in general, and the fact that many Nazi ideals and beliefs were very similar to those expressed by Nietzsche was no accident.[82]

Hitler himself stated that he valued Nietzsche as a genius; however, although Hitler was clearly influenced by Nietzsche, how much in-depth study of Nietzsche's writings Hitler undertook is unknown.[83] We do know that Nietzsche's book *Thus Spake Zarathustra* "became a bible for the goose-stepping, straight-arm-saluting adolescents of the *Hitler-Jugend*," along with *Mein Kampf* and the racist anti-Semitic tome *Myth of the Twentieth Century*. [84]

Hitler also used Nietzsche's ideas in order to help him persuade the German people of the conclusion that the Germans were the "Master Race." Stephen Hicks went beyond the Darwinian Nazi connection and documented that there existed 38 major similarities between the two worldviews, including that both idealized a "brutal, domineering, fearless, cruel youth," words written by Hitler and inspired by Nietzsche, and both were anti-democratic, anti-capitalistic and anti-liberal.[85]

Nietzsche also influenced the so-called race hygiene movement of German professor Alfred Ploetz, the author of *The Fitness of Our Race*, the book that influenced many Nazi leaders and intellectuals.[86] Ploetz even opened his influential book with the following quote from Nietzsche: "upward leads our way from the species to the superspecies."[87]

Viktor Frankl, a Jew who survived the horrors of Auschwitz, also documented the importance of Nietzsche's writings. Frankl, an emi-

---

81 Timothy W. Ryback, *Hitler's Private Library: The Books that Shaped his Life* (New York: Knopf, 2008), 105–106.

82 Staub, *The Roots of Evil*, 111.

83 Ryback, *Hitler's Private Library*.

84 Cate, *Friedrich Nietzsche*, 576.

85 Stephen R.C. Hicks, *Nietzsche and the Nazis* (Roscoe: Ockham's Razer Publishing, 2010), 97–99.

86 Peter Padfield, *Himmler* (New York: Holt, 1990), 32–33.

87 Alfred Ploetz, *Die Tüchtigkeit unsrer Rasse und der Schutz der Schwachen* (*The Fitness of Our Race and the Protection of the Weak*) (Berlin: S. Fischer, 1895).

nent neurologist and psychiatrist, founded the school of psychology called Logotherapy and is considered one of the most important psychologists of the last century. Frankl astutely evaluated the influence of modern European philosophy, especially that of Nietzsche, in helping to prepare the way for the Nazi atrocities, concluding that the

> gas chambers of Auschwitz were the ultimate consequence of the theory that man is nothing but the product of heredity and environment—or, as the Nazis liked to say, of "Blood and Soil." ...the gas chambers of Auschwitz, Treblinka, and Maidanek were ultimately prepared not in some Ministry or other in Berlin, but rather at the desks and in the lecture halls of nihilistic scientists and philosophers.[88]

## DIFFERENCES BETWEEN HITLER AND NIETZSCHE'S PHILOSOPHY

There were, though, some differences between Nietzsche's and Hitler's philosophy. Nietzsche stressed the elevation of superior *individuals*, not the elevation of a specific *race* as Hitler did. They both believed that the source of superior individuals and races was the result of genetics. For this reason, they concluded that, because a race is simply a large number of superior individuals classified together by genetic traits, the differences between superior races and individuals are relatively minor.

## NIETZSCHE'S INFLUENCE IN AMERICA

Nietzsche's influence was also felt in America. One reason William J. Bryan opposed evolution and became involved in the Scopes Trial was because

> Nietzsche carried Darwinism to its logical conclusion and denied the existence of God, denounced Christianity as the doctrine of the degenerate, and democracy as the refuge of the weakling; he overthrew all standards of morality and eulogized war as necessary to man's development.[89]

---

88 Frankl, *Doctor and the Soul*, xxxii.

89 William Jennings Bryan, *Seven Questions in Dispute* (New York: Fleming H. Revell, 1924), 146.

Some twentieth-century Darwinists have attempted to dissociate themselves from Nietzsche, not because they disagreed with his philosophy, but because they thought his views were too extreme. Conversely, many persons, especially those in the eugenics movement, celebrated his work.[90] Nietzsche is still, even today, celebrated and emulated for his wisdom and insight into human nature and morality.[91] Many others regard him as one of the most evil men who has ever lived.[92]

Also of note, is the fact that modern historians of philosophy have tended to ignore the strong relationship between Nietzsche and Darwin, a fact "probably related to the appropriation of Nietzsche's philosophy by the Nazis."[93] Historians have also "tended to ignore the connection between Nietzsche and the Third Reich."[94] The fact is, "Eugenics, grounded as it was in scientific research, appeared to confirm empirically what Nietzsche had grasped philosophically."[95]

## HIS MENTAL BREAKDOWN

Much speculation exists about the relationship between Nietzsche's philosophy and his mental breakdown. One claim is that Nietzsche suffered from the effects of syphilis that caused gradual creeping paralysis and mental problems, producing a manic-depressive disorder, now called bipolar disorder, failing eyesight, and, toward the end of his life, precocious drooling senility. Although Wright claims that this diagnosis is in little doubt,[96] Cate concluded the syphilis claim is "a mystery that will probably never be elucidated."[97]

Wright also claims that, in January of 1889, Nietzsche experienced an "apoplectic fit" that marked the beginning of his end. Nietzsche then "exhibited numerous eccentricities, so grave as to mean but

90 Stone, *Breeding Superman*, 64.

91 Brian Leiter and Neil Sinhabau, ed., *Nietzsche and Morality* (New York: Oxford University Press, 2007).

92 Wiker, *10 Books*.

93 Gayon, "Nietzsche and Darwin," 155.

94 Gayon, "Nietzsche and Darwin," 155.

95 Stone, *Breeding Superman*, 65.

96 Wright, "Introduction," x.

97 Cate, *Friedrich Nietzsche*, 72.

one thing: his mind was seriously affected."[98] Wright claims that the immediate

> cause of Nietzsche's breakdown was due to…his excessive use of chloral which he took for insomnia, the tremendous strain to which he put his intellect, his constant disappointments and privations, his mental solitude, his prolonged physical suffering. We know little of his last days before he went insane.[99]

Others believe that his ideas were a major, if not *the* major factor, that influenced his breakdown.[100] Maximilian Mügge, in a detailed review of Nietzsche's mental breakdown, described his mental state in terms such as the "sorrow"[101] that he "uttered in the fantastic tone of a madman,"[102] "sleep could only be obtained artificially."[103] When it "was ascertained that Nietzsche was insane," he was placed into an institution.[104] In gross contradiction to his philosophy, Nietzsche himself was hardly a superman, either in body or mind.

## CONCLUSION

Nietzsche's philosophy is the antithesis, not only of the biblical teaching that "all men are descendents of Adam," but also of the philosophy of American and many other societies teaching all persons must be treated with respect and dignity. Nietzsche embraced the basic Darwinian concept with "relish" and went beyond Darwin to advocate a philosophy adopted by governments ranging from Nazi Germany to Communist China and the Soviet Union.[105]

Nietzsche's book *Beyond Good and Evil*[106] was rated by Benjamin

---

98 Wright, "Introduction," x.
99 Wright, "Introduction," x.
100 Wiker, *10 Books*.
101 Mügge, *Friedrick Nietzsche*, 85.
102 Mügge, *Friedrick Nietzsche*, 86.
103 Mügge, *Friedrick Nietzsche*, 90.
104 Mügge, *Friedrick Nietzsche*, 85.
105 Cate, *Friedrich Nietzsche*, 355.
106 Friedrick Nietzsche, *Beyond Good and Evil: Prelude to a Philosophy of the Future*, trans. Walter Kaufmann (New York: Vintage Books, 1966).

Wiker as one of the top ten books that "screwed up the world."[107] Nietzsche's work also had a profound influence on the worst slaughter of humans in the history of humankind, the Holocaust and World War II, which cost 55 million lives. It also had a major adverse influence on academia and philosophy and contributed to ushering in post-Christian philosophy. A succinct summary of Nietzsche's philosophy was the "weak and the botched must perish: that is the first principle of our humanity. And they should be helped to perish! ...[A] good war hallows every cause! Barbarous? Ruthless? Unchristian? No doubt. But so is life itself."[108]

---

107  Wiker, *10 Books*, 99–114.

108  Quoted in Henry Lewis Mencken, "The mailed fist and its prophet," *The Atlantic Monthly*, November 1914, 607.

# Social Darwinism leads to murder: The cases of Anders Behring Breivik and Charles Manson

IIIIIIIIIIIIIIIIIIIIIIIIIIIIIIIIIIIIIIIIIIIIIIIIIIIIIIIIIIIIIIIIIIIIIIIIIIIIIIIIIIIIIIIIIIIIIIIIIIIIIIIIIIIIIIIIIIII

## CASE 1: ANDERS BEHRING BREIVIK

Anders Behring Breivik is a young Norwegian who was enamored with Darwinism and his modern-day disciples, such as Princeton University evolutionary biologist Lee Silver. On Friday, July 22, 2011, Behring Breivik set off a powerful homemade bomb in Oslo, Norway, and went on a killing rampage, killing 77 young persons, and injuring many more, at a Youth League meeting. It was the worst terrorist attack in modern Norwegian history, and one of the worst in modern European history.[1] His story and the harm that he caused to his many victims resulted in a best-selling book by noted author Åsne Seierstad.[2]

The bombing of government buildings in Oslo resulted in eight deaths, and the mass shooting at a Workers' Youth League of the Labor Party on the island of Utøya resulted in killing 69 people, mostly teenagers, and injuring at least 96 other persons. His goal was to bring

---

1 Gordon Rayner, et al., "Hunt for Britons linked to Norway killer Anders Behring Breivik," *The Telegraph*, September 23, 2011.

2 Åsne Seierstad. *One of Us: The Story of Anders Breivik and the Massacre in Norway* (New York: Farrar, Straus, and Giroux, 2015).

attention to his belief that modern Darwinian eugenics could create a utopia and eliminate many of the major problems of the world. His 78,000-word manifesto details his motives and goals for his terrorist attack on his own people.

Breivik was born on February 13, 1979, the son of Wenche Behring, a nurse, and Jens David Breivik, a civil economist. He attended Smestad Grammar School, Ris Junior High, Hartvig Nissen High School and Oslo Commerce School. As an intelligent, sensitive, physically strong young man, he opposed bullying others. Since adolescence, Breivik spent a great deal of time weight-training and used anabolic steroids to improve his physique. He cared a lot about his looks and, in his early twenties, underwent cosmetic surgery to look more like what he judged to be pure Aryan. Breivik worked as a customer service representative, working with people from all nations, and reportedly had good relations with his customers, except he seemed to be easily irritated by those of Middle Eastern or South Asian origin.[3]

## HIS TERRORIST KILLINGS

Soon after the murders occurred, the establishment media, including the Australian and Canadian Broadcasting Corporations, claimed that the influence of fundamentalist Christianity and various right-wing groups explained Breivik's ideology and actions.[4] One typical headline read "Norwegian Killer is Conservative Christian Fundamentalist" a claim which was later repeated by several sources.[5] Although, as is true of many persons, he had both rightwing and leftwing views, his detailed manifesto made his views very clear—and they had nothing to do with Christian fundamentalism.

---

3   Chris Slack, "Anders Breivik 'was on Norwegian secret service watchlist' after buying chemical haul from Polish retailer," DailyMail.com, July 26, 2011; http://www.dailymail.co.uk/news/article-2018646/Norway-shooting-Anders-Behring-Breivik-secret-service-watchlist.html; accessed September 13, 2016.

4   Jonathan Sarfati, "Norway terrorist: more media mendacity," August 2011; http://creation.com/norway-terrorist-breivik-not-christian; accessed September 13, 2016.

5   Seierstad, *One of Us.*

## Anders Behring Breivik (b. 1979)

Racism, eugenics and social Darwinism are at the core of Breivik's ideology and his 2011 bombing and mass shooting in Oslo, Norway, was meant to bring his ideology to the forefront of the world's attention.

Photography © REUTERS/Lise Asreud/NTB

To explain his terrorist actions, Breivik produced a 1518-page manifesto titled *2083 – A European Declaration of Independence*. One reason he gave for his killing spree was that he believed "Marriage is not a conspiracy to oppress women, it's the reason why we're here. And it's not a religious thing, either. According to strict, atheist Darwinism, the purpose of life is to reproduce."[6]

The media almost totally ignored his virulent scientific fundamentalism and social Darwinism, including his far-ranging proposal to revive Darwinian eugenics inspired by the writings of Princeton University evolutionary biologist Lee Silver. They also ignored his agnosticism, such as his "if there is a God" proviso when pondering his destiny after death.[7]

Breivik details in this document that he is an unapologetic champion of modern biology and the evolutionary worldview. Breivik's vision of "a perfect Europe" involves social Darwinism, which he identifies with logic and rationalist thought, opining that the application of "national Darwinism" should be at the core of our society.[8] He does not believe that science should be left in private hands, but instead should be lavishly supported by the government. Specifically, he believes that fully 20 percent of all government spending must be devoted to scientific research[9] and that science funding is even more important than aid to the poor: "Welfare expenditure should not take precedence over the 20% fixed sum dedicated to science/technology, research, and development."[10]

Breivik also stresses that science trumps religion: "As for the Church and science, it is essential that science takes an undisputed precedence over biblical teachings."[11] Breivik listed Darwin's *Origin of Species* as one of the more "important" books that he has ever read.[12] He

---

6 Anders Behring Breivik, *2083 – A European Declaration of Independence* (self-published, 2011), 350; https://fas.org/programs/tap/_docs/2083_-_A_European_Declaration_of_Independence.pdf; accessed October 31, 2016.

7 Breivik, *2083*, 1345.

8 Breivik, *2083*, 1386.

9 Breivik, *2083*, 1188, 1386.

10 Breivik, *2083*, 1195.

11 Breivik, *2083*, 1403.

12 Breivik, *2083*, 1407.

lamented that "Social-Darwinism was the norm before the 1950s. Back then, it was allowed to say what we feel. Now, however, we have to disguise our preferences to avoid the horrible consequences of being labeled as a genetical preferentialist."[13]

Social Darwinism is never far below the surface in his extensive social policy discussions. Breivik's social Darwinism is even foundational to the solution of global ecology and overpopulation problems. He argues that "radical policies will have to be implemented" to reduce the human population by, he concludes, more than half, or down to 3.8 billion people.[14] Furthermore, if "second and third world countries" are unable to curb their population growth, "nature will correct their suicidal tendencies because," as Darwin stressed, they will be "unable to feed their populations," a process that he believes Western countries should not interfere with, even if mass starvation results: "If starvation threatens the countries who have failed to follow our [population control] guidelines, we should not support them by...send[ing] any form of aid."[15] Indeed, food "aid to 3rd world countries must stop immediately as it is the primary cause of overpopulation."[16]

The most blatant example of Breivik's radical Social Darwinism is his endorsement of "reprogenetics," a form of "positive" eugenics that enables humans to control their evolution so as to produce better humans through eugenics. Breivik even argues that the "never-ending collective pursuit for scientific evolution and perfection *should become the benchmark and essence of our existence.*"[17]

Breivik's advocation of the "commercialization and state/media encouragement of reprogenetics favoring the Nordic genotype" was similar to the Nazi Lebensborn program used in their attempt to breed superior Aryans. Specifically, he advocates the use of "large scale surrogacy facilities as a secondary reproduction option.... The donors of eggs and sperm will then exclusively carry the Nordic genotypes."[18]

---

13  Breivik, *2083*, 1227.
14  Breivik, *2083*, 1202.
15  Breivik, *2083*, 1202.
16  Breivik, *2083*, 1203.
17  Breivik, *2083*, 1199. Emphasis added.
18  Breivik, *2083*, 1192.

Breivik laments that the Nazi abuses have made implementing eugenics more difficult today:

> We all remember the horrors from WW2 where the Empire of Japan committed atrocities against the Chinese by large scale massacres and by using them as human test subjects.... Nazi Germany and other countries did the same thing in a smaller degree.... Unfortunately, the horrors of WW2 created a stigma associated with all future research and advances in the field of reprogenetics and improving humans biologically by removing negative hereditary factors. Nevertheless, it is common today for Westerners to abort if it is proved that the fetus has Downs syndrome, severe disfigurements (lacking or additional limbs) or other severe physical handicaps like dwarfism.[19]

Nonetheless, he feels compelled "to bring up this topic despite the fact that it is considered political suicide to discuss under the current Marxist regimes. Most of the propagators of these issues are often affiliated with racist or Nazi ideologies."[20] He explains that the Nazis had the proper social Darwinist goals, but unfortunately they

> destroyed the reputation of "eugenics" by combining it to scientific racism and mass extermination. But seeking biological perfection is still a logical concept.... We just have to make sure that we offer it as a voluntary option to everyone or at least start by legalizing it (promotional voluntary reprogenetics or private reprogenetics). We should legalize reproductive technologies that will allow parents to create offspring with biological improvement (reprogenetics). This must be a non-coercive form of biological improvement which will be predominantly motivated by individual competitiveness and the desire to create the best opportunities for children.[21]

---

19  Breivik, *2083*, 1189–1190.
20  Breivik, *2083*, 1189–1190.
21  Breivik, *2083*, 1200.

Noting the social stigma of eugenics, Breivik writes that, unfortunately, eugenics and reprogenetics are now "extremely politically incorrect to discuss" because of "the 'negative eugenics programs' of Nazi Germany," namely

> sterilization and...experimentation of human test subjects are factors used at that time.... Many European countries used to forcefully sterilize Gypsies/Roma up to aprox. 1972 to prevent them from breeding because they used to be considered "subhuman" etc. These programs are today referred to as "negative eugenics" due to these and other factors.[22]

Breivik concludes that we need to get over this taboo

> because it is estimated that the Nordic genotypes will be extinct completely within 200 years. This is mainly due to intermarriage between Nordics and non-Nordics. Multiculturalist doctrines have speeded this "indirect extermination process" up further in many Western European countries so the extinction might happen sooner. For example, the Norwegian cultural Marxist government has created a vast network of asylum camps all over the country (and in historically isolated small towns and villages) which will contribute to accelerate this process substantially. The Nordic genotypes might be wiped out within 200 years and yet not a single counter-measure has been employed to prevent this from happening due to the fact that it is considered politically incorrect.[23]

He adds that the most effective way to prevent this problem is to introduce

> negative eugenics programs combined with ethnic segregation somewhat similar to some policies of the Third Reich. Segregating Nordics and non-Nordic genotypes at this point would be

---

22 Breivik, *2083*, 1190.
23 Breivik, *2083*, 1190.

almost impossible even if you had military and political carte blanche. Even in Norway and Sweden the number of individuals with the Nordic genotype is reduced annually at a drastic rate due to EU open borders program, mass-Asian/African immigration and significantly higher Asian/African (especially Muslim) birthrates.[24]

His solution, which he feels is "the only option which could work in this modern world" is

to commercialize positive reprogenetics programs on a state level. This will obviously not be possible as...[a]nyone who suggests a program like this would immediately be labeled a Nazi and racist, which subsequently would end anyone's career (character assassination). No Western politician, which is a part of the current EUSSR/USASSR hegemony, will take this chance.[25]

Nonetheless, he predicts that those who support reprogenetics will

seize power within 30–70 years. And when we do we should refrain from committing the same mistakes of the past. We must reject negative eugenics and instead focus on positive eugenics or so called reprogenetics. Political correct individuals will say: "Who cares if blonde people with blue eyes are extinct? We are all going to be dark skinned in the future anyway." Wrong. ... [W]e have no intention to allow...the indigenous peoples of Europe to be indirectly exterminated. The hypocritical thing is that the same individuals stating this are likely to support...the preservation of rare species in the animal kingdom etc.[26]

Breivik obsesses about preserving the "Nordic" race, which he believes possess "rare characteristics that have been acquired through

---

24  Breivik, *2083*, 1190.
25  Breivik, *2083*, 1191.
26  Breivik, *2083*, 1191.

an evolutionary process which has taken more than 1 million years" to evolve.[27] Breivik's major concern is that modern liberal attitudes toward "race-mixing" are leading people of Nordic ancestry to act "unnaturally" and undo what a million years of evolution has produced. He echoes in this conclusion the ideas of leading early twentieth-century Darwinian eugenists, including Madison Grant, whom Breivik cited favourably in his manifesto.[28] In his *Passing of the Great Race* (1918), Grant denounced the American "melting pot" ideal because its inevitable result was inter-racial marriage that he believed, as did the Nazis, caused degeneration of the "superior" race. Grant wrote that the "result of the mixture of two races, in the long run, gives us a race reverting to the more ancient, generalized and lower type."[29] Grant especially was concerned about the degradation of the "Nordic races" because he believed that Nordics were naturally the "rulers, organizers, and aristocrats." Grant repeatedly cited the importance of evolution for his theory in his 1918 tome.[30]

## BREIVIK RELIES ON MODERN DARWINISTS

Breivik's calls for a eugenics revolution were not inspired by his own private ideas, but instead, they spring largely from leading mainstream Darwinists, past and present. His social Darwinism was a clear part of the mix that caused his murderous rampage.

Although contemporary scientists now distance themselves from Madison Grant's racism, he was once a highly respected scientist by the American scientific community. His many honours include board member of the prestigious American Museum of Natural History in New York, chairman of the New York Zoological Society and councillor for the American Geographical Society. Some of his articles were published in *National Geographic* magazine. Grant's book, *The Passing of the Great Race*, went through multiple editions, each with a con-gratulatory preface by American Museum of Natural History president

---

27 Breivik, *2083*, 1158.

28 Breivik, *2083*, 1152–1153.

29 Madison Grant, *The Passing of the Great Race, or, the Racial Basis of European History* (New York: Charles Scribner's Sons, 1918), 16.

30 Breivik, *2083*, 11, 27, 33, 88, 95, 105, 121, 135, 152, 228, 234.

(from 1908 to 1933) and Columbia University zoologist, Henry Fair-field Osborn.[31]

Many of Grant's concerns about the negative effects of race-mixing were echoed by leading evolutionary biologists of the era, such as Harvard professor Edward East and the head of the Cold Spring Harbor Research Lab, Charles Davenport. East and Davenport were both members of the elite National Academy of Sciences, and Davenport was a founding father of the "science" of eugenics. Grant, East and Davenport are examples of how past mainstream ideas still can exert a pernicious influence today.

Breivik drew not only on early Darwinian thinkers, but his "repro-genetics" proposal was lifted from a modern, highly respected evolu-tionary biologist, Lee Silver, a Princeton professor and fellow of the American Association for the Advancement of Science. It was Silver who coined the term "reprogenetics," and his 1997 book, *Remaking Eden: How Genetic Engineering and Cloning Will Transform the American Family*, is prominently featured in Breivik's manifesto.

Reprogenetics merges existing reproductive and genetic technolo-gies, all of which Silver predicts will become less costly, more available and increasingly powerful. Reprogenetics involves applying genetic advances currently being perfected, including technological improve-ments in interpreting the effects of specific DNA on morphology, the ability to harvest large numbers of embryos from adult females, and progress to dynamically increase the current rate of successful embryo reinsertion into host mothers. Silver's goal is for parents to be able to select the genetic characteristics of their offspring, which he predicts will trigger major social changes, including reducing genetic diseases and the breeding of superior humans.

Eugenics, the "science" of improving the gene pool, became infa-mous for the brutal policies that its supporters practiced in the twen-tieth century. The major differences between reprogenetics and eugenics is that, in contrast to reprogenetics, eugenics programs were compulsory, imposed by governments attempting to achieve some idealistic utopian goal such as high IQ individuals.

---

31 Henry Fairfield Osborn, "Introduction," in *The Passing of the Great Race, or, the Racial Basis of European History* (New York: Charles Scribner's Sons, 1918), vii-ix.

Unlike Breivik, Silver does not advocate using genetic means to preserve the "Nordic" race, but does argue that reprogenetics will achieve superior human beings by allowing humans to control human evolution. Although Silver is concerned that wholesale genetic engineering could lead to a chasm between those who can afford genetic enhancements and those who cannot, Silver spends much of his book attempting to dismiss what he perceives to be the major objections to his new eugenics. In his prologue, Silver explores

> the ethical arguments that have been raised against the use of this technology. In most instances, I will attribute opposition to conscious or subconscious fears of treading in "God's domain." Indeed, I will argue that nearly all of the objections raised by bioethicists and others ring hollow.[32]

In the chapter titled "The Designer Child," Silver sounds very much like the eugenicists of a century past, arguing that technology now has given us the power to direct our own evolution, and we must seize that power, opining, "While selfish genes do, indeed, control all other forms of life, master and slave have switched positions in human beings, who now have the power not only to control but to create new genes."[33]

He adds, "Why not control what has been left to chance in the past?" We control all other aspects of our children's lives and identities through powerful social and environmental influences as well as by powerful drugs such as Ritalin or Prozac: "On what basis can we reject positive genetic influences on a person's essence when we accept the rights of parents to benefit their children in every other way?"[34]

In his epilogue, Silver offers a utopian vision of the future directed by intelligence that would make some earlier eugenicists envious. Writing a hypothetical history of reprogenetics from some future date, Silver details how humans have utilized genetic engineering to evolve

---

32 Lee M. Silver, *Remaking Eden: Cloning and Beyond in a Brave New World* (New York: Avon Books, 1997), 13.

33 Silver, *Remaking Eden*, 277.

34 Silver, *Remaking Eden*, 277.

themselves into God-like creatures, writing the "critical turning point in the evolution of life in the universe" was

> when the first generation of cognition-enhanced GenRich matured, they produced among themselves scientists who greatly outshone geniuses from all previous epochs. And these scientists made huge advances in further understanding the human mind, and they created more sophisticated reprogenetic technologies, which they then used to enhance cognition even further in the GenRich of the next generation.[35]

By this means, Silver concludes that each generation will achieve quantum leaps of progressive evolution. Silver's conclusion was, although some argued that there exist "limits to mental capacity and technological advances," these prophesied limits were soon swept aside

> as intelligence, knowledge, and technological power continued to rise. A special point has now been reached in the distant future. And in this era, there exists a special group of mental beings. Although these beings can trace their ancestry back directly to homo sapiens, they are as different from humans as humans are from the primitive worms with tiny brains that first crawled along the earth's surface.[36]

He justified achieving his eugenic evolutionary goals by reasoning that it required some

> 600 million years for those worms to evolve into human beings. It has taken far less time for humans to self-evolve into the mental beings that now exist. It is difficult to find the words to describe the enhanced attributes of these special people. "Intelligence" does not do justice to their cognitive abilities. "Knowledge" does not explain the depth of their understanding of both the universe

---

35 Silver, *Remaking Eden*, 293.
36 Silver, *Remaking Eden*, 293.

and their own consciousness. "Power" is not strong enough to describe the control they have over technologies that can be used to shape the universe in which they live.[37]

Professor Silver not only served as a major intellectual mentor to Breivik's chilling demands for a new eugenics, but Breivik also embraced wholesale both Silver's reprogenetics program and his scientific utopianism, again documenting the fact that ideas clearly have consequences.

## BREIVIK CONDEMNS "RACE MIXING"
Breivik openly condemns Norway's policy that encouraged race mixing, which contributed to inter-racial marriage, writing that

> the Ombud for Gender Equality recently became The Equality and Antidiscrimination Ombud. Its duties include combating "discriminatory speech" and negative statements about other cultures and religions. If accused of such discrimination, one has to mount proof of innocence. In effect, this institution is a secular or Multicultural Inquisition: the renunciation of truth in favor of an ideological lie. Galileo Galilei faced the same choice during the Inquisition four hundred years earlier. The Multicultural Inquisition may not threaten to kill you, but it does threaten to kill your career, and that goes a long way in achieving the same result.[38]

When advocating positive eugenics to help justify his ideas, Breivik notes that the Swedish government also "applied German race laws from 1937 onwards" and "any Swede who wanted to marry an Aryan German was forced to sign an affirmation stating that none of the German's grandparents were Jewish."[39] Furthermore, in 1937, despite the evidence that Sweden

---

37 Silver, *Remaking Eden*, 293.
38 Breivik, *2083*, 526–527.
39 Breivik, *2083*, 638.

applied Nazi race laws, party members still got away with denouncing critics of their immigration policies as neo-Nazis, racists or Fascists.... Socialist Professor Gunnar Myrdal and his wife Alva, both highly influential ideologists in developing the Swedish welfare state, had intimate connections with the German academic world during the Nazi age.[40]

Furthermore, according to Huntford:

"The professor was then a Nazi sympathizer, publicly describing Nazism as the movement of...the future. In Myrdal's defense... whatever his other propensities, Hitler did have advanced ideas on social welfare, and that the social ideology of the German Nazis and the Swedish Social Democrats had much in common. Until the mid 1930s, Nazism had considerable attraction for those who favored a benevolent and authoritarian state."[41]

Breivik concluded that the Myrdals

promoted the idea of positive eugenics and forced sterilization programs against those with "weak genes." This started in Sweden even before Nazi Germany, and it continued longer. The Nazis called themselves national Socialists, and they took the Socialist component of their ideology quite seriously.... The Nazis were thus to the left, economically, compared to many of the labor parties in Western Europe today. As Adolf Hitler stated in 1927: "We are Socialists, enemies, mortal enemies of the present capitalist economic system with its exploitation of the economically weak, with its injustice in wages, with its immoral evaluation of individuals according to wealth and money instead of responsibility and achievement."[42]

---

40 Quoted in Breivik, *2083*, 638.

41 Cited in Breivik, *2083*, 638. See Roland Huntford, *The New Totalitarians* (London: Allen Lane/The Penguin Press, 1971).

42 Breivik, *2083*, 638.

## RACISM AT THE CORE OF BREIVIK'S IDEOLOGY

Breivik's major concern, as was Hitler's, is the putative soon to occur "rapid extinction of the Nordic genotypes."[43] An example he cites is the data that shows the prevalence of blue eyes among European-Americans living in the United States was

> 57.4 percent for those born from 1899 through 1905 compared with 33.8 percent for those born from 1936 through 1951. Blue eyes have become increasingly rare among American children, with only one out of every six—16.6 percent, which is 49.8 million out of 300 million (22.4% of European-Americans) of the total United States population having blue eyes.[44]

He is obviously unaware of the fact that blue eyes is a mutation that causes a loss of the important brown iris pigment which protects the eyes from the harmful rays of the sun. Breivik's concern about intermarriage was due to its eugenic implications:

> A century ago, 80 percent of people married within their ethnic group. Blue eyes were routinely passed down, especially among people of Western and Northern European ancestry. About half of Americans born at the turn of the 20th century had blue eyes, according to a 2002 Loyola University study in Chicago. By mid-century that number had dropped to a third. Today only about one 1 of every 6 Americans has blue eyes.[45]

The Loyola research was motivated by the observation that blue eyes were much more prevalent among nursing home elderly patients than in the general population. The researchers at first assumed that blue eyes may be related to increased life expectancy, but it turned

> out it has more to do with marriage patterns. A century ago, 80 percent of people married within their ethnic group.... Blue eyes,

---

43 Breivik, *2083*, 1188.

44 Breivik, *2083*, 1188.

45 Breivik, *2083*, 1188.

a genetically recessive trait, were routinely passed down, especially among people of English, Irish, and Northern European
ancestry. By mid-century, a person's level of education—and not
ethnicity—became the primary factor in selecting a spouse. As
intermarriage between ethnic groups became the norm, blue
eyes began to disappear, replaced by brown.[46]

The problem, Breivik argues, was caused by the immigration of various

> nonwhites into the United States, especially from Latin America
> and Asia, [which] hastened the disappearance [of blue eyes].
> Between 1900 and 1950, only about 1 in 10 Americans was non-
> white. Today that ratio is 1 in 3. With the exception of an increased
> risk of macular degeneration (blue eyes are at greater risk), eye
> color is biologically indicative of almost nothing. Boys are 3 per-
> cent to 5 percent likelier to have blue eyes than girls, but beyond
> that it's a non-issue, physiologically speaking. The cultural impli-
> cations are another story. Preferences for fair skin and blue eyes
> stretch back in Europe to at least the Middle Ages.... For women
> in particular, especially those of European descent, fair skin and
> light eyes have long been seen as indicators of fertility and beauty.
> America adopted those biases early on, and Hollywood reinforced
> them by anointing a long line of blue-eyed blondes such as Marilyn
> Monroe as the nation's sex symbols.[47]

He adds that in the past

> eugenicists used the disappearance of blue eyes as a rallying cry
> to support immigration restrictions. They went so far as to map
> the parts of the country with the highest and lowest percentage
> of blue-eyed people. So consumed were Americans with this
> ideal that in the 70s and 80s the fashion models who exemplified
> the All-American look were typically Scandinavian.... Blue...is

---

46  Breivik, *2083*, 1188.
47  Breivik, *2083*, 1189.

by far the most popular color contact lens sold at 1-800-CON-TACTS, the largest contact lens distributor in the US.[48]

Breivik concludes that saving humanity requires the application of eugenics and his murderous rampage would publicize his concerns as spelled out in his manifesto. In the latter goal he was very successful. He also was successful in showing that Darwinian eugenics is still alive and well in the world.

## SUMMARY

This event illustrates the fact that eugenic ideas are still alive and influential in some areas of society and are, likewise, still very destructive. It also illustrates that rejection of the biblical record, especially the doctrine that all humans descended from the first man and woman, Adam and Eve, leads to Darwinism, and evolution leads to racism and eugenics.

## CASE 2: THE CHARLES MANSON MURDERERS AND DARWINISM

One of the most horrific crimes of the twentieth century was the Charles Manson murders that involved the senseless killing of seven people, including director Roman Polanski's pregnant wife, actress Sharon Tate, on August 9, 1969. Two days later, several members of the Manson family, specifically Charles "Tex" Watson, murdered supermarket executive Leno LaBianca and his wife, Rosemary, in their upscale home. The case made headlines around the world and was the subject of at least five books. The most popular book on the case, *Helter Skelter*, written by the prosecuting attorney Vincent Bugliosi, was the best-selling crime book of the twentieth century.[49]

Charles Milles Manson (b. November 12, 1934) is an American ne'er-do-well who led what became known as the Manson Family, or just The Family, a quasi-commune in California in the late 1960s. At most, fewer than 40 people were part of the movement, some only

---

48 Breivik, *2083*, 1189.

49 Jeff Guinn, *Manson: The Life and Times of Charles Manson* (New York: Simon & Schuster, 2013).

temporarily, and mostly young women. Manson believed in what he called Helter Skelter, an expression he exploited from a Beatles song of the same name. The Helter Skelter involved the belief in a soon to occur apocalyptic race war between blacks and whites. Manson expected the killings that The Family committed would help to precipitate that war.[50]

He attempted to achieve this goal by attempting to blame his family's killings on the Black Panthers by such acts as writing words like "Pig," a common term used by radical blacks to describe the white police, in blood in the homes of his victims. Manson naïvely felt that this act would encourage the race war that he felt was sure to come soon. Manson taught that

the Family were going to descend into a "Bottomless pit," …and remain there until the blacks had decimated the whites. Finding themselves incapable of ruling the world, the victors would call upon the Family to take over while they (the blacks) reverted to their natural servant status.[51]

Those who testified at Manson's trial were adamant that this was Manson's central goal. They testified under oath in court that the reason for the Manson murders was because "a war between the blacks and whites was imminent and he [Manson] called that war Helter Skelter."[52] When Manson developed his Helter Skelter theory, he underwent a complete change of lifestyle. He also began to obtain material things such as firearms, vehicles, money. He said he needed these things, "to go to the desert [and hide] because Helter Skelter was coming."[53] Other court testimony in his murder court case that supported this theory was as follows:

Kasabian: Well, they knew that we were super-aware, much more than other white people, and they knew we knew about them

---

50 Nuel Emmons, *Manson in His Own Words* (New York: Grove Press, 1986), 5.
51 George Victor Bishop, *Witness to Evil* (New York: Nash Publishers, 1972), 353.
52 Bishop, *Witness to Evil*, 352.
53 Bishop, *Witness to Evil*, 352.

## Charles Manson (b. 1934)

Leader of a small commune in the 1960s, Manson and his followers murdered seven people over a few weeks in an attempt to precipitate a race war between blacks and whites, something he termed Helter Skelter. Deeply influenced by Darwin and Nietzsche, Manson's followers zealously did his bidding.

and that they were eventually going to take over, his whole philosophy on the black people, that they wanted to do away with us [whites] because apparently they knew that we were going to save the white race or go out to the hole in the desert.

Q: (By Bugliosi): *Did Mr. Manson mention the term Helter Skelter to you?*

A: (By Miss Kasabian after five separate objections by Kanarek): Yes. It is a revolution where blacks and whites will get together and kill each other and all non-blacks and brown people and even black people who do not go on black people's terms...

Q: *Did he say who was going to start Helter Skelter?*

A: Blackie [was]. He used to say that Blackie was much more aware than whitey and super together, and whitey was just totally untogether, just would not get together; ...and blackie was really together.[54]

When the blacks emerged victorious they would realize that they do "not have the mental capacity to govern properly" and would turn over the government to the whites.[55] Then Manson and his followers could assume their rightful place in the White government.

## NIETZSCHE INFLUENCES MANSON

One court trial witness noted that a philosopher who influenced Manson was Nietzsche, testifying that

Charlie claimed to have read Nietzsche and that he believed in a master race, plus the emergence of a startling number of disturbing parallels between Manson and the leader of the Third Reich, led me [Bugliosi] to ask Poston: "Did Manson ever say anything about Hitler?" Poston's reply was short and incredibly chilling... "He said that Hitler was a tuned in guy who had leveled the karma of the Jews."[56]

---

54 Bishop, *Witness to Evil*, 142.

55 Emmons, *Manson in His Own Words*, 6.

56 Vincent Bugliosi, *Helter Skelter: The True Story of the Manson Murders* (New York: Norton, 1974), 236.

The many comparisons between Hitler and Manson include:

> Both Manson's and Hitler's followers were able to explain away the monstrous acts their leaders committed by retreating into philosophical abstractions. Probably the single most important influence on Hitler was Nietzsche. Manson told Jakobson that he had read Nietzsche.... [B]oth Manson and Hitler believed in the three basic tenets of Nietzsche's philosophy: women are inferior to men; the white race is superior to all other races; [and] it is not wrong to kill if the end is right.[57]

Manson's motivation was "it is a matter of evolution" and "the black people are coming to the top."[58] In another example of racism, Manson got upset at people who listened to black music on the radio. Manson didn't like this music because it "offended their Okie-Aryan racism."[59] And, another incident involving Manson's goal to please a gang of bikers was that

> not all of them passed the race test. For instance, Joe of the Straight Satans once brought a guy to the ranch that was one-half Indian, a guy named Sammy. Charlie would not allow him to make it with the girls. A person named Mark who was only one-quarter Indian was not allowed to commerce with the Aryans at the Spahn Ranch.[60]

Manson also very much opposed interracial marriage because, he believed, it would cause degeneration of the White race, the same view that Hitler held.[61]

---

57 Bugliosi, *Helter Skelter*, 474.

58 Bugliosi, *Helter Skelter*, 420.

59 Ed Sanders, *The Family: The Story of Charles Manson's Dune Buggy Attack Battalion* (New York: E.P. Dutton, 1971), 141.

60 Sanders, *The Family*, 41.

61 Emmons, *Manson in His Own Words*, 172.

## HATRED OF CHRISTIANITY

The Family also openly rejected Christianity and, instead, "believed in reincarnation and in the possibility of monitoring past lives. So the child was the sum culmination of the life-chain of evolution."[62]

Promiscuous sex, which was connected to his racism, also was central to Manson's worldview. Manson used sex to help eradicate what he [Manson] viewed as Christian hang-ups:

> If a person indicated reluctance to engage in a certain [sex] act, Manson would force that person to commit it. Male-female, female-female, male-male, intercourse, cunnilingus, fellatio, sodomy—there could be no inhibitions of any kind. One thirteen-year-old girl's initiation into the Family consisted of her being sodomized by Manson while the others watched. Manson also "went down on" a young boy to show the others he had rid himself of all inhibitions.[63]

Watson, a member of Manson's gang who murdered seven persons, became a born-again Christian in 1975 and, through non-incarcerated associates, operates www.aboundinglove.org. His book about his role in the murders includes his testimony and the fact that, although he now feels enormous remorse for his actions, he believes that God has forgiven him.[64] Watson also supported the conclusions documented in this chapter.

## CONCLUSION

The Helter Skelter theory, as explained by Manson's leading disciple, Charles Watson, was based on the belief that Manson "had always taught" that "blacks were less evolved than whites, and therefore were only fit to be their slaves.... [N]ow that all the centuries of operation and exploitation for blackie were over, his karma had turned, and it was time for him to rise and win."[65] The blacks were going to "launch a

---

62 Sanders, *The Family*, 61.
63 Bugliosi, *Helter Skelter*, 327.
64 Charles Watson, *Will You Die For Me?* (Dallas: Cross Roads Publications, 1978).
65 Watson, *Will You Die For Me?*, 104.

fratricidal that would make the War Between the States look tame by comparison."[66] The blacks would win, but, when in full control of the nation, they would realize that they were less evolved than the whites and, consequently, would then hand over the power to the Whites. Manson thought he would help this inevitable Helter Skelter war along by murdering some rich whites, and leave signs at the murder scene that would point to the Black Panthers as the culprits. This far-fetched scenario was less far-fetched in the time that Manson lived when widespread violence and riots were occurring during the civil rights movement of the 1960s and 1970s. This case is one of many examples where Darwinism has influenced racism and led to criminal behaviour.[67]

---

66 Watson, *Will You Die For Me?*, 104.

67 Jerry Bergman, "Darwinian criminality theory: A tragic chapter in history," *Rivista di Biologia/Biology Forum* 98, No. 1 (Jan–Apr, 2005): 47–70.

## Benjamin Spock (1903-1998)

Affectionately known as the "baby doctor," Dr. Spock authored one of the best-selling books of all time, *Baby and Child Care*. Over time, Spock saw the destructive impact of Darwinism and evolutionary theory on society.

# Benjamin Spock and Chet Raymo: The "baby doctor" and the Catholic turned atheist

||||||||||||||||||||||||||||||||||||||||||||||||||||||||||||||||||||||||||||||||||||||||||||||||||||||||||||||||

## BENJAMIN SPOCK: THE "BABY DOCTOR"

Yale-trained physician Benjamin Spock is the author of one of the best-selling nonfiction books of all time, a guide for parents titled *Baby and Child Care*. First published in 1946, it has sold over 50 million copies and has been translated into 42 languages. His writings and ideas have influenced so many mothers that he has been affectionately called the nation's "baby doctor."[1] His influence in the world has been so profound that Dr. Spock was named by *Life* magazine as one of the most important people in the twentieth century.[2] He also is widely considered the most influential child-care authority of the twentieth century.[3]

During his long and distinguished professional career, Spock taught at several of the nation's leading institutions of higher learning, includ-

1   Benjamin Spock and Mary Morgan, *Spock on Spock: A Memoir of Growing Up with the Century* (New York: Pantheon Books, 1989); D. Bell, "Profile: Dr. Benjamin Spock," *Midwife and Health Visitor* 2, No. 8 (August 1966):323.

2   Thomas Maier, *Dr. Spock: An American Life* (New York: Harcourt Brace, 1998), 298.

3   Raymond G. McInnis, "Dr. Benjamin Spock's baby and child care: Origins, impact, sources," *Reference Services Review* 13, No. 4 (1973):9–15.

ing Cornell University, the University of Minnesota and Case Western Reserve University. Always a superior student, he graduated first in his class from Columbia University Medical School.[4] His lifelong interest in and love for people was one factor that helped him develop into an astute observer of the human condition.[5] His interest in his field motivated him to author a dozen books and hundreds of articles not only on childcare, but also on some of the major social problems of our age.[6] Spock was very active in helping humanity by his involvement in numerous organizations until his death in March 1998, a few weeks shy of his ninety-fifth birthday.[7]

## SPOCK INTRODUCED TO DARWINISM

Spock was first introduced to Darwinism as an undergraduate at Yale University, and he referenced Darwin and his ideas several times in his books. Even his classic work, *Baby and Child Care*, under the subheading "They're repeating the whole history of the human race," teaches evolution. Spock wrote that watching a baby grow is "full of meaning" because the development of each individual child retraces

the whole history of the human race, physically and spiritually, step by step. Babies start off in the womb as a single tiny cell, just the way the first living thing appeared in the ocean. Weeks later, as they lie in the amniotic fluid in the womb, they have gills like fish. Toward the end of the first year of life, when they learn to clamber to their feet, they're celebrating that period millions of years ago when our ancestors got up on all fours. It's just at that time that babies are learning to use their fingers with skill and

---

4    Ray Lewkonia, "Benjamin Spock: The public pediatrician," *The Lancet* 35, No. 9130 (1998):825.

5    T. Philpot, "Profile: Dr. Benjamin Spock. A middle-of-the-road man," *Nursing Mirror* 149, No. 19 (Nov. 8, 1979):20–21.

6    Mary Ellen Hubbard, "Benjamin Spock, MD: The Man and His Work in Historical Perspective." Ph.D. diss. Claremont Graduate School, 1981.

7    Lewkonia, "Benjamin Spock"; Danny Duncan Collum, "The Spock revolution," *Sojourners* 27, No. 4 (Jul/Aug 1998):52.

delicacy. Our ancestors stood up because they had found more useful things to do with their hands than walking on them.[8]

## SPOCK RECOGNIZES THE HARM OF DARWINISM TO SOCIETY

Spock eventually recognized the serious harm that Darwinism caused to people's lives and to society in general.[9] The insight Spock gained is the story of many individuals of our time. His biographer, Lynn Bloom, stated it was inevitable that Spock, "frustrated in his attempts to express fully his views on various social or political issues in magazine columns," would elaborate his conclusions in a book—*Decent and Indecent: Our Personal and Political Behavior*. His book, which Bloom calls "Spock's spiritual autobiography," was "the distillation of a lifetime of his varied thoughts on the problems of modern western man, Americans in particular." In this book, he concluded

that *man has lost his belief in himself and his sense of direction because the concepts of evolution, of psychology, and of sociology have undermined the authority of religion and man's identification with God.* They have induced man to belittle himself, to conceive of himself as merely an animal divisible into a number of mechanical parts and drives.[10]

Dr. Spock writes in his spiritual autobiography that he was reared in a family "with stern morals even by New England standards." He then admitted that he tried to free himself from these strict standards throughout his adolescence and young adulthood because he then believed that a "knowledge of biology, psychology, and sociology should offer sufficient guides for a modern man."[11] His lifetime of reading, practicing as a pediatrician, college teaching, talking with parents and researching the problems of Western society caused him

---

8  Benjamin Spock and Michael Rothenberg, *Baby and Child Care*, 6th ed. (New York: Dutton, 1992), 301.

9  Lynn Z. Bloom, *Doctor Spock: Biography of a Conservative Radical* (New York: The Bobbs-Merrill Company, 1972).

10  Bloom, *Doctor Spock*, 213. Emphasis added.

11  Bloom, *Doctor Spock*, 213.

to "come to realize that the worst problems of America—war, racial injustice, unnecessary poverty, for example—are caused not by lack of knowledge or means [to solve these problems] *but by moral blindness or confusion*."[12]

Table 1 shows the increase in some major social problems that have occurred in the past half century alone. Obviously these problems are due to several factors, a major one being the secularization of society and what Spock called "a moral blindness." Spock concluded this moral blindness that produced many of our modern social problems was the direct result of modern secular teachings resulting from Darwinism, Freudianism and other humanistic philosophies. Spock further concluded a major reason for our most serious social problems was the *weakening of the influence of religion that resulted especially from the influence of Darwinism* and our increasingly secular society:

> The teachers in the early colonial schools and universities of the United States were predominantly Protestant ministers whose principal aim was to teach religious principles and to train more ministers, who became the next leaders of the community.... By the second half of the nineteenth century the *discovery of evolution* and the development of various behavioral sciences further weakened the authority of the churches as educators. As the need for schools and universities mounted, they were established increasingly by towns and states. Now the Supreme Court has forbidden in public schools even the vaguest of prayers.[13]

Spock realized that many of the social movements with which he had once agreed had caused an enormous amount of harm to our society. As a result of his insight, he admitted that in the end he had "come full circle...to a feeling that it is crucial, in all issues, to consider the moral dimension" when trying to solve social and societal problems.[14] He realized the major source of morality in the West was the Judeo-

---

12 Benjamin Spock, *Decent and Indecent: Our Personal and Political Behavior* (New York: McCall, 1970), 207. Emphasis added.

13 Spock, *Decent and Indecent*, 207. Emphasis added.

14 Spock, *Decent and Indecent*, xiii.

## Table 1
## A sample of increases in social problems, 1960 vs. 1992

|  | 1960 | 1992 |
|---|---|---|
| Illegitimate births |  |  |
| Whites | 3% | 22% |
| Blacks | 23% | 68% |
| Total population | 5% | 30% |
| Welfare spending | $29 billion | $212 billion |
| Juvenile crime | 137* (1965) | 431* |
| Violent crime | 16* | 76* |
| Total crime | 189* | 566* |
| Cost of crime | $43 billion | $163 billion |
| Combined SAT scores | 975 | 899 |
| Church membership | 63% | 59% |

*Rate per 100,000 population

*Source: Statistical Abstract of the United States*

Christian heritage, which has been seriously undermined by Darwinism, Freudianism, and the secular humanistic philosophies taught in our schools and by the mass media and society as a whole. In his words, he (Spock) "grew up with the century."[15]

## SPOCK LEARNED TOO LATE TO SOLVE THE PROBLEM
Unfortunately, Spock's insight about these issues came late in his life when there was little he could do to ameliorate them. While he recognized that Darwinism was harmful, he had long assumed that evolution theory was supported by verifiable, scientific facts. His own references to the alleged evidence for Darwinism have been refuted long ago. For example, science has now proven that almost every claim made in the quote from Spock's *Baby and Child Care* book is wrong.

The theory that an embryo repeats its ancient evolutionary history has been shown to be based on forgeries.[16] Furthermore, neither

---

15 Spock and Morgan, *Spock on Spock.*

16 Jonathan Wells, *Icons of Evolution: Why Much of What We Teach About Evolution Is Wrong* (Washington: Regnery, 2000); Bergman, "The rise and fall"; Wayne Frair,

embryos nor fetuses have "gills like fish." Spock had recognized that evolution had done much harm in society, but his belief in the evidence that supported evolutionism blocked him from doing much about the problem. This illustrates the importance of stressing current research, which shows that most of the icons used to support evolution are either outright frauds or are based on extremely tenuous and debatable evidence.[17]

## CHET RAYMO: FROM CATHOLIC TO ATHEIST
Does acceptance of Darwinism lead to rejection of Judeo-Christianity morality and the acceptance of atheism? One case reviewed in some detail, which is all too common, is that of Professor Chet Raymo. The case, and why he became an atheist, sheds light on the relationship between Darwinism and both atheism and morality.

Chet Raymo, a well-known and highly respected popular science writer, is professor emeritus of Physics and Astronomy at Stone Hill College in Massachusetts. Raymo was raised in a very religious Roman Catholic home and attended Catholic schools until he went to graduate school. Raymo wrote that when his father was dying of cancer, his father dealt with his condition by relying, first, on God, then medical science and, last, his own resources.[18] Raymo also wrote that he (Chet) believed his own guardian angel hovered reassuringly at his side until it skipped from his conscience during adolescence and vanished completely when he studied science, specifically Darwinism, in college.[19]

## LIFE UNDER DARWINISM
Raymo concluded that Darwinism has made God irrelevant.[20] In his words, he knew "the primary revelation of the Creator is *the creation*," and once he became convinced that evolution was the creator, God became irrelevant.[21] After Raymo accepted Darwinism, he also con-

---

"Embryology and evolution," *Creation Research Society* 36 No. 2 (1999):62–68.

17  Wells, *Icons of Evolution.*

18  Chet Raymo, *Honey from Stone* (Kerry: Brandon, 1997), 110.

19  Chet Raymo, *Skeptics and True Believers* (New York: Walker, 1998), 265.

20  Raymo, *Honey from Stone*, 108.

21  Chet Raymo, *Climbing Brandon: Science and Faith on Ireland's Holy Mountain* (New York: Walker, 2004), 122.

## Chet Raymo (b. 1936)

Raymo's acceptance of Darwinism has seemingly blinded him to the lack of
empirical evidence to support many of his own claims in the realm of science.
His case is not unusual in the academic world where Darwinian indoctrination
has swept most universities today.

cluded that, if Genesis is wrong, then the entire Bible is unreliable. In Raymo's mind, Darwinism murdered God and, although geologists once "struggled to find a way to make the story of the fossils compatible with the story of the Scriptures," they have failed.[22] After Darwinism destroyed Raymo's theism, he became an evangelical atheist, active in preaching his new beliefs to the world in his college teaching, his writings and his life.

Raymo admits that evolution "is not warm and fuzzy" and can even be "capricious and sometimes cruel."[23] He teaches that we should put aside our "security blankets" and accept the "cold and clammy truths" that we descended from amoebic ancestors and don't live in any kind of a nurturing universe.[24] Evolution is "relentless, inscrutable, and ruthless," an idea Raymo admits came from Darwin:

> Humans are animals, Darwin believed, and like all animals they are locked in a struggle for existence, which, left to itself, eliminates the weak. Twenty-six years after [Darwin's daughter] Annie's death, Dr. Robert Koch took the first photograph ever published of a bacterium, the tuberculosis pathogen, and so confirmed the germ theory of disease. As Charles had guessed, Annie had died so that another creature might live.[25]

Raymo now actively opposes "religious people" who, he claims, see the world in black and white only, are comforted by dogma, and seek simple and certain truths. Raymo also concluded that all religious people are true believers who are not persuaded by either reason or logic. Actually, many people are theists more because they have come to accept the truth claims of Christianity as a result of intense personal study. Raymo adds that Darwin's own theory had caused Darwin himself to conclude the inherent cruelty in nature, which "caused him to doubt the existence of an all-powerful loving

---

22 Raymo, *Honey from Stone*, 108.

23 Raymo, *Skeptics*, 144.

24 Raymo, *Skeptics*, 144.

25 Chet Raymo, *Walking Zero: Discovering Space and Time Along the Prime Meridian* (New York: Walker, 2006), 106.

God" and consequently the "promise of an afterlife."[26]

Raymo contrasts "believers" with "skeptics," who, by his definition, are people that hold their beliefs tentatively, are tolerant of others and are more interested in refining their own views than in proselytizing others. He adds that if a "skeptic" is a theist, he or she must wrestle with God in a continuing struggle to hold onto his theism, and, for this reason, theists often are plagued by doubts.[27] He even concludes that 100 percent of the scientific evidence favours Darwinism, and zero percent favours creationism.[28] Most of the examples he provides to support his Darwinian worldview are clearly incorrect, even irresponsible, such as, "I know of not a single article in the vast body of international, peer-reviewed scientific literature offering evidence for a recent creation."[29]

After noting that humans are staggeringly complex electrochemical machines, Raymo dogmatically adds that there "is no ghost in the machine, no soul that exists independently of the body, and therefore no self that will survive the body's disintegration."[30] How he knows this with such confidence from empirical science is not stated. Statements such as these are littered throughout his writings and argue that he is not a skeptic, but a "true believer" atheist in the full sense of the phrase.

He either is unaware of the vast body of evidence against his position, or he refuses to acknowledge the evidence—likely both of these are true. He now spends much of his time writing books on why the creation worldview is wrong and why only the Darwinian worldview is "scientific." He bemoans the fact that we teach kids Darwinism as fact in school and the myth of creation at home, undermining the teaching of evolution.[31]

It is clear from his writings that Raymo is not a product of objective education, but rather a victim of Darwin indoctrination.[32] What else

---

26 Raymo, *Walking Zero*, 105.

27 Raymo, *Skeptics*, 3.

28 Raymo, *Skeptics*, 124, 125, 156.

29 Raymo, *Skeptics*, 124.

30 Raymo, *Skeptics*, 134.

31 Raymo, *Skeptics*, 266.

32 Chet Raymo and Maureen E. Raymo, *Written in Stone: A Geologic History of the Northeastern United States* (New York: Black Dome Press, 2001).

could explain why Raymo often makes misstatements, such as claiming, "Darwin was not an ardent Skeptic, but neither was he a True Believer. Evolution was *forced* upon him by his meticulous examination of the evidence."[33] In fact, after Darwin lost his theistic beliefs, he developed his theory to help him be an intellectually fulfilled skeptic.

Some of Raymo's statements indicate an appalling lack of knowledge, such as his claim that "the teaching of evolutionary biology is under nationwide assault by fundamentalist Christians, led by the powerful Traditional Values Coalition, a group that represents thousands of conservative churches."[34] Although the Traditional Values Coalition is critical of dogmatic Darwinism teaching, scores of organizations are far more important, including Answers in Genesis, the Institute for Creation Research and the Discovery Institute, to name only three.

An example of Raymo's critique of creation includes an effort to disparage the creationist's conclusions that no viable empirically based theory exists to explain how eyes could have evolved. The "evidence" Raymo presents for his view that eyes evolved purely by natural selection, mutations, time and chance includes the fact that he needs glasses to read—therefore imperfect eyes *can* function. This contrasts with the medical conclusion that a nonfunctioning eye is often worse than no eye. He then concludes that the evolution of human eyes from the euglena eyespot (or some similar progenitor) can be supported scientifically and that creationist conclusions are wrong, such as those of researcher and mathematician I.L. Cohen who, in his 1984 book *Darwin Was Wrong: A Study in Probabilities*, claimed that the human eye is irreducibly complex and could not have evolved by random mutations.

The "proof" Raymo offers is not scientific evidence, but a personal attack on Darwin skeptics. He does this by using Richard Dawkins's "argument from personal incredulity" against creationists. An example of this argument is when creationists argue that "from the goo to you by way of the zoo" evolution teaching is improbable, Dawkins responds by stating that it is foolish to conclude that something is impossible

---

33  Raymo, *Skeptics*, 139.
34  Raymo, *Skeptics*, 141.

just because it "seems impossible" and that the natural world is limited by our human imaginations.[35] This response is not evidence or proof, but a debating tactic.

Of course, much that seems impossible actually is impossible, and in science evidence is required to determine if something is not just possible, but true. Raymo even implies that we cannot rely on the evidence of our senses or our mind, at least if such evidence contradicts Darwinism.[36] This "reasoning" is an assertion that may have merit but, again, is not *scientific* proof. Raymo must first empirically demonstrate the steps of the evolution of, for example, seeing eye/brain system that can process light to produce an image in the brain that evolved from a simple light sensory system that can only differentiate light from darkness. It is not enough to *imagine* in detail a set of changes that achieve this—something that no one has yet managed to do.[37]

Raymo concludes that what

> seemed unlikely to Darwin, and seems impossible to creationists, has been shown to be quite reasonable by high-speed computer modeling. Not only reasonable, but given the proven premises of random mutations and natural selection, virtually inevitable.[38]

The results, Raymo claims, swiftly and decisively demonstrate Darwinism—but the results actually say much more about how these programs help us understand why macroevolution is improbable, if not impossible. No evidence of "the proven premises of random mutations"—an area I have been researching for many years—was forthcoming in Raymo's writings.

The fact is, in spite of enormous efforts, it has not been demonstrated that random mutations are a valid source of significant amounts of new information, and, conversely, it has been empirically docu-

---

35 Raymo, *Skeptics*, 150.

36 Raymo, *Skeptics*, 150.

37 Jerry Bergman, "Did eyes evolve by Darwinian mechanisms?" *Journal of Creation* 22, No. 2 (2008):67–74.

38 Raymo, *Skeptics*, 152.

mented that almost all mutations are either near neutral or harmful.[39] One cannot use intelligently designed computer programs operating on intelligently designed computers that appear to mimic evolution to prove evolution any more than one can rely on computers to prove any other ancient historical set of events.

Raymo repeatedly uses examples of *microevolution* (such as those well-documented in Weiner's 1994 book[40]) as evidence for *macroevolution*, when he knows that microevolution is not in dispute by creationists or anyone else. Raymo's claims—such as that Andrew Dickson White's book, *The History of the Warfare Between Science and Theology in Christendom*, is accurate and that "little has changed since"—are irresponsible.[41] Much has been written by both creationists and noncreationists about the egregious errors and distortions found throughout White's now largely discredited book.

## RAYMO'S WRITINGS AND CLAIMS

Raymo's writings have been reviewed favourably in journals ranging from *Science* to *Publishers Weekly* to *Astronomy* and *Choice*—and even by a Catholic priest! Yet the many major gaps in his knowledge and reasoning were not noted by Raymo's reviewers, which include Steven J. Gould. Those who label others as true believers, and themselves as skeptics, need to use the rules of skepticism to evaluate their own position. Only then can they stand back and understand reality as it is, instead of the way they want it to be, or were indoctrinated to see it.

Raymo's writings, although intelligently designed to show the fallaciousness of the creation worldview, eloquently do the opposite and are pregnant with quotations that support much of what Darwin critics have been saying for decades. His works are for this reason extremely valuable in confirming many creationist conclusions, such as how important Darwinism is in causing people to reject the Christian worldview.

---

39 Jerry Bergman, "Darwinism and the deterioration of the genome," *Creation Research Society Quarterly* 42, No. 2 (September 2005):104–114.

40 Jonathan Weiner, *The Beak of the Finch: A Story of Evolution in Our Time* (New York: Knopf, 1994).

41 Raymo, *Skeptics*, 159.

For example, Raymo concludes that "everything science has learned since Galileo suggests that we are accidental, contingent, ephemeral parts of creation, rather than lords over it."[42] This reasoning illustrates what Darwin critics have been stressing for decades, i.e., macroevolution has clear implications for one's worldview and philosophy of life. Although Raymo claims not to be a critic of religion, his work belies this claim. He dogmatically states that we "are not immortal," but "fleeting," and that our "spirits are the brief efflorescence of complexity."[43]

One wonders how Raymo knows this from materialistic science. He observes that many educated people in the West, including himself, long for something akin to religious faith, but can neither accept the idea of God, nor quite leave it alone. Raymo's religion is that of scientism. He even stated that photographs of the universe to him are "religious" icons that expand our horizon and sharpen our senses about the enormity and beauty of the universe.[44]

Raymo writes that, "skepticism is a critical reluctance to take anything as absolute truth," then dogmatically asserts that humans are the offspring of comets.[45] A page later, he says that "the heron like all birds is a close relative of dinosaurs, and that feathered birds first flapped their wings in Jurassic times," never hinting that bird evolution is very controversial in science for many good reasons.[46]

Even a passing familiarity with paleontology will produce an awareness of the debate between eminent paleontologists over the origin of birds. Some experts argue that birds evolved from dinosaurs, while others argue that they evolved from non-dinosaurian reptiles—a debate that now is ironic in view of the recent discovery of evidence that the DNA of birds may be closer to that of mammals than to that of either reptiles or dinosaurs.[47]

Raymo claims that if there were solid evidence supporting the creation worldview, scientists "would be falling over each other to publish

42 Raymo, *Skeptics*, 163.

43 Raymo, *Skeptics*.

44 Raymo, *Skeptics*, 243.

45 Raymo, *Skeptics*, 251.

46 Raymo, *Skeptics*, 254.

47 S. Blair Hedges, "Molecular evidence for the origin of birds," *Proceedings of the National Academy of Science* 91 (March 1994):2621–2624.

it…. Every scientist I know is as happy to have something proved wrong as proved right. Either outcome advances us toward truth."[48] Surely Raymo cannot be this naïve; in a perfect world this would be true, but it has been well-documented that new ideas often are strenuously resisted, even when the research is very persuasive. Among the many examples include plate tectonics postulated by Alfred Wegner and the discovery by Barry Marshall that *Helicobacter pylori* is the cause of the majority of ulcers—not stress and excess stomach acid as was once universally believed. True, the correct view eventually prevailed, but not without enormous difficulty in spite of abundant scientific support.

---

48 Raymo, *Skeptics*, 146.

# 10

# Academia's Darwinian war against Christian morality

||||||||||||||||||||||||||||||||||||||||||||||||||||||||||||||||||||||||||||||||||||||||||||||||||||||||||||||||||||||||

I
t now is well-documented that academia, in general, teaches Darwinism and secular humanism as fact and openly opposes Christianity.[1] A typical example of academia's war against Christianity is the experience of Derrick McCarson at the University of North Carolina at Chapel Hill. Derrick is a committed Christian who enrolled in a course titled, "Introduction to the New Testament." On the first day of class, Derrick was surprised to see almost 500 students enrolled in this class. Professor Bart Ehrman, the instructor, walked in and abruptly asked for a show of hands to determine, in his words,

> "How many Bible-believing Christians do we have in the auditorium today? Come on. Don't be bashful." After about a half dozen students raised their hands, Ehrman said, "That's good. It looks like we have a few Christians here today. Welcome to Intro to the New Testament. My goal this semester will be to change every-

---

1 George Yancey and David A. Williamson, *So Many Christians, So Few Lions: Is There Christianophobia in the United States?* (Lanham: Rowman & Littlefield Publishers, 2014).

thing you Christians think you know about the Bible and about Jesus."[2]

Dembski added that this same problem occurs in many "universities across North America. Students have likewise told us of atheist professors who have informed their Christian students on the first day of class that their goal was for them to give up their faith by the end of the semester."[3]

Evolution is at the centre of this war against Christian morality. Evolutionists' war against morality is complex, but one aspect is the central doctrine of survival of the fittest. Paul Johnson wrote that

> Darwin's notion of the survival of the fittest was a key element both in the Marxist concept of class warfare and of the racial philosophies which shaped Hitlerism. Indeed the political and social consequences of Darwinian ideas have yet to work themselves out.... So, too, the public response to [moral] relativity was one of the principal formative influences on the course of twentieth-century history. It formed a knife, inadvertently wielded by its author, to help cut society adrift from its traditional moorings in the faith and morals of Judeo-Christian culture.[4]

One of the better examples of the colleges' war against both Christian morals and Christianity is the situation at Yale University. One in-depth study of this problem was completed by a recent graduate of Yale University, Nathan Harden. He added one more book, *Sex and God at Yale*, to the growing number of works that document in detail, the fact that many colleges and universities actively indoctrinate students against Christianity.

---

2   William Dembski and Michael Licona, *Evidence for God* (Grand Rapids: Baker Books, 2010), 11.

3   Dembski and Licona, *Evidence for God*, 11.

4   Paul Johnson, *Modern Times: The World from the Twenties to the Nineties* (New York: HarperPerennial/Modern Classics, 1991), 5.

## YALE'S WAR AGAINST CHRISTIAN MORALITY
Harden learned from his firsthand experience that, in order to survive at Yale, "one must glean pearls from the mire," which is not so different from

> any other university. Only the pearls are more lovely and the mire more vile.... [S]ome [students]...wade through the ideological sludge and come out all the stronger for it. But the big moral vacuum at Yale sucks many others right up. Its leaders are afflicted with ethical apathy. They have allowed sleaze peddlers to stand in a place where, by right great poets, scientists, and statesmen should be. A distinguished university like Yale shouldn't be so morally hollow. ...Out of my great love for Yale flows a desire to expose the flagrant educational irresponsibility I found there.[5]

At Yale, instead of Christianity, "environmentalism functions as the unofficial religion for the nonreligious majority."[6] There is no excuse for what Harden encountered at Yale. In most areas, Yale facilities are excellent. For example "Yale had a library system with...[over] 13 million books."[7]

## RELIGION AT YALE
The position of religion at Yale is illustrated by the observation that "Yale being Yale, it's full of privilege and well-connected people. But the last person I expected to show up at graduation was God."[8] He added that, in view of the atheism dominating Yale, he was surprised that religious elements were part of graduation because normally at Yale

> overt expressions of faith are quite rare. But graduation weekend began with a baccalaureate service, which included scripture readings and several prayers. I almost fell out of my chair when

---

5  Nathan Harden, *Sex and God at Yale: Porn, Political Correctness and Good Education Gone Bad* (New York: Thomas Dunne Books, 2012), 218.

6  Harden, *Sex and God at Yale*, 220.

7  Harden, *Sex and God at Yale*, 217.

8  Harden, *Sex and God at Yale*, 218.

we began singing a hymn to God in the middle of the main ceremony on commencement day, with the president of the university standing right up there onstage. The song we sang was called "Thy Praise Alone." It was first featured in Yale commencement ceremonies in the year 1718, and it has been sung in every century since.[9]

He added the religious elements which were part of their commencement were simply a ceremonial gesture, a nod to tradition, but "if you had experienced how nonreligious and antireligious Yale is most of the time, you would understand why the hymns and prayers came as such a shock to me."[10] Although students are daily exposed to the theme "For God, for country...most Yale students aren't very religious. Yet...most nonreligious students accept that religion is part of Yale's past, even if they don't want it to be part of Yale's present."[11] Furthermore, "Yale's transformation from a religious institution, to an institution defined by public service, to finally an institution that seems no longer aware of any higher purpose other than advancing its own growth and prestige" had clearly occurred.[12]

To understand how and why Yale, and most other secular colleges, have become so anti-Christian requires an examination of how its educational mission had radically changed during its history. For example, its rejection of traditional morality is in the end

a symptom of two underlying problems. The first is Yale's loss of a sense of purpose. The second is Yale's profound moral aimlessness. Yale was founded as a religious seminary. Later it evolved into a training ground for America's political cultural elite. To some degree it still fulfills the latter purpose. But these days, faith and patriotism are not widely viewed as virtues at Yale. Instead, it is fashionable to scoff at the very values that defined Yale for its first two and a half centuries. Yale continues to train leaders,

---

9  Harden, *Sex and God at Yale*, 219.
10  Harden, *Sex and God at Yale*, 220.
11  Harden, *Sex and God at Yale*, 223.
12  Harden, *Sex and God at Yale*, 220.

but it has no clear sense of what it should be teaching them. It has no real sense of why it exists anymore. This is the essence of what is wrong with Yale today.[13]

In short, there exists a major void of purpose in the "carnival of sleaze" at Yale. The main academic goal at Yale's founding in 1701 was to train missionaries. Likewise, Harvard also began as a very conservative missionary school designed to train missionaries, but gradually

> Harvard drifted from its conservative and religious roots. Eventually, a group of Harvard men became disgruntled with the direction Harvard was taking. They decided the colonies needed a new college that would teach more faithful doctrine. So they came down to Connecticut and founded Yale.[14]

## YALE INTOLERANT TO RELIGION AND PUSHES ATHEISM

Of note is that some of the very "same people who condemn religious dogma while promoting the idea of 'free academic inquiry' turn out to be unwilling to extend that free inquiry to religious ideas they don't agree with. Their brand of secularism becomes just another form of repressive dogma."[15] Conversely, campus atheists have become aggressively "evangelical. The Yale Society of Humanists holds weekly church-like meetings and passes out tracts. They are very fervent in their nonbelief. I'm perplexed by the emergence of proselytizing atheists who aggressively evangelize against faith." As an example, a controversial evangelical speaker was once invited to speak on Yale campus

> by a group of Christian students. His visit prompted a protest by students who didn't want the guy to appear. It was a group of people who, paradoxically, wanted to exclude a particular religious viewpoint because they thought that viewpoint was not inclusive enough.[16]

---

13  Harden, *Sex and God at Yale*, 221.
14  Harden, *Sex and God at Yale*, 220–221.
15  Harden, *Sex and God at Yale*, 223.
16  Harden, *Sex and God at Yale*, 224.

An example of Yale's anti-Christian proselytizing that Harden related is " Christianity, which played such a prominent role in Yale's history, seems to get added scrutiny. I once took a class in the Religious Studies Department."[17] The professor informed him

> with great passion how he wished that he could just get his religious students to stop believing that the Bible is divinely inspired—his hands waving in the air dramatically to emphasize his point. This professor actually had a seminary degree, yet I wasn't surprised by his lack of appreciation for his students' religious beliefs.[18]

Harden observed the irony that the Religious Studies Department hires professors to teach about Christianity

> *only if they don't believe in it.* Meanwhile, the standards are different for professors who teach about Hinduism, Buddhism, or Islam—any of the non-Western religions. They tend to be actual believers of what they teach.... [T]he university believes that devout faith is a mark of cultural authenticity for those—and only those—who teach about non-Western religions. It enhances their intellectual credibility. On the other hand, devout faith would count as a mark against the credibility of someone who teaches about Christianity, which, as a religion integral to the development of Western civilization, lacks the multicultural value of the non-Western faiths.[19]

Several years ago, Yale hired a Muslim named Dawood Yasin to teach in the Arabic Studies Department who also served

> as a chaplain to the Muslim student association—this is in spite of the fact that Yasin didn't even have a college degree. His only qualification seemed to be that he spent five years living in Syria

---

17   Harden, *Sex and God at Yale,* 224.
18   Harden, *Sex and God at Yale,* 224.
19   Harden, *Sex and God at Yale,* 224. Emphasis added.

after "embracing Islam." It's very hard for me to imagine the university extending a teaching job or a chaplain position to such an under qualified candidate if he had been a Christian.[20]

Worse, Yale views its "Christian past like a recovering alcoholic views his former life of boozing; Yale doesn't deny where it came from, but it's doing its best to move on." For example, religious beliefs are usually treated as intellectually worthless in the classroom, and if you ignore

the multicultural fascination Yale has with devotees of Eastern religions, the presumption of religious skepticism is pervasive among the faculty. And students take note of it. I took many courses at Yale that incorporated religion, politics, philosophy, or ethics into the subject matter. Yet I never once saw a religious student open up about his faith in class.[21]

The real fear was that, if you open up about your faith in class, your grades may well suffer. Harden added that the religious skepticism climate is "so overwhelming that religious students feel pressure to keep quiet, Yale will be a poorer place for it…. An institution founded for the sole purpose of spreading religious faith has now become a place where certain kinds of faith [specifically the Judeo-Christian faith] are intellectually stigmatized."[22] A great university is supposed to be a haven for the free exchange of ideas, but in the academic world there exists a clear and open antagonism between secular

reason and religion—as if one cannot embrace one without abandoning the other. In reality, religion is a fundamental part of human society, just as it has been throughout human history. If you consider world affairs, it's clear that religion continues to animate much of the geopolitical drama of our time. Clearly, therefore, religion should play a role in the intellectual life if a

---

20 Harden, *Sex and God at Yale*, 225.
21 Harden, *Sex and God at Yale*, 225–226.
22 Harden, *Sex and God at Yale*, 225–226.

university wishes to be relevant to the times. And by "play a role" I mean...religion should have a fair place at the table.[23]

For example, *The Yale Daily News* profiled several

students studying at the divinity school who described themselves as agnostic, atheistic, or even Hindu...despite the fact that the express purpose of the school is to train up Christian ministers. When one reads about atheists taking classes with titles such as "Introduction to Pastoral Care," one begins to wonder if the divinity school is on its way to becoming just another place on campus for disinterested study about religion rather than a place where people of genuine faith engage in serious academic study.[24]

Ironically, there exists an enormous "climate of intellectual conformity at Yale. In keeping with that sense of conformity there exists a popular acceptance of the notion that, at the end of the day, smart people just aren't religious, and religious people, well, most of them, just aren't very smart."[25] Harden added that, as recently as the 1950s, many of Yale's leaders

would have said that humans are worthy of dignity because they are made in the image of God. However, in a post religious intellectual world, it becomes increasingly difficult to answer the question of why humans are worthy of being treated with dignity, or why there is any such thing as human rights.[26]

This fact negates the "*We hold these truths to be self-evident, that all men are created equal, that they are endowed by their Creator with certain unalienable Rights....* Those words made sense to our nation's most learned men more than two centuries ago."[27] This problem relates

---

23 Harden, *Sex and God at Yale*, 225–226.
24 Harden, *Sex and God at Yale*, 226–227.
25 Harden, *Sex and God at Yale*, 226–227.
26 Harden, *Sex and God at Yale*, 228–229.
27 Harden, *Sex and God at Yale*, 228–229.

directly to the theme of this entire book. In contrast, in academia today students are immersed "in the age of scientific materialism, the age of empiricism and reductionism." Conversely, science

> has nothing to say about morality, no insight into the issue of human rights. Science can do many wonderful things; but it cannot answer the greatest questions of human existence—how we should live and love. If you think of women as nothing more than the sum of their cells, how do you even know that they are worthy of equal treatment under the law? How do you know it is wrong to brutalize women sexually? Likewise, if man has no soul, what is the source of his dignity? Why should he seek to rise above his most brutal animalistic urges? Questions of human rights are, ultimately, moral questions. At its most basic level, the moral crisis at Yale is a crisis of lost faith. There is no cohesive moral framework in place to replace the one that was abandoned when God fell out of fashion.[28]

Harden writes that he has researched every worldview

> from natural law to Benthamite utilitarianism and just about every other ethical system in between, and none of them seemed...like anything other than an elaborate attempt to intellectualize the prior-held feelings of a particular philosopher's own conscience—I can choose any system of belief that feels good to me and find a way to explain that system logically. But religion has the power to actually transform the conscience because it points to a standard higher than one's own will.[29]

He concludes that human

> dignity really does emanate from his being created by God, and I can't make sense of the notion of human rights or morality under any other pretext. A critic of this view might ask this: How

---

28 Harden, *Sex and God at Yale*, 228–229.
29 Harden, *Sex and God at Yale*, 229.

can a secular university operate under a premise that man is created by God? Wouldn't this amount to imposing a religious doctrine on nonbelieving students? My answer is this; I don't think acknowledging a source of human dignity rooted in a higher power amounts to an ideological imposition at all.[30]

He notes that the "right to speak freely, the right to assemble peacefully, the right to exercise self-government…are sacred,"[31] but Yale is a

secular university that imposes no specific religious orthodoxy on its students or faculty. But it must…acknowledge mankind's God-given dignity as the basis of human rights. Otherwise it cannot defend those rights. The various moral arguments I make… can be reduced, in large part, to a single argument against institutionalized sexism. The case against sexism has to have some coherent moral grounding. I believe that moral grounding must be derived from an acknowledgement for the fundamental dignity of humanity. When our God-given dignity is denied, the basis for human rights disappears. This is what is happening at Yale, and the consequences speak for themselves.[32]

Harden concluded by saying that, during his four years at Yale, he witnessed "much more than the decline of a great university" but witnessed "nothing less than a prophetic vision of America's descent into an abyss of moral aimlessness, at the hands of those now charged with educating its future leaders."[33] Six decades ago, C.S. Lewis wrote about the problem illustrated by Yale:

[R]ulers have become owners. Observe how the "humane" attitude to crime could operate. …[C]rimes are diseases. …And who but the experts can define disease? One school of psychology regards my religion [conservative Christianity] as a neurosis. If

---

30 Harden, *Sex and God at Yale*, 229.
31 Harden, *Sex and God at Yale*, 230.
32 Harden, *Sex and God at Yale*, 230.
33 Harden, *Sex and God at Yale*, 231.

this neurosis ever becomes inconvenient to Government, what is to prevent my being subjected to a compulsory "cure"? It may be painful; treatments sometimes are. But it will be no use asking, "What have I done to deserve this?" The Straightener will reply: "But, my dear fellow, no one's blaming you. We no longer believe in retributive justice. We're healing you."[34]

## YALE UNIVERSITY NO EXCEPTION

Tobin and Weinberg wrote a report on their research on the question of religion and academia in 2007 that found that American colleges "overwhelmingly assert[ed] their desire to see Christian influence lessened," adding that

it is interesting and even perplexing to see a shared inclination among faculty atheists, those faculty with no religion, and those faculty for whom religion holds no importance: They defend the right of Muslims to express their religious beliefs in American politics, while holding openly hostile views of fundamentalist Christians.[35]

The study finding that professors believe that evangelical Christians are "unthinking bigots" was "the most troubling finding in the survey" and

American faculty "feel less positively about Evangelicals than about any other religious group." The survey responses showed that evangelical faculty were perceived as few to nonexistent… and that tolerance, though regarded as a virtue when applied to other religious groups, was regarded as inappropriate when applied to evangelical Christians. According to the researchers,

---

34 C.S. Lewis, "Willing slaves and the welfare state," *The Observer*, July 20, 1958. Lewis expressed similar views in his novel *That Hideous Strength* as well as in the essay: *The Abolition of Man*. The text quoted is also found in Lewis's book *God in the Dock*.

35 Gary A. Tobin and Aryeh K. Weinberg, "Religious Beliefs and Behavior of College Faculty," in *Profiles of the American University*, vol. 2 (Roseville: Institute for Jewish and Community Research, 2007), 76–77.

these findings raise "serious concerns about how Evangelical Christian faculty and students are treated or feel they are treated on campus."[36]

The research has consistently found this trend. One study by a professor at George Mason University found that close to 75 percent of all faculty at American colleges describe themselves as liberal, and 51 percent seldom or never attend church. Furthermore, this study documents that bias against conservatives exists in both hiring and promotion, and "faculty members who are conservative, religious, and female are less likely to get good jobs on college campuses."[37] The study also found that the "shift to the left among college faculty has become more pronounced in the past 20 years."[38]

The fact is certain moral values have been widely considered persuasive and supported by solid moral arguments, such as those against abortion, sexual promiscuity, homosexuality and divorce. By the twentieth century, however, the secular university has widely undermined these moral values.[39] As a result, these moral absolutes have been lost in our Western society.

## THE RADICAL SHIFT IN SEXUAL MORALITY

The negative influence of college on sexual morality was well put by one mother of a college student who related the sexual behaviour that occurred as part of one of her twenty-year-old daughter's class assignments.[40] Her daughter's textbook for her human sexuality class was a paperback by Crooks and Baur, twelfth edition, that "costs $200, of which [her daughter] Ella will only recoup $12 at semester's end—[the text] boasts ponderous double authorship, but the contents bear no resemblance to rigor of scholarship, notwithstanding a plethora of

---

36 Tobin and Weinberg, "Religion Beliefs," 76–77.

37 Joyce Howard Price, "Study finds liberals dominate faculties, most don't go to church," *The Washington Times,* national weekly edition, April 4–10, 2005, 1, 23.

38 Price, "Study finds liberals dominate faculties," 23.

39 Os Guinness and John Seel, eds., *No God but God* (Chicago: Moody Press, 1992), 192.

40 Andrée Seu Peterson, "Sexual propaganda: What many moms and dads are paying for in higher education," *World,* May 3, 2014, 71.

charts and graphs."[41]

She then notes the book went "from the banal to the blatantly propagandist," quoting sections from the textbook to document this:

> "The religious right in America has long labored to reinforce traditional gender roles through its efforts to shape American politics." "Gender roles are a product of socialization." "The teachings of Jesus emphasized love, compassion, and forgiveness.... 'Neither do I condemn thee.'" "Homophobia can be best thought of as prejudice similar to racism, anti-Semitism, or sexism."[42]

The book includes pictures

> of myriad sexual positions, and a table to educate you on the difference between fetishism, transvestic fetishism, sexual sadism, sexual masochism, autoerotic asphyxia, Klismophilia, Coprophilia and Urophilia, exhibitionism, voyeurism, frotteurism, zoophilia, and necrophilia. Not a moral objection is raised to any of the above "sexual expressions."[43]

Her daughter's October 22 term paper was categorized as an "Experiential Paper," and the professor promised, "This paper is completely confidential.... Pick a project that will challenge you." The choices that they were given are as follows:

- Interview someone whose sexuality is clearly different from yours. Find out about their sexual behaviour and feelings.
- Spend at least two hours in a gay male bar, a lesbian bar, a transgender bar, or a sexually oriented club. If you are having trouble finding one, you can search the internet.
- Attend a Sexual Pleasure Workshop. Write about the experience.
- Visit a sex or novelty shop. What was it like inside?

---

41  Peterson, "Sexual propaganda," 71.
42  Quoted in Peterson, "Sexual propaganda," 71.
43  Peterson, "Sexual propaganda," 71.

Ella's November 19 paper was called a "Sexual History" and included the following instructions: "Students will complete a sex history. Below are listed the components you will need to include in your history. Think about all of these components and write about EVERY SINGLE ONE, including your feelings about these events." The obligatory "components" read:

- Early memories of sexual feelings and experimentation.
- First sexual experience(s) with another person.
- Your favourite sexual fantasies and how you feel about them.

Author Cal Thomas writes that part of the problem with colleges today is the parents. He asks:

[W]hy do so many parents who hold traditional views that worked for them and the country willingly and enthusiastically send their children to academic institutions that frequently undermine everything they believe? And pay for it, too? Is it because of the "prestige" of these historic schools? Isn't it time to stop kidding ourselves about the worth of faded sheepskin and "prestige."[44]

## THE DESTRUCTION OF THE FAMILY

One result of the deterioration of morals in American society is today 74 percent of babies born to Blacks are illegitimate, compared to 54 percent of Hispanics and 29 percent of Whites. Fully 47 million Americans live in poverty, and 42 percent of these are single-mother families. The percent of births to unmarried mothers has risen from 5 percent in 1940 to 18 percent in 1960 and to 40 percent in 2007. Poverty primarily consists of children and their single mothers. The single most important factor in life success is to be reared in a stable family consisting of both a mother and father. The divorce rate has risen from 8 percent in 1900 to 26 percent in 1950 and to 50 percent in 1985. Absent and irresponsible fathers is "one of the best predictors of virtu-

---

44 Quoted in Peterson, "Sexual propaganda," 71.

ally every kind of social pathology."[45] In 1968, the rate of illegitimacy among African Americans was close to 25 percent. In 2015, after spending 15 trillion on the war against poverty, we have about the same level of poverty, but the rate of illegitimacy among African Americans was now three times as high, almost 75 percent.

According to the CDC and the Bureau of the Census, 63 percent of teen suicides, 70 percent of juveniles in state-operated institutions, 71 percent of high-school dropouts, 75 percent of children in chemical-abuse centres, 80 percent of rapists, 85 percent of youths in prison, 85 percent of children who exhibit behavioural disorders and 90 percent of homeless and runaway children are children from fatherless homes. In fact, children born to unwed mothers are ten times more likely to live in poverty as children with fathers in the home. The causal link between fatherless children and crime is so strong that controlling for family configuration erases the relationship between race and crime and between low income and crime.[46]

## THE RAPE CRISIS IN ACADEMIA

It is no surprise that dropping the traditional sexual morality has resulted in major social problems. *Time* magazine recently published a report on the serious problem of rape in American colleges. The study concluded that "America's campuses are dangerous places."[47] Typical, the report claimed, is in the college town of Missoula, Montana, where 80 rapes were reported in the last three years alone. A study of 3,000 women on 32 college campuses by Kent State University psychology Professor Mary Koss found that 19 percent of women undergraduates were victims of sexual assault while in college.[48]

This problem carries over from academia to society at large. Another survey completed by the Center for Disease Control and Prevention National Intimate Partner Violence Survey concluded that 19 percent of women were raped at some point in their life.[49] Another survey by

---

45 Barbara Dafoe Whitehead, *The Divorce Culture* (New York: Alfred A. Knopf, 1997).

46 Whitehead, *The Divorce Culture.*

47 Eliza Gray, "Sexual assault on campus," *Time* 183, No. 20 (2014): 20.

48 Gray, "Sexual assault on campus," 23.

49 Centers for Disease Control and Prevention, "The National Intimate Partner

a major South African Survey Research group found one in four South African Men *admitted* to having committed rape.[50]

This number is likely below the actual statistic because a high percent of rapes are never reported, although, conversely, some rapes that are reported are due to revenge that resulted from a male induced romantic break-up, or generalized anger at men due to the behaviour of one or two males. The problem of false rape charges was well illustrated by the Duke lacrosse rape case involving a stripper hired to entertain students in a private home who later charged some of the students in the audience with rape, charges that were proven false by DNA tests. It is a major problem that we now have a rape culture, which involves an attempt to blend Puritanism with free love. The line dividing rape and seduction is no longer very sharp compared to the past, a major conundrum in any promiscuous society! The fact is, the famous London School of Economics is

> the home of Darwin Seminars devoted to proving that Darwinian perspectives can explain almost everything in the world, and certainly everything in human nature. To a large proportion of intellectuals Darwinism has become what the philosopher Daniel Dennett calls "a universal acid".… Darwin has been called in to…[explain] almost everything about human beings from their shape and preference for copulating face to face to their tendency to depression and eating sweets. There are schools of Darwinian medicine; and of Darwinian psychology; but the new explanations do not stop with humans. There are books about Darwinian cybernetics. William Calvin, an American neuroscientist, has a Darwinian theory of how the brain works; and Gerald Edelman, a biochemist, another one.[51]

---

and Sexual Violence Survey," September 4, 2014; http://www.cdc.gov/violenceprevention/nisvs/; accessed November 3, 2016.

50 Centers for Disease Control and Prevention, "National Intimate Partner."

51 Brown, *The Darwin Wars*, 16.

# 11

# Preaching Darwinism: A history of church support for eugenics

||||||||||||||||||||||||||||||||||||||||||||||||||||||||||||||||||||||||||||||||||||||||||||||||||||||||||||||||||||||||||||

**A** review of the history of the eugenics movement finds that a significant major source of support was from churches and ministers, the very ones who should have opposed it on the grounds that it is contrary both to scientific fact and to foundational Christian moral teaching. In view of the moral harm that the eugenics doctrine caused in Germany, the United States and many other countries, it is obvious to almost all persons today that the campaigns to promote it were not only wrong but harmful to humanity. The extent and reasons for church support of eugenics will now be discussed in some detail.

## DEFINITION OF EUGENICS

Eugenics is the application of Darwinism attempting to produce a "superior race" by state control of human reproduction. The control method called *positive eugenics* involved coercing or bribing those judged more fit to produce more children, and those judged less fit were coerced or bribed to produce fewer children. *Negative eugenics* involved forced sterilization or other means, such as killing the less fit as done by the Nazis. According to a historian at the Ethics and Public Policy Center, Christine Rosen, the goal of eugenics was to move human evolution from the blind slow process of nature to the intelligent, deliberate and purposeful guidance of evolution by intelligent humans.[1]

Although, the most well-known example of the application of this policy was in Nazi Germany, it was also applied in the United States, Sweden and many other countries. The United States passed several laws requiring the sterilization of certain people, which were upheld by the Supreme Court in the 1927 court case *Buck v. Bell*.[2] These laws also restricted the immigration of "inferior races," such as Jews, into the United States.

As a result of this restricted immigration policy, many Jews perished in the German Nazi Holocaust—many who could have found safety in America. Some even arrived at our shores only to be sent back to Germany to perish in the concentration camps.[3] The ship the *St. Louis*, which America, and Canada as well, refused, is the most well-known example.[4]

Eugenics theory relied heavily on not only Darwinism, but also Darwin's "tree of life" view with its "extensive system of branches, representing the ever-increasing complexity of earth's many species."[5] Eugenics was a means to facilitate the further growth of this tree—specifically the advancement and evolution of the human race or, as eugenicists expressed it, the betterment of humankind.

Eugenics theory concluded that hereditary explanations could account for a wide variety of social problems, from crime to laziness, alcoholism and everything in between.[6] The many branches of the eugenics tree included sex hygiene, radical sex reform and birth control. In America, eugenics translated primarily into encouragement, or at times coercion, of the superior humans (white Anglo-Saxon

---

1    Christine Rosen, *Preaching Genetics: Religious Leaders and the American Eugenics Movement* (New York: Oxford University Press, 2004), 5.

2    Harry Bruinius, *Better for All the World* (New York: Alfred A. Knopf, 2006).

3    Bruinius, *Better for All the World*.

4    United States Holocaust Memorial Museum, "Voyage of the *St. Louis*"; http://www.ushmm.org/wlc/en/article.php?ModuleId=10005267; accessed September 19, 2016.

5    Rosen, *Preaching Genetics*, 10.

6    Rosen, *Preaching Genetics*, 26.

Protestants, for example) to have large families, and the encouragement of inferior humans (Poles, Russians and other Slovaks, and blacks) to have small families or no families at all.[7] To enforce this policy, extensive campaigns to restrict immigration and even to sterilize "inferior humans" were carried out to reduce "polluting" the American melting pot with inferior races.[8]

## THE CHURCH'S ACCEPTANCE OF EUGENICS
The church's response to Darwinism and the eugenics movement is not only well documented, but also provides much insight into the results of uninformed and uncritical acceptance of so-called science theory. To understand the creation-evolution conflict, it is imperative to review the history of how and why so many Christian ministers embraced the eugenics movement. Many of the churches that rejected evolution and held to a creation worldview opposed eugenics. Most churches that fall into this category are what Rosen calls evangelical and/or fundamentalist.

Conversely, churches that accepted evolutionary theory, commonly the liberal or mainline churches, not only often readily accepted eugenics, but also actively worked toward eugenic solutions to social problems.[9] Watson concluded that eugenics "was embraced with particular enthusiasm by those who would be termed the 'liberal left.'"[10]

The conservative churches were "not necessarily hostile to reform or to science, but as the materialistic philosophy of evolutionary theory grew, they became more intransigent in their insistence on Biblical infallibility."[11] Rosen defines conservative Protestantism as belief in biblical inerrancy and the new birth, along with a commitment to proselytize others.

Conversely, the so-called liberal and modernist churches viewed conservative churches that rejected Darwinism and eugenics as "the

---

7   Nancy L. Gallagher, *Breeding Better Vermonters: The Eugenics Project in the Green Mountain State* (Hanover: University Press of New England, 1999).

8   Rosen, *Preaching Genetics*, 9.

9   Rosen, *Preaching Genetics*, 18.

10   James D. Watson, *DNA: The Secret of Life* (New York: Alfred A. Knopf, 2003), 20.

11   Rosen, *Preaching Genetics*, 17.

intellectual equivalence of canopic jars; full of the desiccated remains of their elders' views of culture and science," incapable of addressing the major concerns of modern society.[12] The liberals believed, as expressed by Rev. Walter Rauschenbusch, that modern theology "must always embody the best thought of its age or its age will seek religion outside of theology."[13] A common rationalization used by Christians to embrace Darwinism was described by Gallagher as

> a reconciliation in "Christian Darwinism." This interpretation of evolution assumed that natural selection was the instrument of God's creation, and the continuing force of natural selection in the present was evidence of God's ongoing immanence in both human and natural history. The human mind and "soul" became the material expression of selection forces modifying nerve tissue into an organ capable of reason, foresight, and imagination.[14]

Furthermore, understanding life from a Darwinian perspective was for Christian Darwinists, such as Congregationalist George Perkins, as much an expression of their religious faith as their Protestant commitment to human progress by scientific means. He taught Sunday School at the College Street Congregational Church in Burlington, Vermont, and during the week taught

> university students zoology, geology, and anthropology served in complementary ways to fulfill his Christian obligation. ...[T]he Christian Darwinists of George Perkins's generation found the idea of human "creation" by means of natural selection self-validating. ...History, religion, and biology became fused in Christian Darwinism. ...Perkins used classic Christian Darwinian

---

12 Rosen, *Preaching Genetics*, 17.

13 Quoted in Glen C. Altschuler, "Protestantism and Social Christianity: Walter Rauschenbusch: Theology, The Church, and the Social Gospel," in *Modern American Protestantism and Its World: Historical Articles on Protestantism in American Religious Life*, ed. Martin E. Marty (New York: K.G. Saur, 1992), 136.

14 Gallagher, *Breeding Better Vermonters*, 13.

texts in his biology classes and apparently incorporated that perspective into his anthropology course.[15]

Some ministers who were decidedly conservative in doctrine championed what were then considered "liberal causes" such as eugenics.[16] Because a few conservatives, and many mainline Protestants, openly supported eugenics, Rauschenbusch concluded, "Protestants proved the most enthusiastic and numerically powerful group of religious participants in eugenics movements."[17]

Supporters ranged from high-ranking clerics to small town ministers mostly in the Unitarian, Methodist, Congregational, Episcopal and Presbyterian churches. Furthermore, a substantial number of theological leaders embraced Darwinism and what it implied, namely eugenics.[18] Nonetheless, Protestants, Jews and Catholics who became involved in eugenics "overwhelmingly represented the liberal wings of their respective faiths."[19]

Catholics resisted eugenics longer than many Protestant denominations—*Catholic World* magazine published articles condemning eugenics as far back as 1870. One 1870 article reviewed Galton's book, *Hereditary Genius*, concluding that eugenics was defective in logic, insufficient in methods and ignored the central Catholic teaching that "all men are born with equal natural *rights*."[20] Pope Pius XI "unequivocally condemned eugenics."[21] Likewise, many Catholic scholars opposed Darwinism. For example, a 16-page article on evolution in the 1913 edition of the *Catholic Encyclopedia* concluded that:

1. The origin of life is unknown to science.
2. The origin of the main organic types and their principal sub-

---

15  Gallagher, *Breeding Better Vermonters*, 13.

16  Rosen, *Preaching Genetics*, 16.

17  Rosen, *Preaching Genetics*, 15.

18  David N. Livingstone, *Darwin's Forgotten Defenders: The Encounter Between Evangelical Theology and Evolutionary Thought* (Grand Rapids: William B. Eerdmans Publishing, 1987).

19  Rosen, *Preaching Genetics*, 14.

20  Rosen, *Preaching Genetics*, 20.

21  Gallagher, *Breeding Better Vermonters*, 119.

divisions are likewise unknown to science.

3. There is no evidence in favor of an ascending evolution of organic forms.

4. There is no trace of even a merely probable argument in favor of the animal origin of man. The earliest human fossils and the most ancient traces of culture refer to a true *Homo sapiens* as we know him today.

5. Most of the so-called systematic species and genera were certainly not created as such, but originated by a process of either gradual or saltatory evolution. Changes which extend beyond the range of variation observed in the human species have thus far not been strictly demonstrated, either experimentally or historically.[22]

As more Catholics accepted Darwinism, likewise, more accepted eugenics. And, not unexpectedly, the more liberal Catholics were more likely to endorse the eugenic movement.[23]

## WHY CHURCHES ACCEPTED DARWINISM AND EUGENICS

Clergymen embraced Darwinism and, eventually, eugenics, for many reasons. One major reason was the growing power and status of science and the respect that society as a whole, especially the clergy, held for science. A somewhat uncritical acceptance of modern science—and this includes evolution and its natural stepchild, eugenics—was often part of the educated culture of trained ministers. The clergy were very aware of the common light versus darkness, superstition versus reason, label—religion was often seen as darkness and superstition, and science as light and reason.[24]

Some clergy, aware of their own declining prestige, endeavoured to adopt what they believed was a "modern" approach to science because they believed it would result in more respect for Christianity from secular society. They also thought it would increase their respectability

---

22 Muckermann, "Evolution," in *The Catholic Encyclopedia*, Vol. 5 (New York: The Encyclopedia Press, 1913), 670.

23 Rosen, *Preaching Genetics*, 21.

24 Rosen, *Preaching Genetics*, 9.

in general and, as a result, the acceptance of their Christian message.[25] Clergy and laypersons that "clung stubbornly to tradition, to doctrine, and to biblical infallibility opposed eugenics" and became the "objects of derision for their rejection of this most modern science."[26]

Conversely, churches attempting to conform to modern science invited eugenics advocates to preach in their pulpits. Baptist college professor William Lovis Poteat lectured widely on "Heredity and Eugenics." The Baptist Tabernacle in Raleigh, North Carolina, greeted his talks "with enthusiasm equal to that which greeted his scientific lectures at the college."[27] Poteat taught that evolution was the "divine method of creation" and that the apostle Paul may have been a theistic evolutionist.[28] Eugenics allowed humans to use this method of creation to improve the human race.

The clergy who supported eugenics seemed unaware of how utterly opposed Darwinism was to the core Christian belief structure. For example, Francis Galton, Charles Darwin's cousin (who coined the term eugenics and, in many ways, was the father of eugenics) described evolution as a "grand Phantasmagoria," a purposeless process spurred on by natural selection, i.e., survival of the fittest, and extinction of the inferior races and individuals.[29]

Most clergy believed that science had proved Darwinism, even though in the 1920s, the heyday of the eugenics movement, empirical scientific evidence for Darwinism was virtually non-existent. Most evidence was indirect or wrong, such as homology, vestigial organs, geographical distribution, the macromutation theory as illustrated by the Ancon sheep example, Haeckel's embryos and others.[30]

Compassion, empathy and a "deep sense of social responsibility" also all motivated the acceptance of eugenics.[31] Eugenic supporters genuinely wanted a better society and felt that eugenics was the path

25  Rosen, *Preaching Genetics*, 13.

26  Rosen, *Preaching Genetics*, 5.

27  Willard Gatewood, *Preachers, Pedagogues and Politicians* (Chapel Hill: University of North Carolina Press, 1966), 59.

28  Gatewood, *Preachers, Pedagogues and Politicians*, 60–61.

29  Rosen, *Preaching Genetics*, 5.

30  Bergman, "Ancon Sheep."

31  Rosen, *Preaching Genetics*, 23.

to this society. Of course, the same could be said of Hitler and Stalin who likewise applied eugenics to solve social problems.[32]

The most extreme example, Adolph Hitler, believed that humankind would eventually laud him as a saviour for applying science to government policy and felt that, although painful now just as surgery is painful, when the patient has healed, he will acknowledge with gratefulness the sacrifice required to cure the disease.[33] For Hitler, the disease was the inferior races, and once they were eliminated, all of society would be greatly blessed.[34] Hitler preached that the Jews were the vermin of society, the bacillus of health, and must be destroyed so that the society may thrive. For most eugenicists, the vermin was not Jews, but other groups.

## JEWISH ACCEPTANCE OF EUGENICS

From our perspective today, the most paradoxical group that embraced eugenics were the Jews.[35] Reformed Rabbis especially enthusiastically embraced Darwinian evolution and, likewise, widely accepted eugenics.[36] Many Jews and some Christians also utilized biblical accounts to support eugenics. Rabbi Max Reichler cited the Mosaic law as proof of biblical justification for eugenics, even claiming that the "very founder of the Jewish race, the patriarch Abraham, recognized the importance of certain inherited qualities, and insisted that the wife of his 'only beloved son' should [be]...from the seed of a superior stock."[37]

Although Jewish eugenicists concluded that certain non-Jewish groups were inferior, such as Negroes, some American eugenicists, and most German eugenicists, claimed that Jews were racially inferior, and therefore eugenics control should also apply to them.[38] One putative scientific study found that Jews produce a much higher proportion

---

32 Jerry Bergman, "Darwinism and the Nazi race holocaust," *Creation Ex Nihilo Technical Journal* 13, No. 2 (1999):101–111.

33 Bergman, "Darwinism and the Nazi race holocaust."

34 Ian Kershaw, *Hitler 1889–1936: Hubris* (New York: Norton, 1998).

35 John Glad, *Jewish Genetics* (Washington: Wooden Shore, 2011).

36 Rosen, *Preaching Genetics*, 18–19.

37 Max Reichler, *Jewish Eugenics and Other Essays* (New York: Bloch Publishing Company, 1916), 7–9.

38 Kershaw, *Hitler 1889–1936*.

of insane, idiots and mentally and physically defective children "than any of the Nations among which they live."[39]

A problem in the eugenics movement was that most persons thought the group that they were part of was superior, or at least not inferior, but that certain *other* groups were inferior. Those in the putative *inferior* group often concluded that they were the *superior* group (or at least not inferior), and *other* groups were inferior.[40] Many clergy in the eugenics movement viewed eastern Europeans as inferior: Reverend Myron W. Reed of Denver stated that it is "difficult to find in a shipload of Poles or Huns ten men that will make Americans...like the insects under the rotten log, they like darkness and confinement."[41]

Rauschenbusch approved of immigrants from Western Europe, but concluded that people from Southern and Eastern Europe, such as Poland, introduced inferior "strains of blood" into American society and caused social unrest.[42] While Hitler was declaring that Germans, actually what he called Aryans, and Scandinavians were the superior races, Rev. Newell Hillis was lecturing in hundreds of American cities arguing that Germans were "brutes," and "orang-outangs," that "must be cast out of society." Hillis added that some statesmen were even discussing "exterminating the German people."[43]

Others proposed the sterilization of all ten million German soldiers, concluding that "nineteen hundred years of education have not changed the German one whit.... [W]hen this generation of Germans goes, civilized cities, states, and races may be rid of this awful cancer that must be cut clean out of the body of society."[44] This illustrates that politics often determined what group was judged genetically inferior— the rhetoric against Germans occurred when we were at war with Germany and was, no doubt, utilized by some jingoists to help justify war.

---

39 Quoted in Rosen, *Preaching Genetics*, 19.

40 Mark H. Haller, *Eugenics: Hereditarian Attitudes in American Thought* (New Brunswick: Rutgers University Press, 1984).

41 Quoted in Rosen, *Preaching Genetics*, 12.

42 Rosen, *Preaching Genetics*, 16.

43 Ray Hamilton Abrams, *Preachers Present Arms: The Role of the American Churches and Clergy in World Wars I and II, with Some Observations on the War in Vietnam* (Scottsdale: Herald Press, 1969), 109.

44 Abrams, *Preachers Present Arms*, 96, 109.

## THE EXTENT OF THE RELIGIOUS EUGENICS MOVEMENT

The religious eugenics movement was not small—Rosen claims that, by 1926, hundreds of clerics from nearly every major Protestant denomination, as well as reformed rabbis, "preached eugenics" across America, in demographically diverse venues, speaking "vividly of the powerful force of heredity" to improve society.[45] One of these preachers, Reverend Osgood, exclaimed in one sermon that the less fit members of society breed faster, and the more fit breed slower—and eugenics is the solution to this "alarming problem."[46] One reason the religious eugenics movement was so large was because mainline Christian scholars "were among the first to embrace Darwin's theory of evolution, and did so well in advance of its widespread acceptance by the scientific community."[47]

Because ministers, preachers and rabbis had great influence over captive audiences (their congregations) and because of their highly visible public profiles, their influence far outweighed their numbers. Rosen goes even farther, claiming for many religious leaders, "eugenics became a modern Baal, zealously worshiped. In eugenics, these men found a faith stronger than their Christianity, fulfilling Francis Galton's hopes of replacing religion with eugenics."[48] Gallagher, in a detailed study of the state of Vermont's eugenics movement, concluded that "the Protestant country church...had always been a key component" of the eugenics movement.[49]

Many clergy lacked an understanding of eugenics, yet naïvely preached its conclusions, assuming that the experts had worked out the details. They felt it was their proper role as clergy to effectively convey the eugenic conclusions of science to the public. Some churches devoted a large proportion of their budget to supporting eugenics programs. A few ministers even reneged on their pulpit duties and spent their time travelling around America preaching the eugenics

---

45 Rosen, *Preaching Genetics*, 4.

46 Rosen, *Preaching Genetics*, 3.

47 Richard Aulie, "Response to Bennetta's Review of the ASA Booklet," *Creation/Evolution Newsletter* 7, No. 2–3 (1987):10.

48 Rosen, *Preaching Genetics*, 22.

49 Gallagher, *Breeding Better Vermonters*, 119.

## Francis Galton (1822–1911)

Considered the "father of eugenics," Francis Galton was Charles Darwin's second cousin. Galton researched intently the relationship between ability and heredity, publishing *Hereditary Genius* in 1869. He coined the term eugenics in 1883 and believed it was the Christian duty of the "more fit" to have large families and "the duty of the less fit" not to have families at all.

gospel. Many churches in Germany also enthusiastically supported Darwin and eugenics—and their backing accounted for a great deal of the support of Adolph Hitler and his policies that led to the Holocaust.[50] Rosen effectively argued that to "practice eugenics was, in some sense, to play God."[51]

Rosen is keenly aware of the results of Darwinism in the Western world as a whole, America in general, and in Germany in particular. She does not mince words in laying blame where it falls. Neither clergy nor scientists are exempt from her wrath in her highly scholarly study that passionately and effectively tells a story vital for modern clergy (and modern society) to be aware of because, although virtually all clergy except for a very few, such as Reverend Pete Peters, have fully repudiated eugenics today, many still hang on to the framework of eugenics, namely Darwinism.

## HEREDITY VERSUS ENVIRONMENT

Two major problems arose in implementing eugenics programs. First: "How do you determine who are evolutionarily inferior, in contrast to who are evolutionarily superior?" And second, "How do you differentiate environmental from hereditary influences?" It is now well documented that families are successful in a large part because of their environment. Better families typically send their kids to better schools, provide a more nurturing and supportive environment for longer periods of time, provide better health care and a more supportive family environment as a whole. This is in contrast to poor families who are less able to properly provide for these and other needs of their children.

Many clergy, although they eagerly embraced eugenics, challenged the belief that the scientists were the "most qualified judges of human 'fitness.'"[52] Some clergy thought that the clergy should have a say about who were the fittest. For this and other reasons, the marriage between liberal religion and the science community was not always harmonious. There was not only a war between conservative religion and Darwin-

---

50 Lutzer, *Hitler's Cross.*
51 Rosen, *Preaching Genetics,* 22.
52 Rosen, *Preaching Genetics,* 22.

ian science, but some rumblings between liberal religion and Darwinists as well.

Reverend Oscar McCulloch,[53] an early 1880s eugenics movement leader, spent a decade on a now infamous study researching "strains of degeneracy" in Indiana families. The 250 families that he researched included 1,692 people—a feat that Rosen calls remarkable because McCulloch was a full-time minister who did his "research" in his free time. McCulloch concluded that defective heredity accounted for "several generations of murderers, illegitimate children, prostitutes, beggars, thieves, and scores of 'generally diseased' human beings."[54]

The most infamous study of this type was completed by Richard Dugdale published as *The Jukes: A Study in Crime, Pauperism, Disease and Heredity*. This study was freely quoted in American biology textbooks for decades and was also exploited by the Nazi's to justify their racial policies. Reverend McCulloch went even further than Dugdale—Dugdale gave equal weight to environmental factors, but McCulloch argued that heredity was much more important than the environment.[55] He concluded from a "study" of 1,750 "genetically inferior" individuals that, even with expert help, only one person escaped from this "festering mass" of a "decaying stock" and can rarely be helped.[56] McCulloch added that "charitable people who give to begging children and women with baskets have a vast sin to answer for."[57]

Rev. McCulloch also argued from his study that attempts to improve environmental conditions—such as better education, housing, nutrition and sanitation—actually worked against eugenics by helping to ensure the survival, and propagation of the weak.[58] The key to race improvement was the *elimination* of the weak by survival-of-the-fittest

---

53 Oscar C. McCulloch, "The Tribe of Ishmael: A Study in Social Degradation," in *Proceedings of the National Conference of Charities and Correction* (Boston: George H. Ellis, 1888), 155.

54 Rosen, *Preaching Genetics*, 29.

55 Edwin Black, *War against the Weak: Eugenics and America's Campaign to Create a Master Race* (New York: Four Walls Eight Windows Press, 2003), 65.

56 Oscar C. McCulloch, *The Tribe of Ishmael: A Study in Social Degradation*, 3rd ed. (Indianapolis: Charity Organizational Society, 1891),7.

57 McCulloch, *Tribe of Ishmael*, 7.

58 Rosen, *Preaching Genetics*, 31.

laws and to encourage the propagation of the more fit. This was achieved in the United States by sterilizing those judged to be weak, restricting the immigration of races judged to be inferior and encouraging large families by those judged superior.[59] In Germany, it was achieved by encouraging the superior humans to produce large families and by killing those humans judged inferior.

## EUGENICS AND FAMILIES

Eugenic ideas also ended up in many so-called marriage manuals, even those written for Christians. For example, Mary Teats in a book titled *The Way of God in Marriage* wrote that the great and rapidly increasing number "of idiots, insane, imbeciles, blind, deaf-mutes, epileptics, paralytics, the murderers, thieves, drunkards, and moral perverts" are very poor material with which to "subdue the world" and usher in the glad day when "all shall know the Lord, whom to know aright is life everlasting."[60]

She declared that: "Some call it evolution, others call it God. Creation and evolution are both alike of God"[61] and then quoted "Prof. Darwin"[62] approvingly, implying, but not discussing, either Darwinism or eugenics. She also mentioned "the antiquity of man" and claimed that organic evolution was "established" as fact during the wonderful twentieth century.[63]

Churches that supported eugenics also adopted many of the positions developed and propagated by anti-Christians, agnostics and atheists. For example, Francis Galton claimed that the church was largely responsible for many social problems by encouraging celibacy among priests, nuns, monks and other church workers. He argued that the church "drained off the cream" of society by selecting the most intelligent and capable persons for church roles and allowing inferior persons to have large families.[64] From this he concluded the very

---

59 Haller, *Eugenics*, 135.

60 Mary Teats, *The Way of God in Marriage* (Spotswood: Physical Culture Publishing, 1906), 30.

61 Teats, *Way of God in Marriage*, 9.

62 Teats, *Way of God in Marriage*, 189.

63 Teats, *Way of God in Marriage*, 261.

64 Rosen, *Preaching Genetics*, 46.

people that should have large families were not having any families and those who should not have families were having large families.

Galton even tried to appeal to Christian England by "Christianizing" eugenics, proclaiming it was the Christian duty of the "more fit" to have large families and "the duty of the less fit" not to have families at all. The question of who was least fit was usually judged by lifetime achievements, which depended on many factors aside from IQ, including connections, good education, early maturity, luck, the ability to get along well with people and acquiring good social skills in general, and personal drive. Eugenics, though, focused heavily on the results of IQ tests, ignoring many other factors. Some eugenicists even assumed that there was a major hereditary component in almost every human trait, from laziness to the "love of the water."

## WHO OPPOSED EUGENICS?

Many of the theologians, priests and ministers who supported eugenics came from good families, went to Ivy League universities, and often headed large churches, writing widely about many topics. Walter Taylor graduated from Dartmouth College in 1898. After becoming ordained, he rose rapidly through the church leadership, eventually becoming Dean of the Cathedral of St. Peter and St. Paul in Chicago.[65] A rousing speaker, he became a eugenics leader, even developing government supported interventional programs to implement eugenics programs.[66]

The main opposition to not only adopting but enthusiastically embracing and spreading eugenics views, came from the religious groups that rejected Darwinism, including many Catholics; the latter partly because many eugenicists endorsed legislation in favour of sterilization. Nonetheless, some prominent Catholics did support sterilization for eugenic reasons.[67] Others opposed the use of state power to force sterilization on people and to make related family decisions.

---

65 Rosen, *Preaching Genetics*, 65.
66 Rosen, *Preaching Genetics*, 55–57.
67 Rosen, *Preaching Genetics*, 48.

## USE OF RELIGION TO PUSH EUGENICS

Albert Edward Wiggam (1871–1957) was one of the most well-known popularizers of eugenics—his many books sold extremely well and still are commonly found in used bookstores. His syndicated column "Let's Explore Your Mind" had a newspaper audience of nearly twenty million. Asked if every family should read the Bible every day, he answered yes, "no matter what" your religious views.[68] Wiggam was "more persuasive in describing eugenics as God's plan" than almost any other person in America.[69] He tried to make eugenics intelligible and argued that the discoveries of modern science—especially Darwinism—required that the churches change their values and beliefs, an idea which, aside from his eugenics crusade, he preached incessantly.

Rather than citing scientific studies to bolster his conclusions, Wiggam "had a keen sense for the appealing tone of religious rhetoric."[70] He even "invoked Jesus to justify his own revision" of religion.[71] The real golden rule, Wiggam stressed, is a "new commandment" namely "the Biological Golden Rule, the complete Golden Rule of science" which was "Do unto both the born and unborn as you would have both the born and the unborn do unto you."[72] He concluded that eugenics "furnishes the final program for the completed Christianization of mankind.... [T]his, and this only, is the final reconciliation of science and the Bible." Wiggam received support by no less a eugenicist than Charles Darwin's son, Leonard Darwin, as well as leading educators, such as Columbia University professor John Dewey, eugenicist Charles Davenport and biologist Thomas Hunt Morgan.

This appeal to the Bible to support eugenics is not unlike that used by many Darwinists today. Eric J. Hildeman in his book *Creationism: The Bible Says No* argued from Scripture that God did not create life, but he let evolution—Darwinian evolution no less—do the job for

---

68 Albert Edward Wiggam, *Let's Explore Your Mind* (New York: Pocket Books, 1949), 145.

69 Rosen, *Preaching Genetics*, 128.

70 Rosen, *Preaching Genetics*, 130.

71 Rosen, *Preaching Genetics*, 129.

72 Albert Edward Wiggam, *The New Decalogue of Science* (Garden City: Garden City Publishing, 1925), 110–111.

him.[73] Kenneth Miller taught the same idea in his *Finding Darwin's God*.[74] Rosen notes that "depicting Jesus as a supporter of one particular social cause was a favored tactic of reformers" such as eugenicists. Churchmen and professional activists alike adopted Jesus to the "promotional demands of the age," and eugenics was no exception. The level of the marriage is indicated by the fact that each session of the 1914 race-betterment conference opened with prayer.[75]

Others attempting to reconcile eugenics with religion included Princeton University biologist Edwin Grant Conklin. He had a preacher's license from the Methodist Episcopal Church, taught at a southern Methodist institution (Rusk University) and also had credentials as a biologist. In his book *Heredity and Environment in the Development of Man*, Conklin included a section on genetics and ethics[76] that relied on the New Testament parable of the talents[77] to support his claim that an important application of the parable is to use our talents to produce better men through eugenics. Eugenics was even declared a means to bring God's kingdom on earth, and God gave us evolution to achieve this goal. Conklin stresses that "improvement of the species is the highest ethical obligation" of humankind.[78]

## GERMAN CHURCHES

Nowhere did the churches cave in to eugenics more fully than in Nazi Germany. As Douglas explained, using undisguised Nazi racism terms, the German Church confessed its "allegiance to the principles of blood and race" and strongly held that *only* those who possessed the rights of German citizenship, meaning the superior race, the Aryans,

> can be church members. Only those persons of Aryan blood who can hold state offices can be church officials. The Christian of

---

73 Eric J. Hildeman, *Creationism: The Bible Says No* (Bloomington: Author's House, 2004).

74 Kenneth Miller, *Finding Darwin's God* (New York: Cliff Street Books, 1999).

75 Rosen, *Preaching Genetics*, 90.

76 Edwin Grant Conklin, *Heredity and Environment in the Development of Man*, 3rd ed. (Princeton: Princeton University Press, 1920), 301–326.

77 Conklin, *Heredity and Environment*, 316.

78 Conklin, *Heredity and Environment*, 322.

another race is not a Christian of inferior rank but rather one of different kind. Acknowledging race as the creation of God, the church must preserve this pure and healthy. Marriage between races of a different kind is a stab against the will of God.[79]

He added that the church's teaching demanded full commitment to the ideal of the "German Man," i.e., the superior race of Aryans:

As the church of Jesus Christ it has the primary task of proclaiming to the German man, who was created by God as a German, the Gospel of Jesus Christ. The Gospel of Jesus Christ means "that God is our Lord and Father, that this God was revealed in Jesus Christ and that we human beings find the way to the Father *only* through Jesus Christ." God places man in the life order of family, folk, and state. Therefore the folkic church recognizes in the claim to totalitarianism of the National Socialist state the call of God to family, folk, and state.[80]

This justification to support Nazism is tactful but clear and opened up the way for Nazism's eugenic policies.

## OPPOSITION FROM CHURCHES

The churches in general—even many of those opposing Darwinism—did relatively little to *oppose* eugenics. Nonetheless, some of the main opposition that did exist was from churches, mostly the conservative churches, such as certain Baptists, Seventh-Day Adventists and the Wisconsin and Missouri Synod Lutheran churches. Some people in other denominations also opposed eugenics. Lawrence Flick, a Catholic physician, effectively criticized the entire eugenics movement in a 1913 anti-evolution monograph. Referring to the now infamous Juke's family study, he wrote that it was absurd to try to draw hereditary conclusions based on only two lines of progeny as did the Juke's

---

79 Paul F. Douglas, *God among the Germans* (Philadelphia: University of Pennsylvania Press, 1935), 112.

80 Douglas, *God among the Germans*, 112.

research.[81] In the case of the eugenicists, he also concluded that it was naïve to reduce society's many problems to a single cause—such as bad germ plasma, as did the eugenics movement—and it was even more naïve to assume the solution to these problems was sterilization.

Some liberal clerics also opposed eugenics. Reverend Henry Emerson Fosdick concluded that eugenics was dangerous and agreed with eugenicists only on one point, that science made change inevitable. Fosdick's concern was how this change would occur, under whose direction, and his concern over the question how much better the world would be when evolutionists are at the helm of this change.[82]

Of the laymen writing about eugenics, Catholic convert G.K. Chesterton (1874–1936)—who also criticized Darwinism—offered "perhaps the most scathing assessment of the movement."[83] Chesterton asserted that eugenics lacked a consistent body of provable scientific theory.[84] He effectively attacked the conclusion that heredity exercised the all-powerful force over humans that the eugenicists claimed.

The church's attempt to find a "modern, scientific way to grapple with the questions of their age" resulted in an "uneasy compromise."[85] Alfred North Whitehead concluded that traditional religion and science are irreconcilable, requiring "abandoning…the clear teaching of religion," which he believed will eventually result in a gradual demise of religion.[86] By "embracing eugenics, some religious leaders hope to forestall this process of degeneration."[87] The same could be said about why many liberal churches naïvely embrace Darwinism today.

The churches' embrace of Darwinism began with the conversion of individuals in the church, often church leaders. The first step in this direction was the "new scientific approach to Scripture and religion

---

81 Lawrence Flick, *Eugenics* (Philadelphia: John Joseph McVey, 1913), 18.

82 Rosen, *Preaching Genetics*, 131–132.

83 Rosen, *Preaching Genetics*, 146.

84 Gilbert Keith Chesterton, *Eugenics and Other Evils* (New York: Dodd, Mead and Company 1927).

85 Rosen, *Preaching Genetics*, 183.

86 Alfred North Whitehead, *Science and the Modern World* (New York: The Free Press, 1953), 181, 188.

87 Rosen, *Preaching Genetics*, 183.

[that] was sweeping into many congregations, and 'biblical criticism'—as well as Darwin's theory of evolution—[that] was eroding the traditional authority of the Holy Book."[88] Bruinius documents several cases, including Charles Davenport, one of the most important American eugenic leaders. The son of a prominent fundamentalist minister, Charles started on a very different path than his father when he began his studies at the Brooklyn Collegiate and Polytechnic Institute, an elite school that focused on math and science.

Davenport soon became fascinated with biology and evolution, which radically reshaped his view of his place in the world.[89] After graduating first in his class, he went on to complete an M.A. at Harvard where he studied books by Darwin and eugenicists Herbert Spencer, Francis Galton and Karl Pearson.[90] He spent the rest of his life proclaiming "the new gospel of eugenics."[91] Eugenics became his new religion, and he was as devoted to it as his father was to Christianity, actively converting both those in the church and those outside of it to his new gospel.

## SUMMARY

Eugenics produced one of the most embarrassing moral chapters in all of modern American religious history. A major question is, why did religious groups participate for decades "in the eugenics movement...a movement that in hindsight was so clearly wrong" and contrary to biblical moral teaching?[92] Rosen concluded the reason was that the clergy accepted the idea on authority—eugenics was almost universally accepted among biologists as well as many other scientists. In her words "looking back, one might expect to find a little more hesitation from religious leaders before they offered their support to a movement that...replaced God with science as the shaper of the human race."[93]

---

88 Bruinius, *Better for All the World*, 124.

89 Charles Davenport, *Heredity in Relation to Eugenics* (New York: Henry Holt, 1911).

90 Bruinius, *Better for All the World*, 129.

91 Bruinius, *Better for All the World*, 137.

92 Rosen, *Preaching Genetics*, 184.

93 Rosen, *Preaching Genetics*, 184.

Rosen's conclusion applies not only to eugenics, but also to Darwinism. The same is true of those who oppose the modern growth of doubts about Neo-Darwinism, even doubts by many who are philosophically firmly in the Darwin camp and have replaced Christianity with the authority of modern secular science. Eugenics was "a movement that the liberals of its day wholeheartedly embraced...providing justification for a range of state interventions, including immigration restriction and compulsory sterilization."[94] That this chapter of church history was not as tragic in the United States as was the embrace of eugenics by the German clergy was masterfully documented by Erwin Lutzer.[95]

Rosen stressed that the history of the relationship between religion and science in modern times is a relationship "often characterized by cooperation; far from the warfare declared by many in that era, religious participation in eugenics shows that secular scientists and clergymen of all faiths were often willing and able to find common ground."[96] The clergy felt that, to provide answers to life's questions, they had to rely on the "scientists and social scientists whose knowledge came, not from Scripture, but from supposedly impeccable empirical evidence."[97] This was part of a secularization of society—no longer were we to rely on Scripture or God for the answers to life's basic questions, but instead were to rely on current science fads.

The number of people affected by eugenics in the United States was not small—in one state alone, Virginia, about 8,000 citizens were sterilized between 1924 and 1979 for eugenic reasons.[98] A total of 29 states passed sterilization laws after 1907.[99]

Unfortunately, the use of genetics to improve the race is still with us. One example is genetic evaluation to determine if a baby should be aborted.

In the earlier debates, religious leaders were among the most vigorous proponents of eugenics, but today "they are largely marginalized,

---

94 Rosen, *Preaching Genetics*, 185.
95 Lutzer, *Hitler's Cross*.
96 Rosen, *Preaching Genetics*, 185.
97 Rosen, *Preaching Genetics*, 185.
98 Rosen, *Preaching Genetics*, 186.
99 Black, *War against the Weak*, 408.

supplemented by a new class of professional bioethicists who work in the halls of academia, not the sanctuaries of churches or synagogues."[100] The compromise by the clergy regarding eugenics has turned out to be an embarrassing chapter in the history of the church, and it has contributed to the modern marginalization of Christianity. No doubt the same will turn out to be true of the modern church's compromise with Darwinism.

---

100  Rosen, *Preaching Genetics*, 187.

# 12

# Hitler's Darwinian goals for the world

IIIIIIIIIIIIIIIIIIIIIIIIIIIIIIIIIIIIIIIIIIIIIIIIIIIIIIIIIIIIIIIIIIIIIIIIIIIIIIIIIIIIIIIIIIIIIIIIIIIIIIIIII

One of the most significant and tragic examples of the effect of Darwinism on morality was the attempt to murder close to 100 million Polish people in Poland, Germany and Russia and force the rest of the Polish people into slavery. The Polish Holocaust is one example of the fact that a major goal of Hitler was the breeding of a superior human race by the application of both positive and negative eugenics. The extent of the Holocaust in terms of lives and property lost is reviewed in this chapter, as is the official reason for the Polish Holocaust given by Nazi leaders. New research of official Nazi records and files has documented that eugenics was not only a major reason for the existence and extent of the war, but also was a primary reason why Germany lost the war.

## THE FORGOTTEN HOLOCAUST

The Nazis most often are remembered for their war against Jews. Unfortunately, the Holocaust against the Poles and all Slavic peoples is largely ignored today. Historian Richard Lukas calls the treatment of Poles under German occupation the "forgotten Holocaust."[1] Of the

---

1   Richard C. Lukas, *Forgotten Holocaust: The Poles under German Occupation 1939–1944*, rev. ed. (New York: Hippocrene Books, 1997).

five million that died in Poland during World War II, Piotrowski estimated that all but about 600,000 were innocent noncombatant citizens.[2] They died mostly due to the Nazi Darwinian goal of producing a superior race.[3] As Epstein quips, "We live in an era obsessed with the Holocaust and other cases of ethnic cleansing and genocide"[4] but often ignore the millions of other Holocaust victims, including Gypsies and all Slavic peoples. The Nazi leaders made their eugenic goals very clear. To them

> the Poles were *Untermenschen* (subhumans) who occupied a land which was part of the *Lebensraum* (living space) coveted by the superior German race. Thus the Poles were to be subjected to a program of extermination and enslavement. As Hitler made clear even before the German invasion of Poland, "The destruction of Poland is our primary task. The aim is...[their] annihilation.... Be merciless! Be brutal.... It is necessary to proceed with maximum severity.... The war is to be a war of annihilation.[5]

The fact is, although the eventual extermination of all inferior races was the Nazi goal, "no country occupied by Germany in the entire war endured as much [suffering] as Poland. This was the epicenter of Nazi brutality, the place where Nazism achieved its purest and most bestial form."[6] These inferior races included "Poles...Gypsies, Byelorussians, and Ukrainians."[7]

After Poland was conquered in 1939, Hitler gave his authorities enormous freedom to rule Poland with an iron hand. Thus, the claim that they were only following orders is not a valid excuse for the brutality that occurred there. Although Hans Frank and Albert Forster were

---

2   Tadeusz Piotrowski, *Poland's Holocaust: Ethnic Strife, Collaboration with Occupying Forces and Genocide in the Second Republic, 1918–1947* (Jefferson: McFarland, 1998), 1.

3   Bergman, *Hitler and the Nazi Darwinian Worldview*, passim.

4   Catherine Epstein, *Model Nazi: Arthur Greiser and the Occupation of Western Poland* (New York: Oxford University Press, 2010), 11.

5   Lukas, *Forgotten Holocaust*, 4.

6   Laurence Rees, *The Nazis: A Warning from History* (New York: MJF Books, 1997), 125.

7   Lukas, *Forgotten Holocaust*, 24.

also responsible for the massive suffering in Poland, the man "most responsible for the appalling suffering of the Poles" was Arthur Greiser (January 22, 1897–July 21, 1946).[8] In 1939, the Nazis conquered most of the western part of Poland, which they named Wartheland (initially Reichsgau Posen, here called Warthegau). Warthegau was comprised of Greater Poland and adjacent areas. The name was derived from the main river located in the region, Warthe (Warta).

In the Warthegau area, German policies, as directed by Greiser against Poles and Jews, were brutal and inhumane yet they were also often contradictory, partly because of the many unexpected consequences and contingencies in their efforts to implement them. One unwanted consequence of the German social policies against both Poles and Jews was a major disruption in the productive wartime labour pool.

To implement the "Germanization program, Greiser showed a callous disregard for the human costs involved."[9] The so-called Ethnic German Self-Defense Force murdered a total of about 10,000 people, mostly Poles, in the Warthegau.[10] The main reason was that the Nazis saw not only the Jewish, but also the Polish "race" and all other Slavics as fundamentally rude, shifty and deceitful people who drank and gorged themselves like animals.[11] Reichskommissar Erich Koch, in a speech given on March 5, 1943, to the Germans, proclaimed that Germans

> are the Master Race and must govern hard.... I will draw the very last out of this country. I did not come to spread bliss.... The population [all non-Aryans] must work, work, and work again.... We definitely did not come here to give out manna.... We are a master race, which must remember that the lowliest German worker is racially and biologically a thousand times more valuable than the population here.[12]

---

8   Rees, *Nazis*, 125.

9   Epstein, *Model Nazi*, 266.

10  Epstein, *Model Nazi*, 132.

11  Epstein, *Model Nazi*, 195.

12  Quoted in Piotrowski, *Poland's Holocaust*, 30.

Therefore, Greiser concluded, that "it was sheer lunacy to believe that there could be a bridging" of the Poles and Germans. For this reason, Greiser regarded assimilation of the Poles into German society as impossible. He believed that Poles were good only for working as slaves for the German people until they died.[13] Of the twenty-five leaders of the Polish cleansing, fifteen had doctorates, according to historian Elwood McQuade.[14]

As a result, the German *Generalplan Ost* called for the deportation and/or extermination of some 31 million people, mostly Slavs, over a twenty-year period.[15] German extermination plans for non-Jews and all other inferior races, especially Slavic peoples, were extensive, and "Had the Nazis triumphed in World War II, the Third Reich would have seen a wholesale slaughter of many non-German peoples."[16]

## GREISER BECOMES THE HEAD OF THE WARTHELAND

Arthur Karl Greiser was a Nazi German politician. On January 30, 1942, he became SS-Obergruppenführer and Reichsstatthalter (Reich Governor) of the German-occupied territory of Wartheland. Although not well known today, he was the man primarily responsible for organizing the Holocaust in Poland and committing numerous other crimes against humanity. Greiser knew what was expected of him and had a great deal of freedom to carry out the Nazi's Darwinian racial purity goals.[17] He had become a Nazi years earlier, partly because in late 1929 he was bankrupt and did not see a future in Germany until he was introduced to the Nazi movement, which

offered him meaning and purpose—a messianic nationalism— that had eluded him in earlier decades. Through the Nazi Party, Greiser came to believe, he could achieve greatness for both himself and his nation.... In the intervening years he became a Nazi, in every sense of the word. He adopted a Nazi persona—bossy,

---

13 Quoted in Rees, *Nazis*, 142.

14 Elwood McQuade, *Halina: Faith in the Fire* (Bellmawr: The Friends of Israel, 2013), 30.

15 Epstein, *Model Nazi*, 161.

16 Epstein, *Model Nazi*, 12.

17 Ian Kershaw, *Hitler 1936–1945: Nemesis* (New York: Norton, 2000), 250.

## Arthur Greiser (1897–1946)

Greiser was Reich governor of the German-occupied territory of Wartheland (Poland). His relentless campaign to exterminate Poles and Jews in the territory resulted in the death of millions over the course of the war.

Photography © Bundesarchive, Bild 183-E11711 / October 1939

churlish, and aggressive. He adopted a Nazi political agenda, loudly attacking...Poles and Poland, and the League of Nations. He adopted Nazi tenets and categories to interpret his goals and striving. And he adopted dramatic changes in his personal life. In the early 1930s, Greiser refashioned his life—his attitudes, his politics, and his relationships—to fit his movement.[18]

In the end, Greiser was "prepared to do anything to retain favor with Hitler.... [N]o price was too high," even murdering millions of innocent persons.[19] The Nazi decision to murder most European Jews was not finalized until late in December 1941. Furthermore, the treatment of Jewish deaths as an isolated genocide was not generally accepted until some twenty years after World War II ended. Meanwhile, in reality, close to

12,000 Polish people died in the occupied territories as a result of the Nazi euthanasia program. Of this total, 10,000 were from hospitals for the mentally impaired. That this was only the beginning of the Nazi plan for achieving a superior race of human beings is borne out by Gauleiter Arthur Greiser's intention to exterminate 25,000 to 35,000 Poles in Kraj.[20]

## GREISER'S WAR AGAINST CHRISTIANITY

Also often ignored is the Nazi's strong anti-Christianity philosophy. Greiser himself was fanatically anti-Christian. In fact, Greiser's systematic, anti-church policy was not only directed at Polish Catholicism, but also Christianity in general, because he saw it as a threatening alternative to Nazism.[21]

This hostility against Christianity was common in many nations that used the "separation of church and state" claim to justify their hostility.[22] According to historian Ian Kershaw, the result of such mas-

18 Epstein, *Model Nazi*, 50.

19 Kershaw, *Hitler 1936–1945*, 250.

20 Piotrowski, *Poland's Holocaust*, 28.

21 Richard J. Evans, *The Third Reich at War: 1939–1945* (New York: Penguin, 2005), 482.

22 Epstein, *Model Nazi*, 221–230.

sive hostility was "mass-closing of Catholic churches and arrests or murder of clergy."[23]

The responsibility for implementing the war against Christianity and the Holocaust came both from top-down and local policies.[24] This helps to explain why Jews were shot in some locations, and gassed in others, forced into ghettos in some places, and spared for forced labour in some places, but not in others.[25]

The hatred of totalitarian movements toward religion, and the religious, is illustrated by the fact that Nazism, Fascism and Communism all elevated the state to a deity, and they trampled human beings, all who were created in God's image and likeness.[26] Historian Tadeusz Piotrowski writes that the "lot of the Catholic clergy and religious [people] was especially hard" in Poland.[27] And that

> Poles constituted the vast majority of the Christian clergy persecuted by the Nazis; in Dachau, the principal camp employed to imprison clergy from all Europe, Poles constituted 65 percent of the total clergy population, and about 90 percent of those clergymen were put to death. Of all the Christian clergy in Dachau, Polish priests were especially selected for medical experiments.[28]

## THE CRUSADE AGAINST ALL "INFERIOR" RACES

The anti-Semitic aspects of Nazism have far overshadowed the Nazi anti-Christian atrocities. An example of an anti-Christian atrocity is the Nazi war against Catholic priests, not only the Polish priests, but also other Christians.[29] In one incident, the Nazis confiscated a local monastery library and burned all of its books—often Polish, but also German-language books. Their motivations were anti-Christian as

23 Kershaw, *Hitler 1936–1945*, 252.

24 Epstein, *Model Nazi*, 389.

25 Epstein, *Model Nazi*, 182.

26 Henry M. Malak, *Shavelings in Death Camps: A Polish Priest's Memoir of Imprisonment by the Nazis, 1939–1945* (Jefferson: McFarland, 2012), 93.

27 Piotrowski, *Poland's Holocaust*, 28.

28 Zygmunt Zielinski, quoted in Piotrowski, *Poland's Holocaust*, 28.

29 Malak, *Shavelings in Death Camps*, 94.

well as Polonophobic.[30] Polish priests were slandered in Nazi show trials by false claims they were sexual deviants,[31] slander which, in general, is very much part of anti-Christian propaganda today.

In the concentration camps, the Nazis purposely chose *kapos* (capos) from criminal or Communist backgrounds to rule over and, at times, torment the priests. Many of the criminals had an instinctive hatred for priests because the latter represented the laws that many criminals had long flouted. Nazi doctors performed horrific experiments on Polish priests at Dachau, including malarial infection experiments, injections of various toxic chemicals and research on surviving in ice-cold water.[32] In January 1942 alone, 300 Polish priests were dispatched to Dachau's gas chambers.[33] Out of a transport of 500 Polish priests that arrived at Dachau on October 30, 1941, only 70 were still alive on the day of liberation.[34]

Readers accustomed to thinking that only Jews were Nazi Holocaust victims are often surprised to learn about the German's revolting cruelties against the Slavic peoples. For example, in 1939 the Luftwaffe bombed many Slavic churches with parishioners inside and then slaughtered the defenseless parishioners attempting to flee.[35] Actually, some Jewish prisoners were at times better fed than Poles, and some even staffed the Dachau crematorium. As was the case with the *sonderkommandos* in the main death camps, the Nazis periodically killed them to eliminate eyewitnesses.[36]

## ANTI-POLISH CLAIMS

Some "Jewish only" Holocaust proponents have advanced the fallacious argument that, whereas the Jews could do nothing to change their standing in the eyes of the Nazis, the Poles could redeem themselves by accepting Germanization. In fact, "as is well known, the

---

30 Malak, *Shavelings in Death Camps*, 30.

31 Malak, *Shavelings in Death Camps*, 396

32 Malak, *Shavelings in Death Camps*, 271–278.

33 Malak, *Shavelings in Death Camps*, 263.

34 Malak, *Shavelings in Death Camps*, 397.

35 Malak, *Shavelings in Death Camps*, 13–14.

36 Malak, *Shavelings in Death Camps*, 297–298.

Nazis tried to build a society on race."[37] To do this, the Germans "applied racial criteria to discover those with desirable traits for Germanization."[38]

When Germans "Germanized" Polish lands, their goal was not to transform Poles into Germans, but to *replace* Poles with ethnic Germans by ethnic cleansing and genocide.[39] Greiser concluded that since Poles could never be equal to Germans, they must be forced to be slaves to them.[40] Specifically, while

> the Germans intended to eliminate the Jews before the end of the war, most Poles would work as helots until they too ultimately shared the fate of the Jews. Extermination by outright execution was only one method in the Nazi arsenal; extermination by working the Poles to death had the advantage of deriving economic value from them before they died. Martin Bormann, who played an important role in the administration of the forced labor program and thus influenced Nazi policy concerning the Poles and other Slavs...said that "the Slavs are to work for us. Insofar as we don't need them, they may die." Thus the economic value of the Poles was to be only temporary.[41]

Greiser concluded that it was sheer lunacy to believe that there could be a bridging of the Germans and Poles.[42] Thus, the goal was "the deportation and/or extermination of some thirty-one million individuals (primarily Slavs) over a twenty-year period."[43] To achieve this goal, nearly 537,000 Germans were settled into the Warthegau area of Poland alone to displace Poles.[44]

The Germanization of Poles that did occur was not an act of mercy to Poles, but mostly to achieve re-Germanization of Polonized Ger-

37  Lukas, *Forgotten Holocaust*, 24.
38  Lukas, *Forgotten Holocaust*, 24.
39  Epstein, *Model Nazi*, 129–130.
40  Epstein, *Model Nazi*, 129.
41  Lukas, *Forgotten Holocaust*, 4.
42  Epstein, *Model Nazi*, 195.
43  Epstein, *Model Nazi*, 161.
44  Epstein, *Model Nazi*, 174.

mans. The borders between Poland and Germany had changed several times, thus producing many ethnic Germans living in Poland and a large number of intermarriages. Less than 0.5 percent of Warthegau Poles qualified, a mere 17,243 out of 4.2 million Warthegau Poles, compared to the over 700,000 Warthegau Poles who were forced from their homes and deported.[45]

In spite of many contradictions and practical difficulties, Greiser generally attempted to adhere to the following classification scheme developed by the Nazis called *The Racial Register*. People of ethnic German ancestry, who strongly self-identified as Germans were Class I. The weakly self-identified as Germans were Class II. The largely Polonized, but still deemed racially valuable, were Class III. Last, the completely Polonized, but not known to be hostile to Germanization, were Class IV and the completely Polonized and hostile to Germans were Class V.

Of the five types, only classes I, II and III could normally obtain Reich citizenship.[46] This system also facilitated drafting Poles into the Wehrmacht, the Nazi army. In other locations of German-occupied Poland, a somewhat different system was used.[47] The Germans paid an enormous price for their Germanization efforts. For example, many Poles burned their own houses and destroyed their property before fleeing, leaving

> charred embers for the new German residents. Other Polish farmers actively resisted; one group attacked the German settlers in Cieszyn, killed 30 of them, and plundered their property. The raid on Cieszyn so enraged Himmler that he ordered the annihilation of entire Polish villages in reprisal. In response to a German reprisal raid that took the lives of 280 Poles, the AK [Einsatzgruppen or the task forces who were responsible for mass killings, primarily by shooting, during World War II] in June 1943, burned a German-colonized village in which 69 settlers perished. Retaliatory operations included attacks on railroad, military, and government targets.[48]

---

45  Epstein, *Model Nazi*, 178, 192.
46  Epstein, *Model Nazi*, 196–197.
47  Epstein, *Model Nazi*, 208–214.
48  Lukas, *Forgotten Holocaust*, 23.

That the Darwinian race concept was central in the German goals is clear. For example, in May 1940, Heinrich Himmler wrote about his goal for Poland, which involved

> racially screening the entire population so as "to fish out of this broth the racially valuable and to bring them to Germany so as to assimilate them there." All others were to receive an elementary education that consisted of "simple arithmetic up to 500, the writing of one's name, and the teaching that it is a divine command to obey the Germans and to be honest, hard-working and good." Himmler ordered that Greiser and the other eastern Gauleiters were to get copies of this memorandum.[49]

The initial plans to expel all Poles from Reich-annexed territories eventually foundered, owing to wartime difficulties and the need for forced labourers.[50] Instead, in harmony with Germany's eugenic goals, German authorities imposed a strict segregation of Poles from Germans. For this reason, both Poles and Germans were punished for having sexual relations with each other. The objectives of the Nazis were very clear. For example as Himmler wrote

> on May 9, 1940, "It is, therefore, an absolute national-political necessity to screen the annexed Eastern territories…for…persons of Teutonic blood in order to make this lost German blood again available to our own people." The Nazis not only wanted to increase the "racially desirable" growth of the German population but also prevent an increase of the Polish *intelligentsia* which…had been Polonized.[51]

The Nazis believed that Polish resistance leaders had a considerable portion of Nordic blood that enabled "them to be active in contrast to the fatalistic Slavonic elements."[52]

---

49  Epstein, *Model Nazi*, 198.
50  Epstein, *Model Nazi*, 195.
51  Lukas, *Forgotten Holocaust*, 24.
52  Lukas, *Forgotten Holocaust*, 24.

Unlike the Jews, who were forced to wear the Star of David, Poles were not forced to wear any identification of their "racial" status, because this would only heighten their numerical abundance in Warthegau. Ironically, it was local Germans who were required to wear identification for being German—a procedure that they commonly resented.[53]

The Germans imposed cultural genocide on Poles by systematically renaming everything in Poland with German names in an effort to erase all visible traces of Polish culture.[54] They confiscated or destroyed Polish books, art and monuments.[55] The German authorities forbade Poles from attending Polish museums, libraries, theatres and concert halls.[56] They virtually eliminated the use of the Polish language in public life.[57]

The Nazis at first forbade Poles to attend schools, then reopened them only at the elementary level, bereft of Polish teachers and Polish academic content in favour of untrained German instructors.[58] Greiser also made it clear that he did not "want to see any officer showing mildness" to those persons he called "Pollocks."[59] The Nazi leaders reasoned that Poles "do not have the right to put themselves on the same level as a people of culture," namely ethnic Germans.[60] As noted, the borders of Poland and Germany had changed so much throughout history that intermarriage was common, producing children of mixed heritage. As a result:

> Not only were children of ethnic Germans who met the criteria for inclusion in the *Volksliste* Germanized, but also children of Polish families were subjected to the process if they met Nazi racial criteria. On June 18, 1941, Himmler declared, "I would consider it right if small children of Polish families who show

---

53 Epstein, *Model Nazi*, 197.
54 Epstein, *Model Nazi*, 261–262.
55 Epstein, *Model Nazi*, 235.
56 Epstein, *Model Nazi*, 199.
57 Epstein, *Model Nazi*, 200–201.
58 Epstein, *Model Nazi*, 201.
59 Kershaw, *Hitler 1936–1945*, 251.
60 Kershaw, *Hitler 1936–1945*, 251.

especially good racial characteristics were apprehended and educated by us in special institutions and children's homes." [61]

## EFFORTS TO EXTERMINATE POLES

Some 10,000 Poles were murdered by the Germans in the first weeks of German rule in the Warthegau area alone.[62] Greiser informed Joseph Goebbels that there was little left of the Polish *intelligentsia* by the end of 1939.[63] Many Poles were forced into ghettos, and over 194,000 were "displaced" in large camps, where they lived under extremely harsh and inhumane conditions.[64]

Greiser later ordered tens of thousands of additional Poles murdered and "hundreds of thousands were deported or sent to do forced labor."[65] The main long-term goal was application of "*Social* Darwinism—'Life makes him [right] who proves himself morally and physically stronger.'"[66]

Due to the heavy wartime demands, the Germans were unable to systematically completely exterminate the Poles, so they opted for passive forms of biological genocide. One example was reducing the Polish birth rate as a step toward their longtime goal of the elimination of all Poles from Gau.[67] Methods of doing this included freely allowing abortions, imposing a high minimum age for marriage, discouraging marriages under various pretexts and confiscating children of Polish mothers engaged in forced labour for the Reich.[68]

Use of public baths by Poles also was limited, which helped to reinforce the dirty Pole stereotype. They could also buy only low-quality food—which reduced Polish health and vigour.[69] The Nazis reasoned that, as explained by chemist Reichminister Dr. Robert Ley, who was part of Hitler's inner circle, "since Poles were racially inferior, they

---

61 Lukas, *Forgotten Holocaust*, 26.
62 Epstein, *Model Nazi*, 130.
63 Epstein, *Model Nazi*, 130.
64 Epstein, *Model Nazi*, 177
65 Epstein, *Model Nazi*, 206, 266.
66 Piotrowski, *Poland's Holocaust*, 189.
67 Epstein, *Model Nazi*, 215.
68 Epstein, *Model Nazi*, 215–16.
69 Epstein, *Model Nazi*, 199–200.

needed less food."[70] The only reason most Poles did not starve to death was due to the complex black market that developed during the Nazi occupation. To facilitate early "natural" deaths, the Germans also generally deprived Poles of pensions.[71]

SS-Obergruppenführer Greiser was not only fully aware of the Polish holocaust, but actively participated in its implementation. On September 18, 1941, Reichsführer-SS Heinrich Himmler informed Greiser that he intended to transfer 60,000 Czech and German Jews to the Łódz Ghetto until the spring of 1942, when the Nazis claimed they would be "resettled." When the first transport arrived a few weeks later, Greiser received permission from Himmler to kill close to 100,000 Jews in his area.[72]

Greiser then instructed Höhere SS und Polizeiführer Wilhelm Koppe to manage the overcrowding problem by experimenting with gas vans as a far more rapid method to murder large numbers of persons at a country estate at Chełmno nad Nerem. This established the first extermination unit that ultimately carried out the mass murder of approximately 150,000 Jews between late 1941 and April 1942. Furthermore, on October 6, 1943, Greiser hosted a national assembly of senior SS officers in Posen at which the mass executions of civilians was planned.

## POLISH RESISTANCE

Although around 50 Polish resistance groups were formed, resistance to German rule had very limited successes due to the harsh repression by the massive German presence.[73] Passive forms of Polish resistance included blowing up railroad tracks and torching barns located in farmsteads confiscated from Poles and given to German settlers.[74] In the end, the resistance was not very effective.

---

70 Lukas, *Forgotten Holocaust*, 31.
71 Epstein, *Model Nazi*, 201.
72 Kershaw, *Hitler 1936–1945*, 484.
73 Epstein, *Model Nazi*, 206–207.
74 Epstein, *Model Nazi*, 172–173.

## GREISER'S END

After the war ended, Greiser was arrested by the Americans in 1945. He was tried, convicted of war crimes and executed by hanging in Poland on July 21, 1946.[75] He was the last man to be publicly executed in Poland. The crowd of spectators who witnessed his execution were so overjoyed by enthusiasm at his demise that "they were kissing one another, jumping up and down, shouting, and bursting into song." The man "most responsible for the appalling suffering of the Poles" finally was brought to justice.[76]

## WHY GERMANY LOST THE WAR

The events at the end of the war document what author Lucy Dawidowicz called a racial war.[77] In short, at least toward the end of the war, eliminating the inferior human races seemed of greater importance to Hitler and his close associates than winning the war against the Allies. That was "what the war was really about."[78] And that, according to several modern scholars, was a more important reason than any other why Germany lost the war.[79]

The most cited instance of the practical effect of Hitler's goals was his continued refusal to allow redeployment of the troops to re-supply the crumbling front lines in Russia. Instead, they were used both to run the trains used to transport Jews and Poles to the death camps, and also to manage the camps. The trains were crammed full of thousands of Jews and Poles being transported to the death camps, requiring enormous manpower to achieve this goal.[80] As the late historian Raul Hilberg documented, the truth of what went on in those last months can be found in the railway schedules. For Hitler, it was less a matter of making the trains run on time than it was to ensure that the trains continue without let-up to transport the "inferior races" to the death camps at Auschwitz, Treblinka and elsewhere.

---

75  Rees, *Nazis*, 125.

76  Rees, *Nazis*, 125.

77  Ron Rosenbaum, *Explaining Hitler: The Search for the Origins of His Evil*, 2nd ed. (Boston: Da Capo Press, 2014), 397.

78  Rosenbaum, *Explaining Hitler*, 397.

79  Rosenbaum, *Explaining Hitler*, 397.

80  Rosenbaum, *Explaining Hitler*, 398.

Toward the end of the war, train cars, supplies and thousands of soldiers that could have been sent to the front were instead involved in transporting Jews and others to the death camps. The German army was so desperate for soldiers at this time that they were drafting boys as young as age 13 and men as old as age 60, often sending them to fight with very little training.[81]

After the Russians overran the mainly Polish-based camps and the camps disbanded, the large SS and native Polish and Ukrainian guard troops feeding the gas chambers were not redeployed to stave off the Russians in the East. Instead, they were ordered to take all the living and half-dead captives on the road in what became the final phase of the Final Solution: the death marches. At this point in the war, killing Jews and the Nazi's eugenic goals were evidently felt to be more important than military objectives.[82]

From January 1945 to the last months of the Third Reich, about 250,000 concentration camp inmates perished on these death marches from countless incidents of mass slaughter. They were mercilessly beaten or shot when they couldn't keep up, and many starved to death while being forced along icy roads with scant clothing.[83] Although the death marches were inspired partly by a desire to preserve the labour force for the SS, they turned into carnage because the effort was so poorly prepared and organized. Nonetheless, the death march commanders had incorporated Hitler's eugenic goals so deeply that they no longer needed orders to murder because their personal goal became to carry out the killing of as many members of inferior races as possible.

It was not just military men, but also civilians along the way, who took part in murdering the half-dead Jews to help eliminate inferior races, including Jews, Poles and all other Slavic peoples.[84] Even in the bloody annals of the Nazi regime, this final death-act was unique both in its character and scope.

---

81 James Norton, *The Holocaust: Jews, Germany, and the National Socialists* (New York: Rosen Publishing Group, 2008), 6–10.

82 Rosenbaum, *Explaining Hitler*, 398–399.

83 Daniel Blatman, *The Death Marches: The Final Phase of Nazi Genocide*, trans. Chaya Galai (Cambridge: Belknap Press, 2011).

84 Blatman, *Death Marches*.

Historian Hugh Trevor-Roper argued that, at the end of the war, Hitler was a messianic "true believer" in his eugenic goals. As Rosenbaum wrote, there exists a

> connection between Hitler's messianic vision of himself as racial savior and the loss of the war. Hitler's suicidal prohibition against even a tactical retreat, such as the one that might have saved his Sixth Army from capture at Stalingrad, was...a self-inflicted defeat entirely due to Hitler's delusion of his messianic destiny.[85]

## SUMMARY

The Slavic Holocaust is a clear demonstration of the fact that the central motive of the Nazis was not anti-Semitism. Rather, their main goal was to produce a superior race by the use of eugenic Darwinism. The Nazis were not only at war against the Jews, but wanted to destroy *all* "inferior" races.[86] This was their goal and their motivation for carrying out the Holocaust and, to a large extent, for the entire war as documented by their actions toward the end of the war.

The physical differences between Germans and Poles were often minor, thus the Nazi "racial farce would have been laughable if it did not have such tragic consequences on the unfortunate victims involved."[87] In the end, the Nazi victims included 55 million dead, hundreds of millions injured or homeless, and many hundreds of millions of innocent people losing their homes and most of everything else they possessed.

---

85 Rosenbaum, *Explaining Hitler*, 398.

86 Lucy Dawidowicz, *The War Against the Jews: 1933–1945* (New York: Holt, Rinehart and Winston, 1986).

87 Lukas, *Forgotten Holocaust*, 25.

## Karl Pearson (1857-1936)

Pearson was professor of biometrics at University College London and had a
prominent role in legitimizing the eugenics movement.

# 13

# Karl Pearson: Racist, warmonger and white supremacist

|||||||||||||||||||||||||||||||||||||||||||||||||||||||||||||||||||||||||||||||||||||||||||||||||||||||||||||||||||||||||

**P**rofessor Karl Pearson was more influential in the modern development of the science of statistics than any other person. He also played a critical role in the immoral eugenics movement that was one of the most tragic movements in history. Aside from Francis Galton, more than any other early person he put the now recognized pseudoscience of eugenics on a scientific foundation that facilitated its acceptance in the educated social classes, especially among scientists and physicians. The fallout included over 100,000 sterilized in America, mostly uneducated, poor women, and the Nazi Holocaust that cost over 12 million lives.

## PEARSON'S IMPORTANT ROLE IN THE EUGENICS MOVEMENT

The second most important architect of the early eugenics movement was the eminent British mathematician and statistician Karl Pearson (1857–1936). Called the "saint" of biometrika, Pearson made eugenics acceptable in the academic world by translating its nefarious goals into the language of science. In 1879, Pearson graduated with honours from Cambridge University with a degree in mathematics.

Pearson later went to Germany for post-graduate studies, and although critical of the then German Kaiser, he admired Germany so much that he changed the spelling of his name from Carl to the German Karl and sought to marry a German woman. Later appointed the chair of applied mathematics and mechanics at University College London, he soon established an international reputation as a leading mathematician. His publication of *The Grammar of Science* (1900), which covered in detail many areas of science, including an extensive discussion of evolution, also gave him an honoured place in science.

A committed socialist, he often lectured on Marxism to revolutionary clubs and other receptive audiences. Karl Pearson was connected with a variety of well-known socialists that were involved in various "progressive" movements of the time, such as the free love and birth control movements. These included George Bernard Shaw, Margaret Sanger, the founder of Planned Parenthood, and especially free love advocate Havelock Ellis.

Greatly influenced by Darwin's second cousin, Francis Galton, Pearson soon began to apply his mathematical knowledge to biological problems. He attributed this "change in direction to his benefactor Galton."[1] Actually, it was Galton's book *Natural Inheritance* that "won a brilliant disciple in Karl Pearson."[2] Pearson developed the field now known as statistics primarily to research evolution specifically as it related to eugenics.

Pearson also vigorously applied the experimental method to his eugenic research. One study he completed dealt with the ability of teachers to rate their students on such qualities as academic ability, introspection, temper and handwriting. This study found a correlation of between 0.43 and 0.63 between these ratings and certain biological traits, such as height.[3] Pearson concluded from this research that human progress came only through class and race struggles. He wrote that as a result of their superior genetics, the superior races (the Caucasians) won out, supplanting the lower races, such as Negroes, in the Darwinian struggle for life.[4]

---

1 Stephen M. Stigler, *The History of Statistics: The Measurement of Uncertainty before 1900* (Cambridge: Belknap Press/Harvard University, 1986), 305.

2 Haller, *Eugenics*, 12.

3 Haller, *Eugenics*, 13.

4 Haller, *Eugenics*, 14.

## SIMILARITIES BETWEEN PEARSON AND GALTON

Both Karl Pearson and Francis Galton, the founder of the science of eugenics, were products of middle class Quaker families with stern fathers. Karl's father, William Pearson, came to London from Wiltshire to practice law and eventually became a counsel for the Queen. Karl Pearson

> remembered his father as "an iron man" who rose before dawn to prepare his briefs, rushed to the office after a standing breakfast at nine, returned in the evening to hurry taciturnly through dinner, then promptly retired. If Karl entered his father's study, he would be directed to a chair and left to sit for hours entirely ignored.[5]

Both Pearson and Galton became mentally unstable as adults: Pearson's mental health problems were at one point so serious that he had to withdraw from law school. In 1875, he was able to enroll in Cambridge University on a mathematics scholarship, but was soon forced to drop out due to a nervous breakdown.

Daniel Kevles concluded that Pearson was a cold, remote, very driven man and treated pleasure as a weakness. Highly oriented to academic pursuits, he was very critical of his fellow students because, he thought, many of them were in college for reasons other than to learn. He disliked many of the activities that the upper-middle class enjoyed, such as art, literature and poetry. Challenging Pearson on a scientific point invited a "demolishing fire in return." It was primarily in debates about his eugenic theories in which his fire erupted:

> If Pearson responded to criticism with polemics, it was because the dissent struck at his secular church.... When it came to biometry, eugenics, and statistics, he was the besieged defender of an emotionally charged faith [and his research in eugenics and statistics] conformed to the icy distance of his character, reinforcing his propensity for dealing with man in the impersonal group.[6]

---

5   Daniel Kevles, *In the Name of Eugenics* (New York: Knopf, 1985), 21–22.
6   Kevles, *In the Name of Eugenics*, 36.

Pearson and Galton were also both "like so many Victorian under-graduates" in that they were "beset by an agony of religious doubt."[7] Pearson's socialist leanings at first caused him to conclude that Darwinism, especially as expressed in Herbert Spencer's writings, provided justification for *laissez faire* capitalism. When the reformers of his day managed to forge Darwinism into a weapon against *laissez faire* capitalism, Pearson switched sides and joined the Eugenic Darwinists.

Pearson concluded that Darwinism supported socialism because he believed that socialism produced a wealthier, stronger, more productive, and, in short, a superior nation. And Pearson believed that, in the long run, the outcome of the Darwinian struggle resulted in the ascendancy, not only of individuals, but of nations. Achievement of national fitness, Pearson argued, could better be produced by national socialism because socialism produced nations that were better able to survive in the Darwinian struggle for existence both within and between nations.

## HIS IDEAS

Pearson carried his conclusions of heritability far beyond that which was warranted by the data. For example he proclaimed to an audience of professionals at the 1903 anthropological institute that humans "inherit our parents' tempers, our parents' conscientiousness, shyness and ability, even as we inherit their stature, forearm...[and] no training or education can *create* [intelligence], you must breed it."[8]

Kevles claimed that Pearson often displayed a "relentless closed-mindedness," and "frequently took a club to his scientific enemies and slashingly abused even...his...friends who queried his biometry or his eugenics" ideas.[9] Much of the criticism in Pearson's day against the theory of eugenics was also against Darwinism. The two ideas were highly intertwined, and many scientific critics attacked both ideas as a unit.

Danish biologist Wilhelm Johannsen discerned from his empirical research on beans that, barring the use of gene splicing technology, which was unknown in his day, regardless of how it was manipulated,

---

7   Kevles, *In the Name of Eugenics*, 22.

8   Quoted in Kelves, *In the Name of Eugenics*, 32–33.

9   Kelves, *In the Name of Eugenics*, 36.

a pure line of beans could not be bred beyond a maximum limit for a given character. Pearson irrationally responded against this concept, even dismissing two members of his editorial board when they published articles reporting Johannsen's research.

Pearson's only argument against Johannsen's evidence was the fact that reasonable correlational coefficients for intelligence and physical traits existed; therefore the influence of heredity *must* be similar for both; end of argument. As is well-known today, correlations do not prove causation. Pearson also believed that morality was merely the "outcome of Darwinian struggle with the ascendancy of the fittest nation."[10] In other words, might makes right.

## HIS STATURE IN SCIENCE

Pearson was no minor figure in the history of science. His contributions in statistics are crucial to virtually all modern scientific research.[11] He developed not only the Pearson Product Moment Correlational Coefficient, to which his name is attached today, but also regression analysis, multiple correlation and chi square; he also made numerous important contributions in the area of statistical analysis, including the *goodness-of-fit* theory. This technique examines how closely a given set of data corresponds to the mathematical curve that one would expect by chance.

A simple goodness-of-fit test attempts to answer questions such as "Are male sheep more likely to survive to adulthood than female sheep?" One selects a sample of adult animals, then determines the male to female ratio. The expected ratio is the birth ratio, or about 50/50. If the ratio of sheep is found by an empirical research study to be 45/55, the question is then asked: "Could this difference be due to sampling error, i.e., chance, or does it represent a real difference between birth rates of males and females for this particular animal?" This question can, in part, be answered by the goodness-of-fit statistical test.

His motive behind developing these statistical tools was primarily to convince the scientific world of the validity of the eugenic claims. One of Pearson's last contributions, achieved with Dr. Weldon, a pro-

---

10 Kelves, *In the Name of Eugenics*, 23.
11 Stigler, *History of Statistics*.

fessor of comparative anatomy at Oxford, and Galton in *Biometrika*, dealt with statistical theory clothed with biological terminology.

## PEARSON'S WORK WITH GALTON

During most of Pearson's career, Galton was highly involved in the eugenics movement. Galton, also one of the movement's chief financial supporters, awarded a research fellowship of £500 per year, about what a luxury automobile cost then, to study government programs that were designed to improve the racial or mental qualities of future generations. Galton also contributed much of his fortune to the Galton Laboratory for National Eugenics, which was under Pearson's directorship. When Galton died in January 1911, the bulk of his £115,000 estate, an enormous sum of money at the time, was willed to support eugenic studies. The University College London received much of the money and established a Galton eugenics professorship and a new department called *applied statistics* to study eugenics and other "applied" topics.

The fund enabled Pearson to be freed from what he regarded as "burdensome" teaching duties to be able to devote himself to full-time eugenics research. The new department blossomed and drew prominent researchers from around the world. Pearson was then able to select the best scientists and students who were required to completely immerse themselves in the goal of documenting eugenics claims. His students worked on the dozens of eugenics research projects in which Pearson was involved.

Pearson's students, and those who worked under him, were as dedicated as Pearson was, or they were soon forced to leave his lab. Some, in attempting to emulate Pearson's pace of work, suffered nervous breakdowns.[12] The lab's goal was the production of research, and produce they did—between 1903 and 1918 alone, Pearson and his staff published over 300 research articles plus various government reports and popular expositions of eugenics.

Some of his coworkers questioned the idea that the only way to improve a nation was to ensure that its future generations were primarily produced from the putative superior members of the existing

---

12 Kevles, *In the Name of Eugenics*, 39.

generation, but most said nothing—no doubt partly due to fear of losing their career. If

> staff members or students had private reservations about the valid-
> ity of the work, it required rare courage for them to make their
> doubts known.... Pearson chose and assigned the research prob-
> lems, guided their execution, and edited the results. Intellectually,
> he was as domineering in the laboratory as outside of it.[13]

In 1925, Pearson began publishing a journal titled *The Annals of Eugenics*. He continued to contribute both his enthusiasm and his mathematical genius to the eugenic cause until he died in 1936.

## PEARSON'S LEGACY

Pearson's work had profound effects on the world for years after he
died. More than any other person, Pearson put eugenics on what
appeared to be an impressive, solid scientific foundation. Many of
Pearson's eugenic ideas were incorporated in school textbooks, especially biology textbooks, spreading racism throughout the world,
especially in America and Germany.[14]

Pearson actively helped to spread the eugenics movement, first to
Germany and later to the United States, then to the four corners of
the earth. In Munich, Germany, The International Society for Racial
Hygiene was formed in 1910 with Galton as the honourary president.[15]
As Haller states, "Thus eugenics in Germany began its sad history that,
under the Nazis, would justify wholesale sexual sterilization and then
euthanasia for the allegedly unfit and would provide part of the justification for the slaughter of four to six million Jews."[16]

Galton's successor was the son of Charles Darwin, Leonard Darwin,
who was very active in the eugenics movement for many years.[17]

---

13 Kevles, *In the Name of Eugenics*, 40.

14 Allan Chase, *The Legacy of Malthus: The Social Costs of the New Scientific Racism*
(New York: Alfred A. Knopf, 1980), 308.

15 George L. Mosse, *Nazi Culture: Intellectual, Cultural, and Social Life in the Third
Reich* (New York: Schocken Books, 1981).

16 Haller, *Eugenics*, 20.

17 Jerry Bergman, "Darwin's cousin Sir Francis Galton (1822–1911) and the eugenics

Leonard advocated compulsory sterilization to prevent the "danger resulting from unchecked multiplication of inferior types."[18] As Andrew Norman wrote, "Whereas Francis Galton showed a degree of hesitation when it came to the question of eugenics in practice, Pearson was constrained by no such moral scruples."[19]

An example is in a lecture delivered to the Newcastle Philosophical Society in November 1900, in which Pearson claimed that the science of eugenics required ensuring only the physically and mentally fitter were to become parents of the next generation, and this process must be repeated for many generations to produce a superior race. Pearson added that this process alone will not reduce the tendency to produce bad stock because only both conscious and

> unconscious selection can alone bring that about. What I have said about bad stock seems to me to hold for the lower races of man. How many…thousands of years, have the…negro held large districts in Africa undisturbed by the white man? Yet their inter-tribal struggles have not yet produced a civilization in the least comparable with the Aryan. Educate and nurture them as you will, I do not believe that you will succeed in modifying the stock. History shows…one way only, in which a high state of civilization has been produced, namely, the struggle of race with race, and the survival of the physically and mentally fitter race. If you want to know whether the lower races of man can evolve [into] a higher type, I fear the only course is to leave them to fight it out among themselves.[20]

He also wrote that the "white man" who went to Africa to look for the agricultural and mineral resources there could "settle down and live alongside the inferior race," a solution which he condemned, writing that "the only healthy alternative is that he should go and completely

---

movement," *Creation Research Society Quarterly* 39, No. 3 (December 2002):169–176.

18 Chase, *Legacy of Malthus*, 282.

19 Andrew Norman, *Charles Darwin: Destroyer of Myths* (New York: Skyhorse, 2014), 226.

20 Karl Pearson, *National Life from the Standpoint of Science* (London: Adam and Charles Black, 1901), 19–22.

drive out the inferior race."[21] He added that "driving the inferior race out" means "suffering, intense suffering, while it is in progress; but that struggle and that suffering have been the…[means] by which the white man has reached his present stage of development."[22] The scientific view, he wrote, by comparing humans to animals, leads to the conclusion that society will improve only if we ensure that the next generation

> are substantially recruited from the better stocks, and kept up to a high pitch of external efficiency by contest, chiefly by way of war with inferior races, and with equal races by the struggle for trade-routes and for the sources of raw material and food supply. This is the natural history view of mankind.[23]

In the end, he wrote that humankind:

> as a whole, like the individual man, advances through pain and suffering only. The path of progress is strewn with the wreck of nations; traces are everywhere to be seen of the hecatombs [sacrifices] of inferior races and of victims who found not the narrow way to the greater perfection. Yet these dead peoples are, in very truth, the stepping-stones on which mankind has arisen to the higher intellectual and deeper emotional life of today.[24]

Norman concluded from a review of Pearson's writings that he was "a eugenicist, a racist, a warmonger, and a 'white supremacist'" through and through.[25] The fact that the eugenics movement was directly at odds with both Christian and Jewish teachings was not lost on those in the movement: many leading eugenicists including Pearson, were openly critical of Christianity, and large numbers, including Pearson, were open agnostics or atheists.

---

21  Pearson, *National Life*, 21.
22  Pearson, *National Life*, 24.
23  Pearson, *National Life*, 43–44.
24  Pearson, *National Life*, 61–62.
25  Norman, *Charles Darwin*, 227.

## SUMMARY

Pearson's many contributions to research, and especially statistics, are unquestionably first class and so important that he did more than any other person to put the field of research and measurement on a firm foundation.[26] Conversely, he used this science to put eugenics on a respectable footing, leading to the abuses of the Holocaust and the eugenics laws enacted in the United States that ended up sterilizing well over 100,000 young women, a movement that ended only in the 1970s. His work leaves us with an important lesson in science. In Einstein's words, science without religion is not just lame, but dangerous.

---

26 Karl Pearson, *The Grammar of Science* (London: Adam and Charles Black, 1900).

# 14

# Darwinism destroys aesthetic sensibility

||||||||||||||||||||||||||||||||||||||||||||||||||||||||||||||||||||||||||||||||||||||||||||||||||||||||||||||||||||||||||

**B**eth Houston, a professor at the University of California, stresses that science, especially Darwinism, has now become a form of dogmatism that she feels should be challenged. One point she has documented is that Darwin's central ambition was not to explore the world to let it reveal itself, but to become famous. She concluded that, more than anything else, it was partly Darwin's focused ambition for respect that accounted

for his success. It certainly explains his rush to publish the *Origin* …once Wallace arrived on the scene. It is also conceivable that the central role of survival-of-the-fittest competition in his theory of natural selection was a projection of his own ambitious nature. Though he doubted his intellectual agility, he considered his talent for observation and collection of facts to be superior, and his love of natural science, "steady and ardent."[1]

1   Beth Houston, *Natural God: Deism in the Age of Intelligent Design* (Florida: New Deism Press, 2012), 126.

Houston writes that, although Darwin enjoyed being a naturalist, his motivation was, to quote Darwin himself, "much aided by the ambition to be esteemed by my fellow naturalists."[2] Early in his life, "Darwin was less than intellectually inclined. Ambitious as he was, his years at Cambridge [University] were, in his words, a waste of time.... [H]is academic interests were quite limited and his performance well below par."[3]

While still a student at Cambridge, Darwin admitted that reading works by naturalists "stirred up in me a burning zeal to add...to the noble structure of Natural Science."[4] He once explained the reason he wanted to make a contribution to science was due to his drive for fame.

## THE *BEAGLE* VOYAGE

During Darwin's famous HMS *Beagle* voyage, his research was motivated by his drive to investigate, but also by his "strong desire to add a few facts to the great mass of facts in Natural Science...and [Darwin admitted] I was also ambitious to take a fair place among scientific men."[5] When he returned from his *Beagle* voyage "Darwin was most strongly influenced by Sir Charles Lyell, a science mentor who 'was very kind-hearted, and thoroughly liberal in his religious beliefs, or rather disbeliefs.'"[6] Lyell's influence was important in helping Darwin achieve his goal of fame because "it was Lyell's encouragement, advice, and example that most ignited Darwin's aspiration to prove specifically a theory of origin—a topic very much in the air, and one that was sure to impress the impressive Lyell."[7] Furthermore, Darwin knew full well that his one chance at making a major contribution to science

would only be his theory of natural selection. Despite his own grave doubts, by the time the *Origin* was published and barked

---

2   Charles Darwin, *Charles Darwin: His Life Told in an Autobiographical Chapter*, ed. Francis Darwin (New York: D. Appleton, 1892), 55.

3   Houston, *Natural God*, 127.

4   Nora Barlow, ed., *The Autobiography of Charles Darwin 1809–1882* (New York: Norton, 1958), 68.

5   Barlow, ed., *Autobiography of Charles Darwin*, 80–91.

6   Houston, *Natural God*, 127.

7   Houston, *Natural God*, 127.

## Charles Darwin (1809-1882)
In his early thirties, Charles Darwin conceived the idea of evolutionism through natural selection.

by his Bulldog [T.H. Huxley], Darwin was fully invested, if not in his theory's validity, then in the *need* for it to be valid and true, or at least highly esteemed. That need itself evolved.[8]

In the end, Houston concluded that, in spite of Darwin's

tendency toward self-depreciation, Darwin's ambition fueled his vanity and triggered defensiveness toward his "original" theory of natural selection. Though his goal was to impress a few select people, he did relish the fame that came with success. Is ambition vain or humble if the writer cares not about the readers who made him famous? In Darwin's case, perhaps a bit of both.[9]

For example, Darwin wrote, "I think that I can say with truth that... though I cared in the highest degree for the approbation of such men as Lyell and Hooker, who were my friends. I did not care much about the general public."[10]

In contrast to this admission, Darwin once admitted that it was the *public success* of his first work, the *Journal of Researches*, a book that covered his observations made on the volcanic islands that he visited during his *Beagle* voyage, which "always tickles my vanity more than that of any of my other books."[11] Houston concluded, "Vain or not, the fundamental force that drove his work was desire for that high esteem among fellow naturalists that can only be attained by an important contribution to 'the noble structure of Natural Science.'"[12]

## DARWIN'S LOSS OF HIS AESTHETIC SENSIBILITY

Houston has carefully documented her position that evolution theory has caused its developer, Charles Darwin, to lose both his aesthetic sensibility and his appreciation of esthetic beauty. She concluded this by relying on Darwin's own words to support the fact that, as he devel-

---

8  Houston, *Natural God*, 127.

9  Houston, *Natural God*, 127.

10  Barlow, ed., *Autobiography of Charles Darwin*, 82.

11  Darwin, *Charles Darwin: His Life*, 40.

12  Houston, *Natural God*, 127–128.

oped his evolutionary theory, he lost his aesthetic sensibility. After noting that, when still a young man, Darwin loved his dogs and his beetles, but

> he also loved killing and collecting trophies. Early on he believed in God and the Bible and even fervently defended his religion against the taunting crew of the *Beagle*; later his religion gave way to agnosticism which gradually slipped toward atheism. Darwin evolved—he grew up, he changed.[13]

Houston added that Darwin changed in one other significant way. Darwin was able to establish his evolution theory, achieving fame and a place "beside the great scientists of the age" yet he "was aware that something profound and natural in him had been sacrificed: first and foremost, the faculty of aesthetic sensibility."[14] To document this claim, she pointed to Darwin's love of art as a young man, which was clear evidence of his early aesthetic sensibility. She noted that, as a young man, "art brought him 'intense pleasure' and even sometimes 'excited' in him a 'sense of sublimity.'" While a student at Cambridge

> Darwin was, as he put it in his *Autobiography*, "inoculated" by his friends and professors with a taste for quality art. He frequented the Fitzwilliam Gallery and the National Gallery in London, and the intense pleasure he got from the art of Sebastian del Piombo excited in him "a sense of sublimity."[15]

Darwin also "acquired a taste for music from his musician school-mates" in college.[16] He "regularly listened to the daily anthems in King's College Chapel and even hired the chorister boys to sing in his rooms."[17] Later in life, he wrote in his autobiography that he admitted he was: "so utterly destitute of an ear, that I cannot perceive a discord,

---

13  Houston, *Natural God*, 162.
14  Houston, *Natural God*, 162.
15  Houston, *Natural God*, 162.
16  Houston, *Natural God*, 162–163.
17  Houston, *Natural God*, 162–163.

or keep time and hum a tune correctly; and it is a mystery how I could possibly have derived pleasure from music" when younger.[18] In response to this claim, Houston asks: "If Darwin's aesthetic faculty was so severely handicapped, what is the quality of pleasure he derived from flat, distorted sound…. What is the quality of pleasure deprived of the depth and meaning of genuine appreciation?"[19]

Houston also documented that Darwin's loss of his love for literature and poetry occurred later in life. When, as a young man on his five-year-long trip around the world on the *Beagle*, Darwin delighted in reading "the poetry of Wordsworth, Coleridge, and Milton, his favorite at that time and most famously the poet of *Paradise Lost*. But his love of metaphysics and poetry waned during his twenties."[20]

She added that "Though he was informally taught to appreciate art and probably did derive pleasure from it…it's fair to ask whether by looking at art he was actually seeing and appreciating the work itself."[21] Even if Darwin's aesthetic sensibilities were not fully refined as a young man, all of the evidence we have shows that his pleasure in music and poetry that he claimed existed when he was young was evidently genuine.

Darwin's loss of the aesthetic may be part of the reason he rarely attended funerals.[22] In fact "Darwin avoided funerals all his life unless it was absolutely impossible for him not to attend."[23] Darwin had a total of ten children, and three died while Charles was still alive (Anne, age ten; Mary Eleanor, age three weeks, and Charles Waring, age one and a half).[24] He did not attend the funeral of his father, nor even his

---

18 Charles Darwin, *The Life and Letters of Charles Darwin* (New York: D. Appleton, 1896), 43. This has echoes in art such as *Hollow Men* by T.S. Eliot or the lyrics of "The Logical Song" by SuperTramp; http://www.lyricsfreak.com/s/supertramp/the+logical+song_20133850.html; accessed October 14, 2016.

19 Houston, *Natural God*, 163. Italics in original.

20 Houston, *Natural God*, 163. Italics in original.

21 Houston, *Natural God*, 163. Italics in original.

22 Tim M. Berra, *Darwin and His Children: His Other Legacy* (New York: Oxford University Press, 2013), 62.

23 Berra, *Darwin and His Children*, 43.

24 Berra, *Darwin and His Children*, 187.

favourite daughter, Anne, who died at age of ten of tuberculosis.[25] One funeral that he did attend was the September 1, 1881, funeral of his older brother Erasmus.[26]

## WAS DARWIN'S LOSS OF AESTHETIC SENSIBILITY DUE TO HIS EVOLUTION THEORY?

Houston concludes that it is no mere coincidence that, as Darwin developed his theory of evolution, his spiritual and aesthetic faculties both atrophied.[27] Darwin's own assessment of the demise of his personal aesthetics is clear evidence of Houston's view. Darwin openly admitted that his appreciation for aesthetics had dynamically changed, at least in one major respect, during the last twenty or thirty years of his life, writing:

> Up to the age of thirty…poetry…such as the works of Milton, Gray, Byron, Wordsworth, Coleridge, and Shelley, gave me great pleasure, and even as a schoolboy I took intense delight in Shakespeare, especially in the historical plays. I have also said that formerly pictures gave me considerable, and music very great delight. But now for many years I cannot endure to read a line of poetry: I have tried lately to read Shakespeare, and found it so intolerably dull that it nauseated me. I have also almost lost my taste for pictures or music.[28]

He also wrote in his autobiography that his "curious and lamentable loss of the higher aesthetic tastes is all the odder, as books on history, biographies, and travels (independently of any scientific facts which they may contain), and essays on all sorts of subjects" still interested him, but, nonetheless, Darwin acknowledges that his mind had

> become a kind of machine for grinding general laws out of large collections of facts, but why this should have caused the atrophy of that part of the brain alone, on which the higher tastes depend,

25 Berra, *Darwin and His Children*, 43–48.
26 Berra, *Darwin and His Children*, 75.
27 Houston, *Natural God*, 163–164.
28 Darwin, *Life and Letters of Charles Darwin*, 81.

I cannot conceive...if I had to live my life again I would have made a rule to read some poetry and listen to some music at least once every week; for perhaps the parts of my brain now atrophied would thus have been kept active through use.[29]

Darwin then admitted that the "loss of these tastes is a loss of happiness, and may possibly be injurious to the intellect, and more probably to the moral character, by enfeebling the emotional part of our nature."[30] Houston concludes that it strikes her "as a peculiar tragedy worthy of Shakespeare or Milton" that Darwin,

the man most responsible, nominally at least, for the sacrifice of the human spirit on the altar of mechanistic determinism could admit nonchalantly that he had in essence willfully programmed his mind into a machine—a computer—that resulted in loss of happiness, injury to moral character, emotional enfeeblement, and, ironically, severe mental atrophy. Darwin the man created the theory that symbolizes the absurd predicament, perhaps even the tragic flaw, of modern humanity.[31]

## EVIDENCE THAT EVOLUTION WAS PARTLY RESPONSIBLE

The fact is, Darwinism became widely accepted in spite of its many major lethal scientific flaws and its open racism. And when Darwin was shown to be clearly wrong "he would always conclude that, all things considered, he was still right and everyone else was wrong."[32] Houston argued that

Darwin's faith in his theory of evolution reached the pitch of religious conviction even while he expressed his doubts about the theory's validity. The passionate naturalist, cannibalized by the dark lord kill-or-be-killed, leaned toward mechanistic atheism. ...Darwin describes the objects and processes that his close obser-

---

29 Darwin, *Life and Letters of Charles Darwin*, 81–82.

30 Darwin, *Life and Letters of Charles Darwin*, 82.

31 Houston, *Natural God*, 165–166.

32 Bruno Maddox, "Deconstructing Darwin," *Discover Magazine* (November 2009):40.

vation once reckoned as beautiful, yet his stance now seems aloof and flat, as if his enjoyment of nature was like his tone-deaf "enjoyment" of music or his atrophied pleasure in art and poetry.[33]

She concluded that what was wrong with Darwin was the "dimension that gives life lived to the fullest its zing" was gone or

> verged on extinction. By the time he finished the *Origin*, and certainly his later *Autobiography*, beauty had ceased to be beauty at all. Darwin objectified nature into a kind of intellectual pornography for scientific voyeurs; beauty was observed and used like a prostitute for a distant satisfaction of an immediate need, never for love of beauty for its own sake, never for the pleasure of intimate contact [with nature].[34]

Houston then applied this trend that occurred in Darwin to Darwin's followers:

> Darwin, like some neo-Darwinians today, could state the facts of elegance and beauty in an objective, abstract tone even while the descriptions themselves betray the inherent vitality of their own inherent elegant beauty. ...[M]echanistic agnostics like Darwin...know intellectually that nature is beautifully constructed while emotionally denying that it is. The aesthetic atrophies when the spirit does, or when the spirit lies dormant and inactivated. It is...mechanistic determinism and Darwinian natural selection. There is never any death of God, only the murder or suicide of the killer's own God-given faculties.[35]

## DARWIN'S SPIRITUAL DISASSOCIATION
Houston concluded that, even though Darwin had major doubts about his theory, his faith in evolution was still strong enough to cause the atrophy of his aesthetic dimension:

---

33  Houston, *Natural God*, 165.

34  Houston, *Natural God*, 165. Italics in original.

35  Houston, *Natural God*, 165.

Far from scientific treatises proving natural selection, Darwin's writings betray the psychological angst of a man plagued by self-doubt, contradiction, and denial. Read closely, his work becomes a casebook exposing the consequences of spiritual dissociation that has infected modern thought. The atrophy of the aesthetic faculty and its subsequent flattening of perception is a crucial symptom of spiritual dissociation rarely considered when assessing declarations of scientific theory as fact.[36]

Furthermore,

> Darwin realized that his mind had become a machine for grinding out abstractions from collections of facts, but because he had repressed his spiritual faculty and erased the possibility of spiritual dimension from Nature, he was unable to understand why his aesthetic faculty had atrophied.... What Darwin *knew about* he could not truly *know*.[37]

Darwin wrote that he "had always been much struck by such adaptations" as the ability of "a woodpecker or a tree-frog to climb trees, or a seed for dispersal by hooks or plumes" but "until these could be explained it seemed to me almost useless to endeavour to prove by indirect evidence that species have been modified" via evolution.[38] Darwin then

> spent the rest of his life trying to prove that species types have been modified into new types. He never succeeded. To an artist, transcending modifications are perfectly natural. Darwin was unable to process the *creation* in Creation. As any true artist knows, creation is a generous act of love.[39]

---

36  Houston, *Natural God*, 166.
37  Houston, *Natural God*, 166. Italics in original.
38  Houston, *Natural God*, 166–167.
39  Houston, *Natural God*, 166-167. Italics in original.

## WHY EVOLUTION CAUSES LOSS OF AESTHETIC SENSIBILITY

As he developed his theory of evolution, Darwin concluded that he saw nature more and more both brutal and selfish. In one example, he wrote, "Natural selection cannot possibly produce any modification in any one species exclusively for the good of another species; though throughout nature one species incessantly takes advantage of, and profits by, the structure of another."[40]

In short, "Darwin considered life to be a battleground where opposites fight and separate themselves out, but Darwin's 'good' was brute selfishness, the antithesis of anyone else's definition of good."[41] In Darwin's own words, "natural selection can, and does, often produce structures for the direct injury of other animals, as we see in the fang of the adder, and in the ovipositor of the ichneumon, by which its eggs are deposited in the living bodies of other insects."[42] Houston concluded from her detailed study of Darwin's writing that, in

> Darwin's world of fangs and ovipositors, good equals harm successfully inflicted on another. In other words, benefit exists only through harm. ...Darwin knew that his theory was dependent upon the inherent ruthlessness of Nature, not upon something reminiscent of the benevolent God of his abandoned religion.[43]

For example, Darwin wrote if "it could be proved that any part of the structure of any one species had been formed for the exclusive good of another species, it would annihilate my theory, for such could not have been produced through natural selection,"[44] Houston then speculates that

> Darwin's insistence that natural selection is ultimately brutal is a projection of...the brutal side of his own nature. Natural selec-

---

40  Charles Darwin, *On The Origin of Species* (London: John Murray, 1859), 200.
41  Houston, *Natural God*, 167.
42  Darwin, *Origin of Species*, 200–201.
43  Houston, *Natural God*, 167.
44  Darwin, *Origin of Species*, 201.

tion justifies brutality and sanctifies guilt. The brutal cannot face a God who might not condone brutality. Therefore, religions create their gods in the image of their own brutality to justify and sanctify brutality, and science creates its god, natural selection, the shadow of civilized man, for the same purpose.[45]

Furthermore, she concluded that the contrast of Darwinism and Creationism is critical in causing a loss of aesthetic value, writing that

cooperative goodness produced by the God proclaimed by every major religion and recognized by the vast majority of people who have ever lived is an abstract construct to the tone-deaf, spiritually myopic Darwin. Intellectually, abstractly, Darwin understands the facts. ...For Darwin...[l]ife exists only to reproduce itself in an endless loop of brute survival for its own sake.[46]

She generalized that the

Darwinians are like people who visit art museums but are never deeply moved by the art. For them, Nature is a picture of life, a still life produced with paints on a two-dimensional canvas. ... What escapes them is depth, representational meaning, the correspondence between one world and another. ...Reason is diluted by reductive scansion; intuition, emotion, and aesthetic exist like phantom limbs.[47]

## SUMMARY

Professor Houston makes a convincing case that the natural world provides clear evidence for a Creator. She also documents the adverse effects of Darwinism on morality, using as a prime example its destructive effect on aesthetics. Exhibit one was Darwin himself who lost his early love of poetry, music and his aesthetic sensibilities in general when he accepted an evolutionary origin for life. She then proposed

---

45 Houston, *Natural God*, 168.
46 Houston, *Natural God*, 168.
47 Houston, *Natural God*, 168.

a plausible explanation for this loss, namely his changed worldview, when he moved from a theistic creationist to an atheistic/agnostic evolutionist worldview. Last, she carefully documented her case in a convincing manner.

# 15

# The failed attempt to prove Jewish inferiority by a skeleton collection

||||||||||||||||||||||||||||||||||||||||||||||||||||||||||||||||||||||||||||||||||||||||||||||||||||||||||||||||||||||||

The best example of immorality inspired by Darwinism is the quest to apply Darwinism to produce a superior race. And the best example of this is the attempt to exterminate the Jews to help achieve this goal by preventing the pollution of a superior with an inferior race. A common claim is that the Jewish Holocaust was caused purely by anti-Semitism. In fact, as has been well documented, racism based on Darwinism was a central factor in causing the Holocaust.[1] One of many examples of evidence for this fact is the extensive, detailed study of Jewish skeletons that was undertaken by Nazi collaborators in an attempt to prove scientifically the racial inferiority of Jews. What the scientists were looking for is unknown, but they believed that Jews were biologically inferior, so concluded that a careful study of their skeletons would find scientific evidence for this view.

The Nazis were so confident in this view that they attempted to set up a public display of these skeletons to help convince the public of

---

1   Bergman, *Hitler and the Nazi Darwinian Worldview*, passim; Benno Muller-Hill, *Murderous Science: Elimination by Scientific Selection of Jews, Gypsies, and Others in Germany, 1933–1945*, trans. George R. Fraser (New York: Oxford University Press, 1988).

Jewish inferiority as well as that of other inferior races, such as the Slavs.[2] A collection of skeletons of Jews murdered to obtain the collection was only one of many attempts by the Nazis to prove the racial inferiority of the "Jewish race," specifically their conclusion that the Jews were *Untermenschen* ("sub-humans"), in contrast to the Germans, which the Nazis considered *Übermenschen* (superior-humans). The program was sponsored by the German Ahnenerbe office to carry out various scientific studies on race, especially those people that were members of what the leading scientists then determined were inferior races.[3]

The Nazi's anthropological skeleton display was also created and designed to help justify Nazi programs against Jews to the general public. Involved in this project were the nation's leading anthropologists, scientists and medical professionals, all who supported the "innate superiority of the 'Aryan' folk" belief.[4] The collection was originally to be housed where the initial preparation of the corpses was done, namely, at the Anatomy Institute of the University of Strasbourg.

The collection was sanctioned by Reichsführer SS Heinrich Himmler and was under the direction of August Hirt and Rudolf Brandt. Wolfram Sievers was responsible for procuring and preparing the corpses for a display of skeletons of inferior humans. The collection was part of the work of several eminent German anthropologists at the Kaiser Wilhelm Institute. The Kaiser Wilhelm Society was supported by many eminent scientists including

> Otto Hahn, Albert Einstein, Max Planck, and Werner Heisenberg, scientific giants active at a time when Germany was a scientifically dominant nation. That era came to an abrupt end when

---

2    Anton Weiss-Wendt, *Eradicating Differences: The Treatment of Minorities in Nazi-Dominated Europe* (Newcastle-upon-Tyne: Cambridge Scholar Press, 2010); Richard Weikart, *Hitler's Struggle for Existence against Slavs: Racial Theory and Vacillations in Nazi Policy Towards Czechs and Poles* (forthcoming).

3    Robert J. Lifton, *The Nazi Doctors: Medical Killing and the Psychology of Genocide* (New York: Basic Books, 1986), 286.

4    Simon D. Messing, "On Anthropology and Nazi Genocide," *Current Anthropology* 17, No. 2 (June 1976):326.

Hitler rose to power and the Nazis ousted many of the best scientists because they were Jewish.[5]

Soon the Kaiser Wilhelm Institute became a central part of the Nazi war machine, and

through its Institute for Anthropology, Human Heredity, and Eugenics, the Kaiser Wilhelm Society was actively involved in racial science and the crimes that grew out of that. In that institute, based in Berlin, people like Josef Mengele were scientific assistants while performing experiments on inmates at Auschwitz death camp, many of them children. Whereas Mengele was sentenced for his crimes after the war (although he had escaped to South America), his superiors at the Institute for Anthropology were never charged. On the contrary, some of them became professors at universities.[6]

The original plan was to obtain "specimens" for the collection from the Jews originally captured by the Wehrmacht on the Eastern front. The individuals ultimately chosen for the anthropological research were obtained from a pool of 115 Jewish inmates at the Auschwitz concentration camp in occupied Poland. They were known to not be a representative sample of Jews, but were chosen specifically because their appearance conformed to the Jewish stereotypical "inferior" racial characteristics.

The initial selections and preparations were carried out by Bruno Beger and Hans Fleischhacker. The scientists arrived in Auschwitz in the first half of 1943 and completed their preliminary work on the Jewish victims by June 15, 1943. Due to a typhus epidemic among the camp prisoners, the candidates chosen for the skeleton display were quarantined to prevent them from becoming ill and ruining their evolutionary anatomical value. Sievers reported in June 1943 on the preparation status, writing that "115 persons were worked on, 79 were

---

5  Svante Pääbo, *Neanderthal Man: In Search of Lost Genomes* (New York: Basic Books, 2014), 80.

6  Pääbo, *Neanderthal Man*, 80–81.

Jews, 30 were Jewesses, 2 were Poles, and 4 were Asiatics. At the present time these prisoners are segregated by sex and are under quarantine in the two hospital buildings."[7]

The victims selected were then sent to the Natzweiler-Struthof camp near Strasbourg and were only a few of the thousands of men murdered at this concentration site. The complex was

> surrounded by electrified barbed wire, its barracks overrun with lice and typhus, the chimney above its crematorium constantly belching acrid smoke into the mountain air…. Between 1941 and 1945, disease, hunger, routine barbarity, and the gas chamber claimed nearly twenty-two-thousand lives. It was at Natzweiler that eighty-six Jewish men and women were gassed to provide anatomical specimens for the Jewish skeleton collection, an exhibit the Nazis hoped to display at the planned Reich University of Strasbourg to highlight the physical inferiority of the Jewish race.[8]

The delegate in charge of securing the victims was instructed to take a series of photographs, anthropological measurements, and, in addition, as far as possible to determine the background, date of birth, and other relevant information required for their racist research.[9] To properly complete their "anthropological research" on race, measurements "of all the parts of the body" were taken.[10]

Ultimately, a total of 86 persons, 57 men and 29 women, were sent to Natzweiler-Struthof. Of the specimens, 46 were originally from Thessaloniki, Greece. The deaths of these inmates were "induced" in an improvised gassing facility. The corpses were then sent to Strasbourg for disposal. Josef Kramer, who became the commandant at Auschwitz and was the last commandant of Bergen Belsen, personally

---

7    Viven Spitz, *Doctors from Hell: The Horrific Account of Nazi Experiments on Humans* (Boulder: Sentient Publications, 2005), 231.

8    Simon Read, *Human Game: The True Story of the "Great Escape" Murders and the Hunt for the Gestapo Gunmen* (New York: Berkley Caliber, 2012), 132.

9    Spitz, *Doctors from Hell*, 232.

10    Robert J. Lifton, *The Nazi Doctors* (New York: Basic Books, 1986), 284. See also Robert J. Lifton "Nazi Medical Experiments," in *The Holocaust*, ed. Mitchell Bard (San Diego: Greenhaven Press, 2001), 90–96.

carried out the gassing of 80 of the 86 victims. The researchers had installed a one-way mirror in the gas chamber to allow the scientists to observe the deaths of the subjects, "as part of the necessary research," evidently to determine if inferior races die differently than superior races. One male victim fought so vociferously to keep from being gassed that he was ultimately shot.

The first step of the process of preparing for the display was to make anatomical casts of the bodies prior to reducing them to skeletons. Then, following the murder of the "specimens," their heads were not to be damaged, but separated from the body and forwarded to its proper "destination in a hermetically sealed tin can, especially produced for this purpose and filled with a conserving fluid" to preserve them for racial research.[11]

The plan was to complete various comparison tests and detailed anatomical research on the skulls in an attempt to document the form and size of the brain to prove their racial inferiority and other pathological features. The photos, measurements, and other data on the head, and tests on the skull itself, were to be used to help document the anthropologist belief in the inferiority of this race.

As the allies approached in 1944, concern existed over the possibility that the corpses, which had not been defleshed, could be discovered. As a solution, in September 1944, Sievers telegrammed Brandt that the collection must immediately be defleshed to be rendered unrecognizable, This would result in this collection being "lost to science, since it would now be impossible to make plaster casts."[12]

The following extract from a report that Sievers submitted to Himmler was read at the Nuremberg Doctors Trial by General Telford Taylor, chief counsel for the prosecution at Nuremberg. This report shows that, in spite of using a biased sample, the scientists realized that their research failed to prove that Jews were *Untermenshen*: "We have a nearly complete collection of skulls of all races and peoples at our disposal. Only very few specimens of skulls of the Jewish race, however, are available with the result that it is impossible to arrive at precise conclusions from examining them."[13] The solution to this problem was the following:

---

11  Quoted in Spitz, *Doctors from Hell*, 232.

12  Spitz, *Doctors from Hell*, 233.

13  Spitz, *Doctors from Hell*, 231–232.

The war in the East now presents us with the opportunity to overcome this deficiency. By procuring the skulls of the Jewish-Bolshevik Commissars, who represent the prototype of the repulsive, but characteristically subhuman, we have the chance now to obtain a palpable, scientific document.[14]

In other words, their sample failed to prove their theory, so they planned to obtain another sample that they felt would help them to achieve their Darwinian racist goal. The report further added the best "method for obtaining and collecting this skull material could be handled by directing the Wehrmacht to turn over all captured Jewish-Bolshevik Commissars alive to the Field Police.[15]

## THE OUTCOME OF THE JEWISH SKELETON RESEARCHERS

Brandt and Sievers were both indicted, tried and convicted in the Doctors' Trial in Nuremberg for murdering 112 Jews for the skeleton collection to be displayed at the Reich University.[16] Both were hanged in Landsberg Prison on June 2, 1948.[17] Josef Kramer, Commandant of Natzweiler-Struthof concentration camp, was convicted of war crimes and hanged in Hamelin prison by the British on December 13, 1945. Other scientists involved in the Jewish skeleton fiasco, including Otto Bickenbach, Friedrich Bickenbach and Helmut Ruehl, were accused of committing war crimes at this camp. Rather than face the hangman, August Hirt, chairman at the Reich University in Strasbourg, committed suicide by a gunshot to the head in Schönenbach, Austria, on June 2, 1945.

In 1974, Bruno Beger was convicted by a West German court as an accessory to 86 murders for his role in procuring the victims for the Jewish skeleton collection. Although sentenced to the minimum term, three years imprisonment, he ended up not serving any time in prison

---

14  Spitz, *Doctors from Hell*, 231–232. Italics in original.

15  Spitz, *Doctors from Hell*, 232.

16  Spitz, *Doctors from Hell*, 231.

17  Gabrielle Kirk McDonald, *Substantive and Procedural Aspects of International Criminal Law: The Experience of International and National Courts*, 1st ed. (Netherlands: Springer, 2000).

and died in Königstein im Taunus on October 12, 2009. Ironically, during the trial "none of the defendants evinced any remorse...and many defended their work as 'good science.'"[18]

Researchers have since learned the identity of these 86 men and women and learned that most had a family and a successful career. One example was successful Berlin dairy merchant Menachem Taffel, a Polish born Jew who, along with his wife and child, was deported to Auschwitz in March 1943. His wife and child were murdered by gassing on arrival, and Menachem was chosen to be an anatomical specimen. He was then shipped to Natzweiler-Struthof concentration camp and murdered in the gas chamber there in August 1943.

Taffel was positively identified through the efforts of Serge and Beate Klarsfeld. In 2003, University of Tübingen professor Hans-Joachim Lang succeeded in identifying all the rest of the victims by comparing a list of inmate numbers of the 86 corpses at Strasbourg, surreptitiously recorded by Hirt's French assistant, Henri Henrypierre, with a list of inmate numbers vaccinated at Auschwitz. The names and various background data and other biographical information of the murdered victims were published in the book *Die Namen der Nummern (The Names of the Numbers)*.[19]

In 1951, the remains of all 86 victims were reinterred in one location in the Cronenbourg-Strasbourg Jewish Cemetery. On December 11, 2005, memorial stones engraved with the names of the 86 victims were placed in the cemetery. A plaque honouring the victims was placed outside the Anatomy Institute at Strasbourg's University Hospital. Thus ended the attempt to use Darwinian science to prove the inferiority of the Jewish race.[20]

---

18 A. Mark Clarfield, "Nazi medicine," Review of *Nazi Medicine and the Nuremberg Trials: From Medical War Crimes to Informed Consent* by Paul Julian Weindling, *Journal of the American Medical Association* 295, No. 22 (June 14, 2006): 2668.

19 Hans-Joachim Lang, *Die Namen der Nummern: Wie es gelang, die 86 Opfer eines NS-Verbrechens zu identifizieren* (Hamburg: Hoffmann und Campe, 2004).

20 Kenneth Mellanby, "Medical experiments on human beings in concentration camps in Nazi Germany," *British Medical Journal* 1, No. 4490 (January 25, 1947): 148–150; Clarfield, "Nazi medicine."

# 16

## Darwinism motivated Japanese sadism during World War II

||||||||||||||||||||||||||||||||||||||||||||||||||||||||||||||||||||||||||||||||||||||||||||||||||||||||||||||

O ne of the best examples of immorality inspired by Darwinism is the extreme Japanese sadism exhibited during World War II. During the ninteenth century, the Japanese believed they were the "master race of Asia," superior to, not only non-Orientals, but also all people of Chinese, Korean, Filipino, Mongolian, Pacific Islander/Polynesian and those of other Asian descent.[1] The fact is:

> Race was absolutely part of Japanese ideology during the war; they saw themselves as the "master race" of Asia, much as Hitler saw the Germans as the "master race" of Europe. As such, they presented themselves as the champions of Asia against European imperialism, but imposed their own imperialism on the "lesser" Asian peoples, and could be very brutal in doing so.[2]

---

1 Otto D. Tolischus, ed. *Through Japanese Eyes* (New York: Reynal and Hitchcock, 1945).

2 "Was Japan racist during World War II?" Yahoo! Answers; https://answers.yahoo.com/question/index?qid=20110226195227AAfbHKm; accessed October 14, 2016,

## THE INTRODUCTION OF DARWINIAN RACISM INTO JAPAN

In the late 1800s Japan was modernized, a process that included the introduction of Darwinism by inviting several leading Darwinist professors to lecture in Japanese universities.[3] One example was Harvard-trained Darwinist Edward Morse who lectured on evolution at the leading Japanese university, the University of Tokyo, from 1877 to 1879. Morse was an excellent and persuasive lecturer and attracted many Japanese who "smoothly accepted the facts and the theory of evolution."[4] He also "made Darwinism fashionable among the public."[5]

One reason the "Japanese people readily accepted the concept of evolution [was] because, lacking Christianity, there was no religious opposition."[6] The objections that did surface in Japan mostly "came from Christian communities," which numbered less than 9,000 people.[7] In addition, evolution theory,

> especially in the form of Social Darwinism developed by Herbert Spencer, was extremely popular in Japan at the turn of the century, as it was in the United States, though Japanese theorists were more inclined to stress the idea of survival of the fittest among nations rather than among individuals.[8]

Historians have "widely believed that Darwinian evolutionary theory is one of the most important contributions...to human thought in general"—a belief largely accepted in Japan.[9] Consequently, Darwinism, including its racist teachings, had a critical influence on Japan.

Darwinism was also used to oppose Christianity. One part of Morse's Darwinism "lecture was its antagonism to Christianity.... There was also an anti-Christian feeling in Japan in those days, and Darwinism

---

3  Osamu Sakura, "Similarities and varieties: A brief sketch on the reception of Darwinism and sociobiology in Japan," *Biology and Philosophy* 13 (1998): 342.

4  Sakura, "Similarities and varieties," 343.

5  Eikoh Shimao, "Darwinism in Japan, 1877–1927." *Annals of Science* 38 (1981): 93.

6  Sakura, "Similarities and varieties," 341.

7  Sakura, "Similarities and varieties," 343.

8  Sharon H. Nolte, *Liberalism in Modern Japan: Ishibashi Tanzan and His Teachers, 1905–1960* (Berkeley: University of California Press, 1987), 44.

9  Sakura, "Similarities and varieties," 343.

was used to reject Christianity."[10] Furthermore, "Christian intellectuals were a minority who treated Darwinism critically in those days when most of the people received it uncritically."[11]

This, combined with the "many instruments of indoctrination in Japan" included "the state school, the press, and radio," all of "which monotonously preached a morbid nationalism and a chauvinism both as potent and poisonous as Nazi racism," which proved to be a lethal combination that produced the horrors of World War II in the East.[12] The Japanese also had a "contempt for the West and...a 'race hate' that 'many Japanese nourish deep down in their viscera.'"[13]

One example that illustrated both the Darwinian theory and the Nazi philosophy, which teaches natural selection of the superior race by elimination of the inferior races, was a pamphlet published in 1934 by the Japanese Imperial Army. It described war as "the father of creation and the mother of culture."[14] Furthermore, "one of the fundamental tenets of the wartime Kyoto School of philosophers and historians was that [war] is eternal" and should be recognized as being "creative and constructive." War was central to the ongoing historical process of "purification" and part of their "philosophical struggle."[15]

This Darwinian idea was borrowed from the "survival of the fittest," or rather "survival of the strongest" philosophy, as Spencer's original phrase was commonly interpreted. No success could be greater than a triumph in war. Only a few decades after the onset of its modernization, Japan accepted this notion and took it to its extreme.[16] As a result, after Japan's

---

10  Shimao, "Darwinism in Japan," 93–94.

11  Shimao, "Darwinism in Japan," 95.

12  E. Herbert Norman, "Militarists in the Japanese State," *Pacific Affairs* 16, No. 4 (December 1943): 475.

13  Norman, "Militarists in the Japanese State," 475.

14  Quoted in Robert Olson Ballou, *Shinto: The Unconquered Enemy—Japan's Doctrine of Racial Superiority and World Conquest* (New York: The Viking Press, 1945), 185.

15  John Dower, *War without Mercy: Race and Power in the Pacific War* (New York: Pantheon Books, 1993), 216.

16  Rotem Kowner and Walter Demel, eds., *Race and Racism in Modern East Asia* (Boston: Brill, 2013).

victory in the first Sino-Japanese War (1894 to 1895) Japan joined the imperialist race in East Asia in earnest, but during a time ruled by racial ideology, it could not assert its new position as long as it did not win a war with a Western power. The final confirmation of Japan's regional position came exactly a decade later when it won the war with Russia—Europe's most populated nation and the possessor of its largest army.[17]

Another factor was that both

naturalism and pragmatism regarded science as a means to the emancipation of the self. ...Naturalism and pragmatism, both strongly influenced by Darwin, viewed evolutionary change as an opportunity for the assertion of human will rather than a sentence of subjugation to blind natural law.[18]

Although, for purposes of war propaganda, the Japanese claimed to be "liberating Asia for the Asians," they were, in fact, enslaving them. Although some Japanese social groups were racist before, during and even after World War II, one result was the Japanese military worked to death those that they judged to be inferior races, or allowed them to starve or die from diseases brought on by malnutrition. Many putative "inferior" races were even tortured to death. Japanese soldiers were deliberately indoctrinated in the belief that "the Japanese race was superior to all others," including other Asian races and even "the inferior Americans."[19] They even believed that racism to the point that the women from conquered territories were forced to "service" Japanese soldiers. If these raped women became pregnant, they were disemboweled or murdered "for fear of diluting the purity of the Japanese race with the blood of a mixed-race child."[20]

As German racism resulted in the death of millions of Jews, Russians and Poles, likewise, in the end, Japanese racism was responsible

17 Kowner and Demel, *Race and Racism in Modern East Asia*, 117.

18 Nolte, *Liberalism in Modern Japan*, 82–83.

19 Bill O'Reilly and Martin Dugard, *Killing the Rising Sun* (New York: Henry Holt, 2016), 12.

20 O'Reilly and Dugard, *Killing the Rising Sun*, 234.

for the death of millions of Chinese and other Asians, plus an estimated 150,000 Allied prisoners of war (POWs) that were treated like
the Japanese judged them to be, namely members of an inferior race.[21]

During World War II, Japan believed that, as the superior race, there
was no such thing as "surrender" or "capture," because all Japanese
POWs were considered not only inferior persons, but also traitors to
Japan. This is why thousands of Japanese soldiers committed suicide
rather than surrender. They also treated American POWs cruelly,
indiscriminately killing them due to their belief that they were an
inferior race. They were also believed to be less than human for sur-
rendering or allowing themselves to be captured, rather than dying in
combat or by suicide. The Asian nations used Darwinian

> evolutionary theories to represent the world as a battlefield in
> which different "races" struggled for survival. But while they
> appealed to such foreign luminaries as Charles Darwin and
> Herbert Spencer, their understanding of "race" was also informed
> by their own background. They did not simply copy what they
> read from these authors, but instead endowed "race" with indig-
> enous meanings.[22]

It is no wonder that the typical Japanese soldier was "encouraged by
his officers to slaughter, rape and terrorize to impress the unhappy
neighbours of Japan with the 'superiority' of the Yamato race."[23] An
example of the Japanese racism included the fact that the Japanese
believed

> that they are a pure and superior race and looked at other people
> with contempt. Before and during WW II this led a lot of Japa-
> nese soldiers to act with arrogance to people they had conquered
> or prisoners they had taken. This arrogance...resulted in many
> atrocities (the Rape of Nanjing [now spelled Nanking] being just
> the largest single example) and beheading POWs for little or no

---

21 O'Reilly and Dugard, *Killing the Rising Sun*, 235.
22 Kowner and Demel, *Race and Racism in Modern East Asia*, 356.
23 Norman, "Militarists in the Japanese State," 475.

reason except to demonstrate their superiority. The American attitude taken into WW II is often claimed to have been racist, but the Japanese made the worst American racists seem like Sunday School teachers.[24]

In addition, another problem was that the "Japanese were not the only racists in the Pacific War." Some Americans were as well, resulting in some American soldiers taking "trophies or "souvenirs" of the heads or ears of slain Japanese, sometimes even

> sending them home to their girlfriends—desecration of bodies that they would never have done (and did not do) to dead Germans. Reports of this behavior horrified the Japanese and persuaded them that the Americans were demons who had to be resisted to the last, so that mutual racism made the war far more bloody and vicious than it might otherwise have been.[25]

The similarity of the Japanese racial views to the Nazi racial views is illustrated by the writings of Nakajimi Chikuhei, a major industrialist and political party leader. He wrote in 1940 that there exist "superior and inferior races in the world," and "it is the sacred duty of the leading race to lead and enlighten the inferior ones."[26] The reason why many Japanese believed they were "the sole superior race in the world," Nakajima explained, was that

> the Japanese were pure-blooded, and...[t]he Greater East Asia War was thus no ordinary conflict.... Many other such statements could be quoted...where they were presented as proof that the Japanese, like the Nazis, regarded themselves as a master race.[27]

Although Japan resisted Nazi attempts to force the Holocaust on the Jews, the Japanese government sent most of the approximately

---

24 "Was Japan racist during World War II?"
25 "Was Japan racist during World War II?"
26 Dower, *War without Mercy*, 217.
27 Dower, *War without Mercy*, 217.

3,000 Indonesian Jews to work camps. Very few survived.[28] University of Hawaii political science professor R.J. Rummel estimates that between 1937 and 1945, the Japanese military murdered nearly 10 million people, most likely 6 million Chinese, Indonesians, Koreans, Filipinos and Indochinese, among others.[29]

## AN EXAMPLE OF THEIR BRUTALITY

The broad details of the Rape of Nanking are not in dispute by historians today. In November 1937, the Japanese launched a massive attack on the then capital of the Republic of China, Nanking, and when

> the city fell on December 13, 1937, Japanese soldiers began an orgy of cruelty seldom if ever matched in world history. Tens of thousands of young men were rounded up and herded to the outer areas of the city, where they were mowed down by machine guns, used for bayonet practice, or soaked with gasoline and burned alive. For months the streets of the city were heaped with corpses and reeked with the stench of rotting human flesh.[30]

The fact is, if "one event can be held up as an example of the unmitigated evil lying just below the surface of unbridled military adventurism, that moment is the Rape of Nanking."[31] Furthermore, "even by the standards of history's most destructive war, the Rape of Nanking represents one of the worst instances of mass extermination."[32] Specifically, between 260,000 and 350,000 Chinese were murdered in the span of only a few weeks.[33] The Rape of Nanking is notorious not only for the enormous number of innocent people slaughtered, but also for

---

28 Gil Ronen, "Japanese scapegoated Indonesia's Jews in WW2," *Arutz Sheva*, April 27, 2010; http://www.israelnationalnews.com/News/News.aspx/137244; accessed November 4, 2016.

29 Rudolf J. Rummel, *Death by Government* (New Brunswick: Transaction Publishers, 2008), 146–149, 153.

30 Iris Chang, *The Rape of Nanking: The Forgotten Holocaust of World War II* (New York: BasicBooks, 1997), 4.

31 Chang, *Rape of Nanking*, 4.

32 Chang, *Rape of Nanking*, 4.

33 Chang, *Rape of Nanking*, 5.

the inhumane and cruel manner in which many of the Chinese were murdered. Furthermore, an

> estimated 20,000–80,000 Chinese women were raped. Many soldiers went beyond rape to disembowel the women, slice off their breasts, nail them alive to walls. Fathers were forced to rape their daughters, and sons their mothers, as other family members watched. Not only did live burials, castration, the carving of organs, and the roasting of people become routine, but more diabolical tortures were practiced, such as hanging people by their tongues on iron hooks or burying people to their waists and watching them get torn apart by German shepherds. So sickening was the spectacle that even the Nazis in the city were horrified, one proclaiming the massacre to be the work of "bestial machinery."[34]

One infamous incident that caused the deaths of thousands of Chinese in Nanking involved two Japanese officers who forced their men to gather hundreds of Chinese civilians. The reason was for a contest to determine who could decapitate the most people during a set time span. The Japanese determined the men's success by measuring the height of the stack of heads.

A 1945 study prepared by the Japanese cabinet "attempted to demonstrate with extensive historical data that war was constructive, and protracted war was inevitable—and, indeed, that protracted war required the thorough-going exercise of a nation's 'unique racial power.'"[35]

This was the same rationale given by the Nazi Darwinists to justify war. The Japanese, as did the Nazi's, invariably regarded themselves alone as the superior race. The Japanese, as also did the Nazi's, "nationalized and racialized purity, treating this ultimate ideal as if it could only be truly appreciated, and attained, by the Japanese."[36] Once one accepts Darwinism, the next step is to inquire about the characteristics of man that

---

34 Chang, *Rape of Nanking*, 6.

35 Dower, *War without Mercy*, 216.

36 Kowner and Demel, *Race and Racism in Modern East Asia*, 53.

make him different from apes… Are there ape-men or are at least some varieties of mankind more ape-like than others? Do "monstrous races" really exist, as had been assumed since antiquity? Does the outer appearance of men or certain groups of men reflect their inner values, their characters…?[37]

## THE INFLUENCE OF DARWINISM IN JAPAN

The large influence of Darwinism and racial superiority beliefs in Japan is well documented.[38] Even during the war years, "the theory of biological evolution" was taught in the public schools, and Japanese scholars continued to publish on the subject in spite of war rationing. The evolution taught in the schools was a mixture of Darwin, Haeckel and other Western Darwinian theories. An example of Haeckel's influence was the teaching that "the ancestor of all humankind was not a human being," but rather

some kind of creature living in water. The human fetus, floating in its own fluid, seemed to be a reenactment of these ancient origins, and in many other ways as well the evolution of life appeared to be recapitulated in the human experience. Thus, the fetus was monkey like, the first cry of the child was catlike, infants crawled like animals before walking, babies sometimes had tail-like protuberances when born, and the ability of humans to wiggle their ears suggested the persistence of an animal muscle.[39]

The way in which some

Japanese handled scientific theories of evolution and the question of physical differences among races during this period of ultranationalism can be found in a collection of essays published for popular audiences in the spring of 1944 by the well-known Japanese anatomist, Professor Buntaro Adachi.

---

37 Kowner and Demel, *Race and Racism in Modern East Asia*, 53.
38 Ballou, *Shinto*.
39 Dower, *War without Mercy*, 220.

The essays were titled *Studies in the Physical Constitution of the Japanese People*.[40] The new edition included a short "preface by the author condemning Europeans and Americans for...arrogance concerning their own racial superiority."[41] As Michael Weiner wrote, the critical

> impact on Japan of Social-Darwinist assumptions concerning the competitive capacities of different populations cannot be underestimated. As transmitted to Japan during the late nineteenth century, theories of "race" and scientific racism incorporated assumptions which extended beyond boundaries of biological determinism. Darwinian theories of natural selection were introduced by Edward Morse...in a series of lectures of evolutionary theory given in 1877. A Japanese edition of Thomas Huxley's *Lectures on the Origin of Species* appeared two years later.[42]

Also, Japanese intellectuals were exposed to the evolutionary theories of both Haeckel and Lamarck, but neither the writings of Haeckel nor Lamarck

> achieved the immense popularity of Herbert Spencer. A Japanese translation of Spencer's evolutionary theory first appeared in 1884, and, in total, some thirty translations of his works had appeared by the turn of the century. The Social-Darwinian vocabulary...provided a scientific gloss to the idea that social development in all its manifestations occurred through the aggressive interplay of natural forces.[43]

It is now clear that the adverse influence of Darwinism, especially as elaborated by Herbert Spencer, was critical in Japan in influencing the Japanese sadistic war behaviour.

---

40 Buntaro Adachi, *Nipponjin taishitsu no kenkyu* (*Studies of the Physical Constitution of the Japanese People*) (Tokyo: Ogiwara, 1944).

41 Dower, *War without Mercy*, 217–218.

42 Michael Weiner, "Discourses of race, nation and empire in pre-1945 Japan." *Ethnic and Racial Studies* 18, No. 3 (July 1995):442.

43 Weiner, "Discourses," 442–443.

## DARWINISTS INFLUENCED EMPEROR HIROHITO

Hirohito (1901–1989) became emperor of Japan at age 13 after the death of his father. Educated both in Europe and Japan, Hirohito became very aware of the Darwinist beliefs in science, an area of special interest to him. This philosophy had a major influence on him later in life. For example, at the Peer's School in Japan, his teachers, including Sugiura Shigetake, "were influenced by Herbert Spencer's social Darwinism" that was much in vogue in Japan at that time. One of his teachers, Dr. Sugiura, "studied agricultural science at Owens College (later, the University of Manchester), and chemistry at London University" and exposed Hirohito to a wide variety of subjects including Darwinism.[44] Emperor Hirohito had a great interest in history, but

> biological research became Hirohito's greatest lifelong intellectual passion, dating from his studies…under the scientist, Dr. Hattori…. In 1919 Hirohito made his first scientific discovery, of a new species of prawn. He made a great many other discoveries over the years and wrote many scientific articles and books, mostly on marine life as a distinguished marine biologist.[45]

Hattori often accompanied Hirohito "on expeditions to collect marine specimens in Sagami Bay, Tokyo Bay, and elsewhere" and "he was happiest 'when working with a microscope, absorbed in a factual world quite different from that normally inhabited by a Crown Prince or Emperor.'" [46] Furthermore, aside from

> encouraging Hirohito's interest in science, Hattori taught him about Darwin's theory of evolution which Hattori had recently encountered in the publications of the zoologist, Oka Asajiro. It was natural, therefore, that a bust of Charles Darwin would be found in the library of the Showa Emperor, together with busts

---

44 Stephen S. Large, *Emperor Hirohito and Showa Japan: A Political Biography* (New York: Routledge, 1992), 17.

45 Large, *Emperor Hirohito and Showa Japan*, 19.

46 Large, *Emperor Hirohito and Showa Japan*, 19.

of Lincoln and Napoleon which reflected Hirohito's interest in history.[47]

Hirohito greatly admired Lincoln for liberating the oppressed and Darwin for his scientific work.[48] Critically, it was through the Darwinist Hattori that Emperor Hirohito accepted

the widespread belief that nature was governed by the laws of evolution which Darwin had described.... Hirohito and his teacher also shared the general assumption that the concept of evolution, and its core notion of progressive development through the adaptive process of natural selection, could be applied to the values and institutions of contemporary society.[49]

It was also under "Hattori's guidance that Hirohito read Darwin's theory of evolution as interpreted by the popular writer Oka Asajiro" and also, evidently, a Japanese translation of Darwin's *Origin of Species*.[50] Furthermore, "[a]mong thinkers everywhere who were influenced by Darwin, such ideas were commonplace at the time" in Japan.[51] From a study of Japan and Emperor Hirohito, it is very apparent today that

this confidence in the efficacy of knowledge, applied to all fields of human endeavor, including politics and government, was the most important legacy of Hirohito's education at the Togu-goga-kumonsho. ...[I]t was during this phase of his education that he acquired...a "scientific rational spirit" of inquiry, whether from Sugiura's intellectual eclecticism, Shiratori's historical skepticism, or Hattori's lessons on Darwin and scientific methodology.[52]

---

47 Large, *Emperor Hirohito and Showa Japan*, 19.

48 Albert Axell and Hideaki Kase, *Kamikaze: Japan's Suicide Gods* (New York: Longman, 2002), 198–199.

49 Large, *Emperor Hirohito and Showa Japan*, 19.

50 Herbert Bix, *Hirohito and the Making of Modern Japan* (New York: HarperCollins, 2000), 60.

51 Large, *Emperor Hirohito and Showa Japan*, 19.

52 Large, *Emperor Hirohito and Showa Japan*, 19.

## Emperor Hirohito of Japan (1901-1989)

Hirohito was well versed in Darwinian evolutionary theory and embraced the view of the Japanese as a "superior race."

One irony is that Japan's "National Congress's tacit affirmation of the Emperor's divinity must be a great annoyance to the Emperor, who is a biologist and an admirer of Darwin." [53]

## JUSTIFYING RACISM

The more moderate Japanese scholars, such as Adachi, acknowledged that some races may have superior traits in one area, yet inferior traits in other areas: "'race A may be superior to race B in certain points,' but, he emphasized, 'in certain other respects race A may be inferior to race B. It can never be argued that race A is superior or inferior to race B in all respects.'"[54]

This may at first sound like an equalitarian view, but when examined further, this Darwinian view implied that some traits of race A which are superior to race B, may be much more important, such as intelligence. This egalitarian sounding view was actually a way of justifying racism because the implications include the view that each race should be put in its "proper place" and be given "suitable work" in accordance with its specific abilities and qualities. Adachi

> also emphasized the necessity of giving "superior races" special support, including encouragement in increasing their population. In this, he was perfectly consistent with official government policy, in which it was made clear that in the final analysis the most superior race was the Japanese, and the "proper place" of the Japanese was one of absolute leadership.[55]

Adachi described human beings as *Mammalia* like the apes" that can be "compared to the orangutan, gorilla, chimpanzee, and gibbon. Blood tests...not only showed a relationship between humans and apes, but also revealed that certain races had a closer blood relation-

---

53 Ikuhiko Hata, "The Japanese-Soviet Confrontation, 1935–1939," in *Deterrent Diplomacy: Japan, Germany, and the U.S.S.R. 1935–1940*, ed. J.W. Morley (New York, Columbia University Press, 1976), 77.

54 Quoted in Dower, *War Without Mercy*, 219.

55 Dower, *War without Mercy*, 220.

ship to the apes than others."[56] Adachi then discussed what he judged as the many comparisons of certain human races to our ape ancestors, such as the claim that Malay blood was the closest to monkey blood, Dutch blood the most dissimilar and Chinese blood was somewhere in between the two.

He added that if "one took the orangutan as the standard by which to measure the development of different races—relative 'superiority'... indicated by greater departure from the apish norm—then in the overall picture the Japanese...demonstrated superior development." [57] Adachi also claimed to have discovered that

the irregular profile of Westerners was closer to that of the apes [and]...their shorter ratio of arm length to body length (longer Western arms again being more apish); their lack of a peculiar bone spur in the upper arm which Westerners and animals both possess; their relative lack of body hair; and their relatively mild body odor (he equated the body smell of Caucasians, and even stronger odor of Negroes, with animalistic sexual desires).[58]

Another almost identical argument was made in one popular Japanese book on race, [59] which "placed the Europeans closer to monkeys and other animals than the Japanese" due to such traits as "'high' noses, hairiness, relatively long arms, lower brain-to-body-weight ratio, thick fingers, and strong body odor of the sort associated with the generative function in certain animals."[60]

Although Adachi wrote that the Japanese race "traced their origin, or at least the origin of their imperial line, back to the gods," the educated classes, the evolutionists and scientists often knew better, as likely did many other Japanese, than to believe that the Japanese people traced their origins back to the gods because the

---

56 Dower, *War without Mercy*, 218.

57 Dower, *War without Mercy*, 219.

58 Dower, *War without Mercy*, 219.

59 Kiyono Kenji, *A History of Changing Theories About the Japanese Race* (Tokyo: Koyama Shoten, 1944).

60 Dower, *War without Mercy*, 219.

theory of evolution was endorsed even in popularized science books directed to young readers during the war. A text entitled *Evolution of Life* that was published a year after Pearl Harbor, for example, informed young Japanese that virtually all reputable biologists accepted evolution [as the origin of humans].[61]

Dower added that, although many Japanese felt the idea "of evolution from lesser creatures repugnant..., [n]onetheless, following Darwin, it seemed entirely natural to view such a development as honorable and deserving of pride, for it showed the human race to be advancing in a progressive and positive direction."[62] Despite exposure to evolution theories that stressed the Japanese were superior in some areas, less so in other areas,

> even well-educated Japanese did not hesitate to proclaim...that Japan's destiny as the "leading race" in the world was...genetically preordained. The government's doctrinaire teachings on this score were couched in vague and often extremely ambiguous language...but the orthodoxy unmistakably encouraged an assumption of inherent racial superiority.[63]

As a result, the widely disseminated official beliefs about what it means to be Japanese as

> issued by the Thought Bureau of the Ministry of Education in 1937—explicitly declared that the Japanese were 'intrinsically quite different from the so-called citizens of Occidental [Western] countries,' but were at the same time superior to other Asians as well.[64]

One reason for this superior race view was that, in its long history, Japan was never conquered by another nation. In fact, the "imperial

---

61 Dower, *War without Mercy*, 220.
62 Dower, *War without Mercy*, 220.
63 Dower, *War without Mercy*, 220–221.
64 Dower, *War without Mercy*, 220–221.

virtue" of the Japanese "had attracted other races to Japan and then completely absorbed them."[65] Furthermore, the

> fact that Japan alone had survived like a great rock in the turbu-lent seas of history, one nation and one people, was proof that the country "did not exist only for itself, but rather for the two billion people of the world." Both Japan and the Japanese, state and people together, bore the heavy responsibility of being "the model, the pattern, the standard for the world." It was Japan's destiny "to lead the whole world along the path of virtue."[66]

## THE JAPANESE HOLOCAUST

Darwinism was introduced to Japan in the late 1870s by Western Dar-winists and was rapidly accepted by the educated elite. In the end, it had a major influence on the Japanese racist worldview and propa-ganda led ultimately to the mistreatment of those they considered inferior races, such as not only Westerners, but also the Chinese and other Asians.[67] The parallels between Japan's racism and that of the Nazis was striking, no doubt because they both had their origin in Darwinism. A major problem was that "The strong nationalistic trend in the Meiji period was inevitably reflected in a nationalistic interpre-tation of Darwinism."[68] In the hell that Japan created, Japan

> brought atrocity and death on a scale that staggers the imagina-tion. In the midst of it were the prisoners of war. Japan held some 132,000 POWs from America, Britain, Canada, New Zealand, Holland and Australia. Of those, nearly 36,000 died, more than one in every four. Americans fared particularly badly; of the 34,648 Americans held by Japan, 12,935—more than 37 percent— died. By comparison, only 1 percent of Americans held by the Nazis and Italians died. Japan murdered thousands of POWs on

---

65 Dower, *War without Mercy*, 224.

66 Dower, *War without Mercy*, 224.

67 Saul Padover, "Japanese Race Propaganda," *Public Opinion Quarterly* 7, No. 2 (1943):191–204.

68 Shimao, "Darwinism in Japan."

death marches and worked thousands of others to death…includ-
ing some 16,000 POWs who died alongside as many as 100,000
Asian laborers forced to build the Burma-Siam Railway.[69]

In addition,

> [t]housands of other POWs were beaten, burned, stabbed, or
> clubbed to death, shot, beheaded, killed during medical experi-
> ments, or eaten alive in ritual acts of cannibalism…. [T]housands
> more died of starvation and easily preventable diseases. Of the
> 2,500 POWs at Borneo's Sandakan camp, only 6…made it to
> September 1945 alive.[70]

Furthermore, the above does not include the numbing statistics
involving the

> men who were captured and killed on the spot or dragged to
> places like Kwajalein, to be murdered without the world ever
> learning their fate. In accordance with the kill-all order, the
> Japanese massacred all 5,000 Korean captives on Tinian, all of
> the POWs on Ballale, Wake, and Tarawa, and all but 11 POWs at
> Palawan. They were evidently about to murder all the other
> POWs and civilian internees in their custody when the atomic
> bomb brought their empire crashing down.[71]

In the end, the fact of human "[i]nequality was attributed by the
Japanese to differences in national or 'racial' characteristics; differences which marked some peoples as [less fit, or even] unfit to survive
in the struggle for existence."[72]

---

69 Laura Hillenbrand, *Unbroken: A World War II Story of Survival, Resilience, and
Redemption* (New York: Random House, 2010), 314–315.

70 Hillenbrand, *Unbroken*, 314–315.

71 Hillenbrand, *Unbroken*, 314–315.

72 Frank Dikötter, ed., *The Construction of Racial Identities in China and Japan:
Historical and Contemporary Perspectives* (Honolulu: University of Hawaii Press, 1997),
115.

# 17

# Some brief conclusions

||||||||||||||||||||||||||||||||||||||||||||||||||||||||||||||||||||||||||||||||||||||||||||||||||||||||||||||||||||||||||||||||||||||||||

T he most common response to the material presented in this book is this: if evolution, as defined by leading scientists, is true, the effects of the acceptance of the theory do not matter. In fact, this book was not written with the intent of disproving evolution. Obviously, no matter how much harm it has caused, this does not affect the truth of Darwinism. Conversely, if evolution, given the standard definition of evolution of progression from simple molecules by random combinations of molecules to the first cell, and then eventually to humans by mutations and natural selection, is false, the harm caused by this erroneous idea was enormous. The strictly atheistic evolutionary materialistic worldview does not provide a basis for a morality based on the classic view of humans being created in the "image of God." So even though Darwinism has shed its racism since the Holocaust, most Darwinists are advocates of certain parts of the philosophy documented in the chapters in this book, such as liberal rules regarding abortion.

## WHAT IS EVOLUTION?

The theory of evolution postulates that a single cell eventually evolved into humans as a result of random changes in the DNA code, the outworking of natural laws, such as gravity, plus genetic damage or errors in chromosomes called mutations, and natural selection, plus an enormous amount of time. The concern is not variations within the Genesis kinds called microevolution by many evolutionists, but the source of new information that enables evolution "from goo to you by way of the zoo" to occur. Even in Darwin's day the fundamental problem was never the *survival* of the fittest but the *arrival* of the fittest. According to the modern synthetic theory of evolution, the main source of the new genetic information required for evolution is mutations that are selected by natural selection.

This view is easy to refute by noting that the vast majority of mutations (over 99.9 percent of all mutations) are either near-neutral, mildly deleterious or clearly harmful. Near-neutral mutations do not cause any perceptual damage; but as they accumulate, they eventually cause major damage, resulting in genetic entropy. A common example is aging. As a result, the genome will in time be swamped with near-neutral and harmful mutations, eventually causing mutational meltdown and extinction. Thus, evolution is true, but is going the wrong way.

Another response to our thesis is that evolutionists today do not accept racism or immorality. Although largely true, this does not negate the enormous damage that the evolutionary view of the world has caused in the past to people and society and is still causing, even today. Examples include abortion and the modern hemorrhaging of churches and the resultant deterioration of the moral social fabric of society, especially the family. Another example is the termination of the careers of many students and scientists who do not accept the orthodox evolutionary worldview, a problem of intolerance that has been well documented.

# Bibliography

Abrams, Ray Hamilton. *Preachers Present Arms: The Role of the American Churches and Clergy in World Wars I and II, with Some Observations on the War in Vietnam.* Scottsdale: Herald Press, 1969.

Adachi, Buntaro. *Nipponjin taishitsu no kenkyu (Studies of the Physical Constitution of the Japanese People).* Tokyo: Ogiwara, 1944.

Adams, Grace. *Psychology: Science or Superstition?* New York: Covici Frede, 1931.

Adams, Stephen. "Killing babies no different from abortion, experts say." *The Telegraph,* March 1, 2012.

Agin, Dan. *Junk Science.* New York: St. Martin's Press, 2006.

Alexander, Franz G., and Sheldon T. Selesnick. *The History of Psychiatry: An Evaluation of Psychiatric Thought and Practice from Prehistoric Times to the Present.* New York: Harper & Row, 1966.

"Alfred Kinsey: The swinging detective—He opened their eyes to sex." *London Sunday Times,* April 7, 2005.

Altschuler, Glenn C. "Protestantism and Social Christianity: Walter Rauschenbusch: Theology, The Church, and the Social Gospel." In *Modern American Protestantism and Its World: Historical Articles on Protestantism in American Religious Life,* edited by Martin E. Marty. New York: K.G. Saur, 1992.

Andrews, Pat. "Margaret Sanger: Women and the New Race." In *Voices of Diversity: Perspectives on American Political Ideals and Institutions,* 100–102. Guilford: Dushkin Publishing Group, 1995.

Aulie, Richard. "Response to Bennetta's Review of the ASA Booklet." *Creation/Evolution Newsletter* 7, No. 2–3 (1987): 9–11.

Axell, Albert, and Hideaki Kase. *Kamikaze: Japan's Suicide Gods.* New York: Longman, 2002.

Bagemihl, Bruce. *Biological Exuberance: Animal Homosexuality and Natural Diversity.* New York: St. Martin's Press, 1999.

Bagge, Peter. *Woman Rebel: The Margaret Sanger Story.* New York: Drawn and Quarterly, 2013.

Baker, Jean. *Margaret Sanger: A Life of Passion.* New York: Hill and Wang, 2012.

Ballou, Robert Olson. *Shinto: The Unconquered Enemy—Japan's Doctrine of Racial Superiority and World Conquest.* New York: The Viking Press, 1945.

Barlow, Nora, ed., *The Autobiography of Charles Darwin 1809–1882.* New York: Norton, 1958.

Barrett, David B., George T. Kurian and Todd M. Johnson. *World Christian Encyclopedia.* 2nd ed. New York: Oxford University Press, 2001.

Begin, John. "Abortion should be legal through infancy, medical ethicists argue." Policy. mic, August 9, 2012. http://www.policymic.com/articles/12443/abortion-should-be-legal-through-infancy-medical-ethicists-argue. Accessed September 4, 2016.

Begley, Sharon. "Get shrunk at your own risk." *Newsweek,* June 18, 2007, 49.

Bell, D. "Profile: Dr. Benjamin Spock." *Midwife and Health Visitor* 2, No. 8 (August 1966): 323.

Bergler, Edmund, and William Kroger. *Kinsey's Myth of Female Sexuality: The Medical Facts.* New York: Grune and Stratton, 1954.

Bergman, Jerry. "Ancon Sheep: A now disproven example of microevolution." *Rivista di Biologia/Biology Forum* 98, No. 3 (Sep.–Dec. 2005): 435–448.

_____. "Birth control leader Margaret Sanger: Darwinist, racist and eugenicist." *Journal of Creation* 22, No. 3 (2008): 62–67.

_____. *The Darwin Effect. Its influence on Nazism, Eugenics, Racism, Communism, Capitalism & Sexism.* Green Forest: Master Books, 2014.

_____. "Darwin is the universal acid that affects everything: A review of *The Political Gene: How Darwin's Ideas Changed Politics* by Dennis Sewell," *Journal of Creation* 25, No.1 (2011): 19–21.

_____. "Darwinian criminality theory: A tragic chapter in history." *Rivista di Biologia/Biology Forum* 98, No. 1 (Jan.-Apr. 2005): 47–70.

_____. "Darwinism and the deterioration of the genome." *Creation Research Society Quarterly* 42, No. 2 (September 2005): 104–114.

_____. "Darwinism and the Nazi race holocaust." *Creation Ex Nihilo Technical Journal* 13, No. 2 (1999): 101–111.

_____. "Darwin's cousin Sir Francis Galton (1822–1911) and the eugenics movement." *Creation Research Society Quarterly* 39, No. 3 (December 2002): 169–176.

_____. "Did eyes evolve by Darwinian mechanisms?" *Journal of Creation* 22, No. 2 (2008): 67–74.

_____. *Hitler and the Nazi Darwinian Worldview: How the Nazi Eugenic Crusade for a Superior Race Caused the Greatest Holocaust in World History.* Kitchener: Joshua Press, 2012.

_____. "The rise and fall of Haeckel's biogenetic law." *Creation Research Society Quarterly* 37 No. 2 (September 2000): 110–122.

_____. *Understanding Educational Measurement and Evaluation*. Boston: Houghton Mifflin, 1981.

Berra, Tim M. *Darwin and His Children: His other Legacy*. New York: Oxford University Press, 2013.

Bethell, Tom. "Kinsey as pervert." *The American Spectator* 38, No.3 (April 2005): 42–44.

Bishop, George Victor. *Witness to Evil*. New York: Nash Publishers, 1972.

Bix, Herbert. *Hirohito and the Making of Modern Japan*. New York: HarperCollins, 2000.

Black, Edwin. *War against the Weak: Eugenics and America's Campaign to Create a Master Race*. New York: Four Walls Eight Windows Press, 2003.

Blackstone, William. *Commentaries on the Laws of England, A Facsimile of the First Edition of 1765–1769*. Chicago: The University of Chicago Press, 2002.

Blatman, Daniel. *The Death Marches: The Final Phase of Nazi Genocide*. Translated by Chaya Galai. Cambridge: Belknap Press, 2011.

Blechschmidt, Erich. "Human Being from the Very First." In *New Perspectives on Human Abortion*, edited by Thomas W. Hilgers (author), Dennis J. Horan, and David Mall, 6–28. Washington: University Publications of America, 1981.

Bloom, Lynn Z. *Doctor Spock: Biography of a Conservative Radical*. New York: The Bobbs-Merrill Company, 1972.

Bobgan, Martin, and Deidre Bobgan. *Psychoheresy: The Psychological Seduction of Christianity*. Santa Barbara: East Gate, 1987.

_____. *The Psychological Way/The Spiritual Way: Are Christianity and Psychotherapy Compatible?* Minneapolis: Bethany House, 1979.

Bock, Walter. "Evolution by orderly law." *Science* 164 (May 1969): 684–685.

Boteach, Shmuel. *Moses of Oxford: A Jewish Vision of a University and Its Life*. Vol.2. London: André Deutsch, 1994.

Brandom, Robert B., ed. *Rorty and His Critics*. Oxford: Blackwell, 2000.

Breivik, Anders. *2083: A European Declaration of Independence*. Self-published, 2011. https://fas.org/programs/tap/_docs/2083_-_A_European_Declaration_of_Independence.pdf. Accessed October 31, 2016.

Browder, Sue Ellin. "Kinsey's secret: The phony science of the sexual revolution." *Crisis* 22, No. 5 (May 2004): 12–17.

Brown, Andrew. *The Darwin Wars: How Stupid Genes Became Selfish Gods*. New York: Simon & Schuster, 1999.

Bruinius, Harry. *Better For All the World*. New York: Alfred A. Knopf, 2006.

Bryan, William Jennings. *Seven Questions in Dispute*. New York: Fleming H. Revell, 1924.

Bugliosi, Vincent. *Helter Skelter: The True Story of the Manson Murders*. New York: Norton, 1974.

Call, Lewis. "Anti-Darwin, anti-Spencer: Friedrich Nietzsche's critique of Darwin and "Darwinism." *History of Science* 36 (1998): 1–21.

Carroll, Sean B. *Remarkable Creatures: Epic Adventures in the Search for the Origins of Species*. Boston: Houghton Mifflin Harcourt, 2009.

Carson, Ben. *One Nation: What We Can All Do To Save America's Future.* New York: Sentinel, 2014.

Cashill, Jack. *Hoodwinked: How Intellectual Hucksters Have Hijacked American Culture.* Nashville: Nelson Current, 2005.

Castle, William E. *Genetics and Eugenics.* Cambridge: Harvard University Press, 1930.

Cate, Curtis. *Friedrich Nietzsche.* Woodstock: Overlook Press, 2005.

Centers for Disease Control and Prevention. "The National Intimate Partner and Sexual Violence Survey," September 4, 2014. http://www.cdc.gov/violenceprevention/nisvs/. Accessed November 3, 2016.

Chang, Iris. *The Rape of Nanking: The Forgotten Holocaust of World War II.* New York: BasicBooks, 1997.

Chase, Allan. *The Legacy of Malthus: The Social Costs of the New Scientific Racism.* New York: Alfred A. Knopf, 1980.

Chesen, Eli. *Religion May be Hazardous to Your Health.* New York: Peter H. Wyden, 1972.

Chesler, Ellen. *Woman of Valor: Margaret Sanger and the Birth Control Movement in America.* New York: Simon and Schuster, 1992.

Chesterton, Gilbert Keith. *Eugenics and Other Evils.* New York: Dodd, Mead and Company, 1927.

Christenson, Cornelia V. *Kinsey: A Biography.* Bloomington: Indiana University Press, 1971.

Clarfield, A. Mark. "Nazi medicine." Review of *Nazi Medicine and the Nuremberg Trials: From Medical War Crimes to Informed Consent* by Paul Julian Weindling. *Journal of the American Medical Association* 295, No. 22 (June 14, 2006): 2668–2669.

Clough, Michael. "Diminish students' resistance to biological evolution." *The American Biology Teacher* 56, No.7 (1994): 409–415.

Collum, Danny Duncan. "The Spock revolution." *Sojourners* 27, No. 4 (Jul./Aug. 1998): 52.

Conklin, Edwin Grant. *Heredity and Environment in the Development of Man.* 3rd ed. Princeton: Princeton University Press, 1920.

Cooper, David. *Psychiatry and Anti-Psychiatry.* London: Paladin, 1967.

Cox, Vicki. *Margaret Sanger: Rebel for Women's Rights.* Philadelphia: Chelsea House, 2005.

Crozier, Ivan. "Havelock Ellis, eugenicist." *Studies in History and Philosophy of Biological and Biomedical Sciences* 39, No.2 (2008): 187–194.

Daniels, Cynthia R. *Lost Fathers: The Politics of Fatherlessness in America.* New York: St. Martin's Press, 1998.

Daniels, E.J. *I Accuse Kinsey.* Orlando: Christ For The World Publishers, 1954.

Darwin, Charles. *Charles Darwin: His Life Told in an Autogiographical Chapter.* Edited by Francis Darwin. New York: D. Appleton, 1892.

_____. *On the Origin of Species.* London: John Murray, 1859.

_____. *The Descent of Man, and Selection in Relation to Sex.* London: John Murray, 1871.

_____. *The Life and Letters of Charles Darwin.* New York: D. Appleton, 1896.

Davenport, Charles. *Heredity in Relation to Eugenics: A Textbook for Students of Biology and a Reference Books for Animal and Plant Breeders*. New York: Henry Holt, 1911.

Dawidowicz, Lucy. *The War against the Jews: 1933–1945*. New York: Holt, Rinehart, and Winston, 1986.

Dawkins, Richard. "The Descent of Man (Episode 1: The Moral Animal)." A series of radio broadcasts in January and February 2000 by the Australian Broadcasting Corporation, produced by Tom Morton. http://www.abc.net.au/science/descent/trans1.htm. Accessed August 16, 2016.

De Marco, Donald, and Benjamin D. Wiker. *Architects of the Culture of Death*. San Francisco: Ignatius Press, 2004.

Dembski, William, and Michael Licona. *Evidence for God*. Grand Rapids: Baker Books, 2010.

De Tavernier, Johan. "Morality and nature: Evolutionary challenges to Christian ethics." *Zygon* 49, No. 1 (March 2014): 171–189.

Dikötter, Frank, ed. *The Construction of Racial Identities in China and Japan: Historical and Contemporary Perspectives*. Honolulu: University of Hawaii Press, 1997.

Dolan, Eric W. "Richard Dawkins on the men's rights movement: Really? That's a thing?" *Rawstory*, December 8, 2014. http://www.rawstory.com/rs/2014/12/richard-dawkins-on-the-mens-rights-movement-really-thats-a-thing/. Accessed August 15, 2016.

Douglas, Emily Taft. *Margaret Sanger: Pioneer of the Future*. Garrett Park: Garrett Park Press, 1975.

Douglass, Paul F. *God among the Germans*. Philadelphia: University of Pennsylvania Press, 1935.

Dower, John. *War without Mercy: Race and Power in the Pacific War*. New York: Pantheon Books, 1993.

Dowling, Claudia Glenn. "Sarah Blaffer Hrdy: The scientist who destroyed our quaint concept of what a mother ought to be comes to terms with her own life." *Discover* 24, No. 3 (March 2003): 40–45.

Dugdale, Richard. *The Jukes: A Study in Crime, Pauperism, Disease and Heredity*. New York: Putnam, 1910.

Durant, Will. *The Story of Philosophy: The Lives and Opinions of the Greater Philosophers*. Garden City: Garden City Publishing, 1926.

Ehrlich, Paul R., and Anne H. Ehrlich. *Population Resources Environment: Issues in Human Ecology*. San Francisco: W.H. Freeman, 1970.

Elkins, Caroline. *Imperial Reckoning: The Untold Story of Britain's Gulag in Kenya*. New York: Henry Holt, 2005.

Ellis, Havelock. "Birth-control and eugenics." *The Eugenics Review* 9, No. 1 (1917): 32–41.

———. *Die Gattenwahl beim Menschen: mit Rücksicht auf Sinnesphysiologie und allgemeine Biologie (The mate selection in humans: with regard to sensory physiology and general biology)*. Würzburg: Stuber Verlag, 1906.

———. "Eugenics in Relation to War." In *The Philosophy of Conflict and Other Essays in War-Time*, 110–127. London: Constable, 1919.

_____. *Psychology of Sex: A Manual for Students*. New York: Emerson Books, 1938.

_____. *Sexual Selection in Man and The Problem of Race-Regeneration*. London: Moffat Yard, 1911.

_____. *The Task of Social Hygiene*. Boston: Houghton Mifflin, 1912.

Ellis, Havelock, and John Addington Symonds, *Das konträre Geschlechtsgefühl (Sexual Inversion)*. Leipzig: George H. Wigand's, 1896.

Emmons, Nuel. *Manson in His Own Words*. New York: Grove Press, 1986.

Engelman, Peter. "Foreword" to *The Pivot of Civilization* by Margaret Sanger, 9–29. Amherst: Humanity Books, 2003.

Engs, Ruth Clifford. *The Eugenics Movement: An Encyclopedia*. Westport: Greenwood Press, 2005.

Eppstein, Victor. "When destroying life is morally justified." *The New York Times*, October 9, 1980, A34.

Epstein, Catherine. *Model Nazi: Arthur Greiser and the Occupation of Western Poland*. New York: Oxford University Press, 2010.

Evans, Richard J. *The Third Reich at War: 1939–1945*. New York: Penguin, 2005.

Eysenck, Hans J. *The Effects of Psychotherapy*. New York: International Science Press, 1966.

_____. "The Effects of Psychotherapy: A Reply." *Journal of Abnormal Psychology* 50 (1955): 147-148.

_____. *Uses and Abuses of Psychology*. Middlesex: Penguin Books, 1953.

Fisher, Seymour, and Roger Greenberg. *The Scientific Evaluation of Freud's Theories and Therapy*. New York: Basic Books, 1978.

Flew, Antony. *A Dictionary of Philosophy*. New York: St. Martin's Press, 1979.

Flick, Lawrence. *Eugenics*. Philadelphia: John Joseph McVey, 1913.

Flynn, Daniel J. *Intellectual Morons: How Ideology Makes Smart People Fall for Stupid Ideas*. New York: Crown Forum, 2004.

Frair, Wayne. "Embryology and evolution." *Creation Research Society* 36, No. 2 (1999): 62–68.

Frankl, Victor. *The Doctor and the Soul: From Psychotherapy to Logotherapy*. 3rd ed. New York: Vintage Books, 1986.

Franks, Angela. *Margaret Sanger's Eugenic Legacy*. Jefferson: McFarland, 2005.

Freud, Ernst L., and Heinrich Meng, ed. *Psychoanalysis and Faith: The Letters of Sigmund Freud & Oskar Pfister*. Translated by Eric Mosbacher. New York: Basic Books, 1963.

Freud, Sigmund. *The Standard Edition of the Complete Psychological Works of Sigmund Freud: Volume XIX (1923–1925) The Ego and the Id and Other Works*. Edited by James Strachey. London: The Hogarth Press and The Institute of Psycho-Analysis, 1961.

Gallagher, Nancy L. *Breeding Better Vermonters: The Eugenics Project in the Green Mountain State*. Hanover: University Press of New England, 1999.

Gairdner, William. *The War against the Family*. Toronto: Stoddard, 1992.

Gardner, Martin. *Undiluted Hocus-Pocus: The Autobiography of Martin Gardner*. Princeton: Princeton University Press, 2013.

Gatewood, Willard. *Preachers, Pedagogues and Politicians*. Chapel Hill: University of North Carolina Press, 1966.

Gathorne-Hardy, Jonathan. *Sex the Measure of All Things: A Life of Alfred C. Kinsey*. Bloomington: Indiana University Press, 1998.

Gay, Peter. *Freud: A Life for Our Time*. New York: W.W. Norton & Company, 1998.

Gayon, Jean. "Nietzsche and Darwin." In *Biology and the Foundation of Ethics*, edited by Jane Maienschein and Michael Ruse, 154–197. Cambridge: Cambridge University Press, 1999.

Giubilini, Alberto and Francesca Minerva. "After-birth abortion: Why should the baby live?" *Journal of Medical Ethics* (February 2012): 1–4.

Glad, John. *Jewish Genetics*. Washington: Wooden Shore, 2011.

Gledhill, Ruth. "Scandal and schism leave Christians praying for a 'new Reformation.'" *The Times* (UK), April 2, 2010.

Goddard, Henry. *The Kallikak Family: A Study in the Heredity of Feeble-mindedness*. New York: MacMillan, 1912.

Goldberg, Isaac. *Havelock Ellis: A Biographical and Critical Survey*. London: Constable and Company, 1926.

Gordon, Linda. *Woman's Body, Woman's Right: A Social History of Birth Control in America*. New York: Grossman Publishers, 1976.

Grant, George. *Grand Illusions: The Legacy of Planned Parenthood*. Brentwood: Wolgemuth and Hyatt, 1988.

_____. *Killer Angel: A Biography of Planned Parenthood's Margaret Sanger*. Franklin: Standfast Books, 2014.

_____. *Killer Angel: A Short Biography of Planned Parenthood's Founder, Margaret Sanger*. Franklin: Standfast Books, 2001.

Grant, Madison. *The Passing of the Great Race, or, the Racial Basis of European History*. New York: Charles Scribner's Sons, 1918.

Gray, Eliza. "Sexual assault on campus." *Time* 183, No. 20 (2014): 20–29.

Gray, Madeline. *Margaret Sanger: A Biography of the Champion of Birth Control*. New York: Richard Marek Publishers, 1979.

Greenhouse, Linda. "Constitutional question: Is there a right to abortion?" *The New York Times Magazine* (January 25, 1970): 30–31, 88–91.

Gross, Leonard. *God and Freud*. New York: David McKay, 1959.

Gross, Neil, and Solon Simmons. "How religious are America's college and university professors?" Social Science Research Council web forum on "The Religious Engagements of American Undergraduates." February 6, 2007. http://religion.ssrc.org/reforum/Gross_Simmons.pdf. Accessed September 6, 2016.

Grosskurth, Phyllis. *Havelock Ellis: A Biography*. New York: Knoph, 1980.

Guinn, Jeff. *Manson: The Life and Times of Charles Manson*. New York: Simon & Schuster, 2013.

Guinness, Os. "America's Last Men and Their Magnificent Talking Cure." In *No God but God: Breaking with the Idols of Our Age*. Edited by Os Guinness and John Steel, 111–116. Chicago: Moody, 1992.

Hackett, David. "Indiana University shuns Kinsey biographer." *The Journal Gazette,* March 11, 2003, 2C.

Haller, Mark H. *Eugenics: Hereditarian Attitudes in American Thought.* New Brunswick: Rutgers University Press, 1984.

Harden, Nathan. *Sex and God at Yale: Porn, Political Correctness and Good Education Gone Bad.* New York: Thomas Dunne Books, 2012.

Hartmann, Heinz. "Comments on the Scientific Aspects of Psychoanalysis." Reprinted from *The Psychoanalytic Study of the Child.* Vol. 13, 127–146. New York: International Universities Press, 1958.

Hata, Ikuhiko. "The Japanese-Soviet Confrontation, 1935–1939." In *Deterrent Diplomacy: Japan, Germany, and the U.S.S.R. 1935–1940,* edited by J.W. Morley. New York, Columbia University Press, 1976.

Hausheer, Herman. "Superman." In *Dictionary of Philosophy,* edited by Dagobert Runes, 307. Totowa: Littlefield Adams, 1962.

Hedges, S. Blair. "Molecular evidence for the origin of birds." *Proceedings of the National Academy of Science* 91 (March 1994): 2621–2624.

Hicks, Stephen R.C. *Nietzsche and the Nazis.* Ockham's Razer Publishing, 2010.

Hildeman, Eric J. *Creationism: The Bible Says No.* Bloomington: Author's House, 2004.

Hillenbrand, Laura. *Unbroken: A World War II Story of Survival, Resilience, and Redemption.* New York: Random House, 2010.

Hollingdale, Richard J. *Nietzsche: The Man and His Philosophy.* New York: Cambridge University Press, 1999.

Holmes, Jr., Oliver Wendell. "The path of the law." *Harvard Law Review* 10 (1897): 457.

Holt, Robert R. "Freud's Impact on Modern Morality and Our World View." In *Darwin, Marx and Freud: Their Influence on Moral Theory,* edited by Arthur L. Caplan and Bruce Jennings, 147–200. New York: Plenum, 1984.

Hopwood, Nick. *Haeckel's Embryos: Images, Evolution and Fraud.* Chicago: University of Chicago Press, 2015.

Houston, Beth. *Natural God: Deism in the Age of Intelligent Design.* Florida: New Deism Press, 2012.

Hrdy, Sara Blaffer. *Mother Nature: Natural Selection and the Female of the Species.* London: Chatto & Windus, 1999.

Hubbard, Mary Ellen. "Benjamin Spock, MD. The Man and His Work in Historical Perspective." Ph.D. diss. Claremont Graduate School, 1981.

Humes, Edward. *Monkey Girl.* New York: HarperCollins, 2006.

Jessop, T.E. "Friedrich Nietzsche." In *Dictionary of Christian Ethics,* edited by John Macquarrie, 233. Philadelphia: Westminster Press, 1967.

Johnson, Dirk Robert. *Nietzsche's Anti-Darwinism.* New York: Cambridge University Press, 2010.

Johnson, Paul. *Modern Times: The World from the Twenties to the Nineties.* New York: HarperPerennial/Modern Classics, 1991.

Jones, Ernest. *The Life and Work of Sigmund Freud, Volume 1: The Formative Years and The Great Discoveries 1856–1900.* New York: Basic Books, 1981.

_____. _The Life and Work of Sigmund Freud, Volume 2: Years of Maturity 1901–1919._ New York: Basic Books, 1981.

_____. _The Life and Work of Sigmund Freud, Volume 3: The Last Phase 1919–1939._ New York: Basic Books, 1981.

Jones, James H. _Alfred Kinsey: A Private Life._ New York: Norton, 1997.

Joseph, Dan. "Nearly 50 million abortions have been performed in U.S. since _Roe v. Wade_ decision legalized abortion." January 25, 2011. http://cnsnews.com/news/article/nearly-50-million-abortions-have-been-performed-us-roe-v-wade-decision-legalized. Accessed September 2, 2016.

Kandel, Eric. "Does psychotherapy work?" _Discover_ 27, No. 4 (April 2006): 58–61.

Kenji, Kiyono, _A History of Changing Theories About the Japanese Race._ Tokyo: Koyama Shoten, 1944.

Kennedy, David. _Birth Control in America: The Career of Margaret Sanger._ New Haven: Yale University Press, 1970.

Kenyon, Frank. _Psycho-Analysis: A Modern Delusion._ London: Secular Society/The Pioneer Press, 1949.

Kershaw, Ian. _Hitler 1889–1936: Hubris._ New York: Norton, 1998.

_____. _Hitler 1936–1945: Nemesis._ New York: Norton, 2000.

Kevles, Daniel. _In the Name of Eugenics._ New York: Knopf, 1985.

Kiefer, Otto. _Sexual Life in Ancient Rome._ London: Abbey Library, 1971.

Kilpatrick, William Kirk. _Psychological Seduction: The Failure of Modern Psychology._ Nashville: Thomas Nelson, 1983.

Kinsey, Alfred C. _An Introduction to Biology._ Philadelphia: J.B. Lippincott, 1926.

_____. _New Introduction to Biology._ Philadelphia: J.B. Lippincott, 1933.

_____. _Methods in Biology._ Chicago: J.B. Lippincott, 1937.

_____. _Sexual Behavior in the Human Male._ Philadelphia: Saunders, 1948.

Kischer, C. Ward, and Dianne N. Irving. _The Human Development Hoax: Time to Tell the Truth._ Clinton Township: Gold Leaf Press, 1997.

Knauer, Kelly. _Great People of the 20th Century._ New York: Time Books, 1996.

Koenig, Harold. _Is Religion Good for Your Health?_ New York: Hayworth, 1997.

Koster, John P. _The Atheist Syndrome._ Brentwood: Wolgemuth & Hyatt, 1989.

Kowner, Rotem, and Walter Demel, eds. _Race and Racism in Modern East Asia._ Boston: Brill, 2013.

Kubizek, August. _Young Hitler: The Story of Our Friendship._ London: Allan Wingate, 1954.

Kuntz, Dieter, and Susan Bachrach, ed. _Deadly Medicine: Creating the Master Race._ Chapel Hill: The University of North Carolina Press, 2006.

Lang, Hans-Joachim. _Die Namen der Nummern: Wie es gelang, die 86 Opfer eines NS-Verbrechens zu identifizieren._ Hamburg: Hoffmann und Campe, 2004.

Large, Stephen S. _Emperor Hirohito and Showa Japan: A Political Biography._ New York: Routledge, 1992.

Laumann, Edward O., and Robert T. Michael. _Sex, Love and Health in America: Private Choices and Public Policies._ Chicago: The University of Chicago Press, 2001.

_____, John H. Gagnon, Robert T. Michael, and Stuart Michaels. _The Social Organiza-_

*tion of Sexuality: Sexual Practices in the United States*. Chicago: The University of Chicago Press, 1994.

Lavrin, Janko. *Nietzsche: A Biographical Introduction*. New York: Scribner, 1971.

*Lawrence v. Texas*. 593 U.S. 588 (2003). https://supreme.justia.com/cases/federal/us/539/558/case.html. Accessed August 22, 2016.

Leiter, Brian, and Neil Sinhabau, eds. *Nietzsche and Morality*. New York: Oxford University Press, 2007.

Leo, John. "Singer's final solution." *U.S. News and World Report*, October 4, 1999, 17.

Lewis, C. S. "Willing slaves and the welfare state." *The Observer*, July 20, 1958.

Lewkonia, Ray. "Benjamin Spock: The public pediatrician." *The Lancet* 35, No. 9130 (1998): 825–826.

Licht, Hans. *Sexual Life in Ancient Greece*. London: Abbey Library, 1971.

Lichtenberger, Henri. *The Gospel of Superman: The Philosophy of Friedrich Nietzsche*. London: T.N. Foulis, 1910.

Lichtheim, George. "Freud and Marx." In *Freud: The Man, His World, His Influence*, edited by Jonathan Miller, 58–69. Boston: Little, Brown, and Company, 1972.

Lifton, Robert J. *The Nazi Doctors: Medical Killing and the Psychology of Genocide*. New York: Basic Books, 1986.

_____. "Nazi Medical Experiments." In *The Holocaust*, edited by Mitchell Bard, 90–96. San Diego: Greenhaven Press, 2001.

Lilienfeld, Scott O. "Psychological treatments that cause harm." *Perspectives on Psychological Science* 2, No. 1 (2007): 53–70.

Livingston, David N. *Darwin's Forgotten Defenders: The Encounter Between Evangelical Theology and Evolutionary Thought*. Grand Rapids: William B. Eerdmans Publishing, 1987.

Loftus, Elizabeth F. "Creating false memories." *Scientific American* 277, No. 3 (1997): 70–75.

_____, Maryanne Garry, and Julie Feldman. "Forgetting sexual trauma: What does it mean when 38% forget?" *Journal of Consulting and Clinical Psychology* 62, No. 6 (1994): 1177–1181.

_____, and Hunter G. Hoffman. "Misinformation and memory: The creation of new memories." *Journal of Experimental Psychology* 118, No. 1 (1989): 100–104.

Luborsky, Lester. "A note on Eysenck's article 'The effects of psychotherapy: An evaluation.'" *British Journal of Psychology* 45 (1954): 129–131.

Luhan, Mabel Dodge. *Movers and Shakers: Volume Three of Intimate Memories*. New York: Harcourt, Brace, 1936.

Lukács, Georg. *Von Nietzsche zu Hitler oder Der Irrationalismus und die Deutsche Politik*. Frankfurt am Main: Fischer Bücherei, 1966.

Lukas, Richard C. *Forgotten Holocaust: The Poles under German Occupation 1939–1944*. Rev. ed. New York: Hippocrene Books, 1997.

Lutz, Donald, and Charles Hyneman. "Toward a theory of constitutional amendment," *American Political Science Review* 88 (1994): 355–370.

Lutzer, Erwin W. *Hitler's Cross*. Chicago: Moody Press, 1995.

Maddox, Bruno. "Deconstructing Darwin." *Discover Magazine* (November 2009): 39–41.

Maier, Thomas. *Dr. Spock. An American Life.* New York: Harcourt Brace, 1998.

Major, Trevor. "Haeckel: The legacy of a lie." *Reason and Revelation* 14 (September 1, 1994): 68–70. http://www.apologeticspress.org/APContent.aspx?category=9& article=596. Accessed September 2, 2016.

Malak, Henry M. *Shavelings in Death Camps: A Polish Priest's Memoir of Imprisonment by the Nazis, 1939–1945.* Jefferson: McFarland, 2012.

Marshall, Robert, and Charles Donovan. *Blessed Are the Barren: The Social Policy of Planned Parenthood.* San Francisco: Ignatius, 1991.

Maybury-Lewis, David. *Millennium: Tribal Wisdom and the Modern World.* New York: Viking, 1992.

Mayer, Ernst. "What evolution is," *Edge*, December 31, 1999. http://edge.org/conversation/what-evolution-is. Accessed August 15, 2016.

McCulloch, Oscar C. "The Tribe of Ishmael: A Study in Social Degradation." In *Proceedings of the National Conference of Charities and Correction*, 154–159. Boston: George H. Ellis, 1888.

_____. *The Tribe of Ishmael: A Study in Social Degradation.* 3rd ed. Indianapolis: Charity Organizational Society, 1891.

McDonald, Gabrielle Kirk. *Substantive and Procedural Aspects of International Criminal Law: The Experience of International and National Courts.* 1st ed. Netherlands: Springer, 2000.

McInnis, Raymond G. "Dr. Benjamin Spock's *Baby and Child Care*: Origins, impact, sources." *Reference Services Review* 13, No. 4, (1973): 9–15.

McQuade, Elwood. *Halina: Faith in the Fire.* Bellmawr: The Friends of Israel, 2013.

_____. "New survey shows extent of worldwide anti-Semitism." *Israel My Glory* 72, No. 4 (2014): 25.

Means, Cyril C., Jr. "Eugenic abortion." *The New York Times*, April 16, 1965, 28.

_____. "A fetus as person." *The New York Times*, March 17, 1972, 40.

Medawar, Peter. "Further Comments on Psychoanalysis." In *Pluto's Republic: Incorporating The Art of the Soluble and Induction and Intuition in Scientific Thought*, 62–72. New York: Oxford, 1982.

Mellanby, Kenneth. "Medical experiments on human beings in concentration camps in Nazi Germany." *British Medical Journal* 1, No. 4490 (January 25, 1947): 148–150.

Mencken, Henry Lewis. "The mailed fist and its prophet." *The Atlantic Monthly* (November 1914): 598–607.

Menninger, Karl. *Whatever Became of Sin?* New York: Hawthorn Books, 1974.

Messall, Rebecca. "The long road of eugenics: From Rockefeller to *Roe v. Wade*." *The Human Life Review* (Fall 2004): 33–96.

Messing, Simon D. "On Anthropology and Nazi Genocide." *Current Anthropology* 17, No. 2 (June 1976): 326–327.

Miller, Jonathan, ed. *Freud: The Man, His World, His Influence.* Boston: Little, Brown, and Company, 1972.

Miller, Kenneth. *Finding Darwin's God.* New York: Cliff Street Books, 1999.

Milner, Richard. *The Encyclopedia of Evolution: Humanity's Search for Its Origins.* New York: Facts on File, 1990.

Moore, John S. "Nietzsche's Anti-Darwin." Presented at The 11th annual conference of the Friedrich Nietzsche Society, Emmanuel College, Cambridge, September 8, 2001.

Mosher, William, Anjani Chandra, and Jo Jones. "Sexual behavior and selected health measures: Men and women 15–44 years of age, United States, 2002." *Advanced Data from Vital and Health Statistics* 362 (September 15, 2005). http://www.cdc.gov/nchs/data/ad/ad362.pdf. Accessed August 17, 2016.

Mosse, George L. *Nazi Culture: Intellectual, Cultural, and Social life in the Third Reich.* New York: Schocken Books, 1981.

Moxon, Cavendish. "Freud's denial of religion." *British Journal of Medical Psychology* 11 (1931): 150–157.

Muckermann, H. "Evolution." In *The Catholic Encyclopedia*, Vol. 5, 654–670. New York: The Encyclopedia Press, 1913.

Mügge, Maximilian A. "Eugenics and the superman: A racial science, and a racial religion." *The Eugenics Review* 1, No. 3 (October 1909): 184–193.

_____. *Friedrick Nietzsche: His Life and Work.* London: Fisher Unwin, 1914.

Muller-Hill, Benno. *Murderous Science: Elimination by Scientific Selection of Jews, Gypsies, and Others in Germany, 1933–1945.* Translated by George R. Fraser. New York: Oxford University Press, 1988.

Neel, James. In *The Human Life Bill: Hearings Before the Subcommittee on Separation of Powers of the Committee on the Judiciary. United States Senate, Ninety-Seventh Congress, First Session, on S. 158, a Bill to Provide that Human Life Shall be Deemed to Exist from Conception.* Serial No. J-97-16, May 20, 1981. Washington, D.C.: U.S. Government Printing Office, 1982.

Newberg, Andrew, Eugene D'Aquili, and Vince Rause. *Why God Won't Go Away: Brain Science and the Biology of Belief.* New York: Ballantine Books, 2001.

Nietzsche, Friedrich. *Beyond Good and Evil: Prelude to a Philosophy of the Future.* Translated by Walter Kaufmann. New York: Vintage Books, 1966.

_____. *Thus Spake Zarathustra.* New York: Modern Library, 1950.

Nolte, Sharon H. *Liberalism in Modern Japan: Ishibashi Tanzan and His Teachers, 1905–1960.* Berkeley: University of California Press, 1987.

Norman, Andrew. *Charles Darwin: Destroyer of Myths.* New York: Skyhorse, 2014.

Norman, E. Herbert. "Militarists in the Japanese State." *Pacific Affairs* 16, No. 4 (December 1943): 475–481.

Norton, James. *The Holocaust: Jews, Germany, and the National Socialists.* New York: Rosen Pub Group, 2008.

Oesterreicher, John M. "Abortion, evolution and an untenable biogenetic law." *The New York Times*, October 24, 1980, A32.

Olasky, Marvin. "Darwin matters" *World* (July 2, 2011): 96.

_____. "Non-selective." *World* (December 31, 2011): 8.

Ordover, Nancy. *American Eugenics*. Minneapolis: University of Minnesota Press, 2003.

O'Reilly, Bill and Martin Dugard. *Killing the Rising Sun*. New York: Henry Holt, 2016.

Osborn, Henry Fairfield. "Introduction," in *The Passing of the Great Race, or, the Racial Basis of European History*, vii-ix. New York: Charles Scribner's Sons, 1918.

Overstreet, Harry. "The philosophy of materialism." In Volume 5 of *The Popular Educator Library*. New York: National Educational Alliance Incorporated, 1940.

Pääbo, Svante. *Neanderthal Man: In Search of Lost Genomes*. New York: Basic Books, 2014.

Padfield, Peter. *Himmler*. New York: Holt, 1990.

Padover, Saul K. "Japanese Race Propaganda." *Public Opinion Quarterly* 7, No. 2 (1943): 191–204.

Patterson, C.H. *Theories of Counseling and Psychotherapy*. New York: Harper and Row, 1966.

Paul, Robert A. "Did the primal crime take place?" *Ethos* 4, No. 3 (1976): 311–352.

Pazol, Karen, Andreea A. Creanga, and Denise J. Jamieson. "Abortion surveillance – United States, 2012: Surveillance summaries," *Centers for Disease Control and Prevention, Morbidity and Mortality Weekly Report*, November 27, 2015). http://www.cdc.gov/mmwr/preview/mmwrhtml/ss6410a1.htm. Accessed November 3, 2016.

Pearson, Karl. *National Life from the Standpoint of Science*. London: Adam and Charles Black, 1901.

———. *The Grammar of Science*. London: Adam and Charles Black, 1900.

Peterson, Andrée Seu. "Sexual propaganda: What many moms and dads are paying for in higher education." *World* (May 3, 2014): 71.

Phillips, Roderick. *Putting Asunder: A History of Divorce in Western Society*. New York: Cambridge University Press, 1988.

Philpot, T. "Profile: Dr. Benjamin Spock. A middle-of-the-road man." *Nursing Mirror* 149, No. 19 (November 8, 1979): 20–21.

Pichot, André. *The Pure Society: From Darwin to Hitler*. New York: Verso, 2009.

Pinckney, Edward, and Cathey Pinckney. *The Fallacy of Freud and Psychoanalysis*. Englewood Cliffs: Prentice-Hall, 1965.

Piotrowski, Tadeusz. *Poland's Holocaust: Ethnic Strife, Collaboration with Occupying Forces and Genocide in the Second Republic, 1918–1947*. Jefferson: McFarland, 1998.

Ploetz, Alfred. *Die Tüchtigkeit unsrer Rasse und der Schutz der Schwachen (The Fitness of Our Race and the Protection of the Weak)*. Berlin: S. Fischer, 1895.

Pomeroy, Wardell B. *Dr. Kinsey and the Institute for Sex Research*. New York: Harper and Row, 1972.

Price, Joyce Howard. "Study finds liberals dominate faculties, most don't go to church." *The Washington Times National Weekly Edition*, April 4–10, 2005.

"Psychoanalysis: In search of its soul" *Time* 93, No. 10 (March 7, 1969): 68–70.

Rachels, James. *Created from Animals: The Moral Implications of Darwinism*. New York: Oxford University Press, 1990.

Ravitch, Diane, ed. "Margaret Sanger: The Right to One's Body." 249–252. In *The American Reader: Words that Moved a Nation*. New York: Harper Collins Publishers, 1990.

Raymo, Chet. *Climbing Brandon: Science and Faith on Ireland's Holy Mountain.* New York: Walker, 2004.

_____. *Honey from Stone.* Kerry: Brandon, 1997.

_____. *Skeptics and True Believers.* New York: Walker, 1998.

_____. *Walking Zero: Discovering Space and Time Along the Prime Meridian.* New York: Walker, 2006.

_____, and Maureen E. Raymo. *Written in Stone: A Geologic History of the Northeastern United States.* New York: Black Dome Press, 2001.

Rayner, Gordon, Duncan Gardham, and John Bingham. "Hunt for Britons linked to Norway killer Anders Behring Breivik." *The Telegraph*, September 23, 2011.

Read, Simon. *Human Game: The True Story of the "Great Escape" Murders and the Hunt for the Gestapo Gunmen.* New York: Berkley Caliber, 2012.

Rees, Laurence. *The Nazis: A Warning from History.* New York: MJF Books, 1997.

Reichler, Max. *Jewish Eugenics and Other Essays.* New York: Bloch Publishing Company, 1916.

Reisman, Judith. *Kinsey: Crimes and Consequences.* Arlington: The Institute for Media Education, 1998.

Richardson, Michael, J. Hanken, M.L. Gooneratne, C. Pieau, A. Raynaud, L. Selwood, and G. M. Wright. "There is no highly conserved embryonic stage in the vertebrates: Implications for current theories of evolution and development." *Anatomy and Embryology* 196 (1997): 91–106.

Rifkin, Jeremy. *Algeny.* New York: Viking Press, 1983.

Ritvo, Lucille B. *Darwin's Influence on Freud: A Tale of Two Sciences.* New Haven: Yale University Press, 1990.

Roche, Claire M. "Reproducing the Working Class: Tillie Olsen, Margaret Sanger, and American Eugenics." In *Evolution and Eugenics in American Literature and Culture, 1880–1940: Essays on Ideological Conflict and Complicity*, edited by Lois A. Cuddy and Claire M. Roche, 259–275. Danvers: Rosemont Publishing, 2003.

Ronen, Gil. "Japanese scapegoated Indonesia's Jews in WW2." *Arutz Sheva*, April 27, 2010. http://www.israelnationalnews.com/News/News.aspx/137244. Accessed November 4, 2016.

Rorty, Richard. "Universality and Truth." In *Rorty and His Critics*, edited by Robert B. Brandom, 21–22. Oxford: Blackwell, 2000.

Rosen, Christine. *Preaching Genetics: Religious Leaders and the American Eugenics Movement.* New York: Oxford University Press, 2004.

Rosenbaum, Ron. *Explaining Hitler: The Search for the Origins of His Evil.* 2nd ed. Boston: Da Capo Press, 2014.

Rummel, Rudolph J. *Death by Government.* New Brunswick: Transaction Publishers, 2008.

Rutter, Virginia. "Oops! A very embarrassing story." *Psychology Today*, March/April 1994, 12–13, 95.

Ryback, Timoty W. *Hitler's Private Library: The Books That Shaped His Life.* New York: Knopf, 2008.

Sacks, Jonathan. *The Great Partnership: God, Science and the Search for Meaning*. New York: Hodder & Stoughton, 2011.

Sagan, Carl, and Ann Druyan. "The question of abortion: A search for answers." *Parade Magazine*, Sunday, April 22, 1990, 4–8.

Sahakian, William S. *History of Psychology*. Itasca: Peacock Publishers, 1968.

Sakura, Osamu. "Similarities and varieties: A brief sketch on the reception of Darwinism and sociobiology in Japan." *Biology and Philosophy* 13 (1998): 341–357.

Sanders, Ed. *The Family: The Story of Charles Manson's Dune Buggy Attack Battalion*. New York: E. P. Dutton, 1971.

Sanger, Margaret H. "Individual and Family Aspects of Birth Control," given at Kingsway Hall, London, on July 11–14, 1922. In *Report of the Fifth International Neo-Malthusian and Birth Control Conference*, edited by Raymond Pierpoint, 30–32. London: Heinemann, 1922.

———. *Margaret Sanger: An Autobiography*. New York: Norton, 1938.

———. *The Pivot of Civilization*. Amherst: Humanity Books, 2003.

———. *What Every Girl Should Know*. New York: Belvedere Publishers, 1980.

———. *Women and the New Race*. New York: Blue Ribbon Books, 1920.

Sarfati, Jonathan. "Norway terrorist: More media mendacity." August 2011. http://creation.com/norway-terrorist-breivik-not-christian. Accessed September 13, 2016.

Sarolea, Charles. *German Problems and Personalities*. London: Chatto & Windus, 1917.

Schofield, William. *Psychotherapy: The Purchase of Friendship*. Englewood Cliffs: Prentice-Hall, 1964.

Schultz, Duane. *A History of Modern Psychology*. New York: Academic Press, 1972.

Sedgh, Gilda, Susheela Singh, Iqbal Shah, Elisabeth Ahoam, Stanley Henshaw, and Akinrinola Bankole. "Induced abortion: Incidence and trends worldwide from 1995 to 2008." *The Lancet* 379 (2012): 625–632.

Sedgwick, Adam. "Letter to Charles Darwin dated November 24, 1859." Darwin Correspondence Project. https://www.darwinproject.ac.uk/letter/?docId=letters/DCP-LETT-2548.xml;query=sedgwick;brand=default. Accessed August 15, 2016.

Seierstad, Åsne. *One of Us: The Story of Anders Breivik and the Massacre in Norway*. New York: Farrar, Straus, and Giroux, 2015.

Shields, Stephanie A. "Functionalism, Darwinism, and the psychology of women: A study in social myth." *American Psychologist* 30, No. 7 (July 1975): 739–754.

Shimao, Eikoh. "Darwinism in Japan, 1877–1927." *Annals of Science* 38 (1981): 93–102.

Silver, Lee M. *Remaking Eden: Cloning and Beyond in a Brave New World*. New York: Avon Books, 1997.

Simpson, George Gaylord. "The world into which Darwin led us." *Science* 131, No. 3405 (1960): 966–974.

Singer, Peter. "Peter Singer FAQ." http://www.petersinger.info/faq/. Accessed September 4, 2016.

———. *Rethinking Life and Death: The Collapse of Our Traditional Ethics*. New York: Oxford University Press, 1995.

_____, and Helga Kuhse. *Should the Baby Live? The Problem of Handicapped Infants.* New York: Oxford University Press, 1986.

Skinner, B.F. *Beyond Freedom and Dignity.* Westminster: Random House, 1971.

Slack, Chris "Anders Breivik 'was on Norwegian secret service watchlist' after buying chemical haul from Polish retailer." DailyMail.com, July 26, 2011. http://www.dailymail.co.uk/news/article-2018646/Norway-shooting-Anders-Behring-Breivik-secret-service-watchlist.html. Accessed September 13, 2016.

Small, Robin. "What Nietzsche Did During the Science Wars." In *Nietzsche and Science,* edited by Gregory Moore and Thomas H. Brobjer, 155–170. Burlington: Ashgate Publishing Company, 2004.

Smith, J. David, *Minds Made Feeble: The Myth and Legacy of the Kallikaks.* Rockville: Aspen, 1985.

Sommers, Christina Hoff. *The War against Boys.* New York: Simon and Schuster, 2000.

Spitz, Vivien. *Doctors from Hell: The Horrific Account of Nazi Experiments on Humans.* Boulder: Sentient Publications, 2005.

Spock, Benjamin. *Decent and Indecent: Our Personal and Political Behavior.* New York: McCall, 1970.

_____, and Mary Morgan. *Spock on Spock. A Memoir of Growing Up with the Century.* New York: Pantheon Books, 1989.

_____, and Michael Rothenberg. *Baby and Child Care.* 6th ed. New York: Dutton, 1992.

Staub, Ervin. *The Roots of Evil: The Origins of Genocide and Other Group Violence.* New York: Cambridge University Press, 1992.

Steinem, Gloria. "Margaret Sanger: Her crusade to legalize birth control spurred the movement toward women's liberation." In *Time 100. Leaders & Revolutionaries/Artists and Entertainers.* New York: Time Books, 1998.

Stewart-Williams, Steve. *Darwin, God and the Meaning of Life: How Evolutionary Theory Undermines Everything You Thought You Knew.* New York: Cambridge University Press, 2010.

Steiner, George, *Nostalgia for the Absolute.* Toronto: House of Anansi Press, 1997.

Stigler, Stephen M. *The History of Statistics: The Measurement of Uncertainty before 1900.* Cambridge: Belknap Press/Harvard University,1986.

Stone, Dan. *Breeding Superman: Nietzsche, Race and Eugenics in Edwardian and Interwar Britain.* London: Liverpool University Press, 2002.

Stuart, Richard B. *Trick or Treatment: How and When Psychotherapy Fails.* Champaign: Research Press, 1970.

Sundberg, Norman, and Leona Tyler. *Clinical Psychology.* New York: Appleton Century Crofts, 1973.

Sundberg, Norman, Julian Taplin, and Leona Tyler. *Introduction to Clinical Psychology.* Englewood Cliffs: Prentice-Hall, 1983.

Teats, Mary. *The Way of God in Marriage.* Spotswood: Physical Culture Publishing, 1906.

Tennov, Dorothy. *Psychotherapy: The Hazardous Cure.* New York: Abelard-Schuman, 1975.

Thornton, E.M. *The Freudian Fallacy.* Garden City: The Dial Press/Double Day, 1983.

Tobin, Gary A., and Aryeh K. Weinberg. "Religious Beliefs and Behavior of College Faculty." In *Profiles of the American University.* Vol. 2. Roseville: Institute for Jewish and Community Research, 2007.

Tolischus, Otto D., ed. *Through Japanese Eyes.* New York: Reynal and Hitchcock, 1945.

Tone, Andrea. *Devices and Desires: A History of Contraceptives in America.* New York: Hill and Wang, 2002.

_____. "Historical Influences on Women's Sexual and Reproductive Health." In *Handbook of Women's Sexual and Reproductive Health,* edited by Gina M. Wingood and Ralph J. DiClemente, 7–19. New York: Kluwer Academic/Plenum, 2002.

Torrey, E. Fuller. *The Death of Psychiatry.* Radnor: Chilton, 1974.

Trombley, Stephen. *The Right To Reproduce: A History of Coercive Sterilization.* London: Weidenfeld and Nicolson,1988.

United States Holocaust Memorial Museum. "Voyage of the *St. Louis.*" https://www.ushmm.org/wlc/en/article.php?ModuleId=10005267. Accessed September 19, 2016.

Vitagliano, Ed. "Sir William Blackstone and the long war against law." *afa Journal* (January 2015). http://www.afajournal.org/past-issues/2015/january/sir-william-blackstone-and-the-long-war-against-law/. Accessed August 16, 2016.

Vitz, Paul C. *Faith of the Fatherless: The Psychology of Atheism.* Dallas: Spence, 1999.

_____. *Psychology as Religion: The Cult of Self Worship.* Grand Rapids: Eerdmans, 1977.

_____. *Sigmund Freud's Christian Unconscious.* New York: The Guilford Press, 1988.

Vuitsch, Milan M. "Letter to Senator John East dated April 22, 1981." In *The Human Life Bill Appendix: Hearings Before the Subcommittee on Separation of Powers of the Committee on the Judiciary, United States Senate, Ninety-Seventh Congress, First Session, on S. 158, a Bill to Provide that Human Life Shall be Deemed to Exist from Conception, April 23, 24; May 20, 21; June 1, 10, 12, and 18.* Serial No. J-97-16. Washington: U.S. Government Printing Office, 1982.

"Was Japan racist during World War II?" Yahoo! Answers. https://answers.yahoo.com/question/index?qid=20110226195227AAfbHKm. Accessed October 14, 2016.

Washington, Harriet A. *Medical Apartheid: The Dark History of Medical Experimentation on Black Americans from Colonial Times to the Present.* New York: Doubleday, 2006.

Watson, Charles. *Will You Die For Me?* Dallas: Cross Roads Publications, 1978.

Watson, James D. *DNA: The Secret of Life.* New York: Alfred A. Knopf, 2003.

Weikart, Richard. *Hitler's Struggle for Existence against Slavs: Racial Theory and Vacillations in Nazi Policy Towards Czechs and Poles.* Forthcoming.

_____. "The Impact of Social Darwinism on Anti-Semitic Ideology in Germany and Austria, 1860–1945." In *Jewish Tradition and the Challenge of Darwinism,* edited by Geoffrey Cantor and Marc Swetlitz, 93–115. Chicago, University of Chicago Press, 2006.

Weiner, Jonathan. *The Beak of the Finch: A Story of Evolution in Our Time.* New York: Knopf, 1994.

Weiner, Michael. "Discourses of race, nation and empire in pre-1945 Japan." *Ethnic and Racial Studies* 18, No. 3 (July 1995): 433–456.

Weiss-Wendt, Anton. *Eradicating Differences: The Treatment of Minorities in Nazi-Dominated Europe.* Newcastle-upon-Tyne: Cambridge Scholar Press, 2010.

Wells, Harry K. *The Failure of Psychoanalysis.* New York: International Publishers, 1963.

Wells, Jonathan. "Haeckel's embryos & evolution." *The American Biology Teacher* 61, No. 5 (1999): 345–349.

———. *Icons of Evolution: Why Much of What We Teach About Evolution Is Wrong.* Washington: Regnery, 2000.

West, John G. *Darwin Day in America: How Our Politics and Culture Have Been Dehumanized in the Name of Science.* Wilmington: ISI Books, 2007.

White, Kevin. *Sexual Liberation or Sexual License? The American Revolt against Victorianism.* Chicago: Ivan Dee, 2000.

Whitehead, Alfred North. *Science and the Modern World.* New York: The Free Press, 1953.

Whitehead, Barbara Dafoe. *The Divorce Culture.* New York: Alfred A. Knopf, 1997.

Wiggam, Albert Edward. *Let's Explore Your Mind.* New York: Pocket Books, 1949.

———. *The New Decalogue of Science.* Garden City: Garden City Publishing, 1925.

Wiker, Benjamin. *10 Books that Screwed up the World.* Washington: Regnery, 2008.

Williams, Robert H. "Our role in the generation, modification, and termination of life." *Archives of Internal Medicine* 124, No. 2 (August 1969): 215–237.

Wolpe, Joseph. "Introduction." In *Trick or Treatment: How and When Psychotherapy Fails* by Richard B. Stuart. Champaign: Research Press, 1970.

Wolpert, Lewis. *The Triumph of the Embryo.* Oxford: Oxford University Press, 1992.

Wright, Willard Huntington "Introduction." In *The Philosophy of Nietzsche*, vii–xi. New York: Modern Library, 1954.

Yancey, George, and David A. Williamson. *So Many Christians, So Few Lions: Is There Christianophobia in the United States?* Lanham: Rowman & Littlefield Publishers, 2014.

Zindler, Frank R. "An acorn is not an oak tree." *American Atheist* 27, No. 8 (1985): 27–30.

Visit us online at
**www.joshuapress.com**

*Other titles available from Joshua Press...*

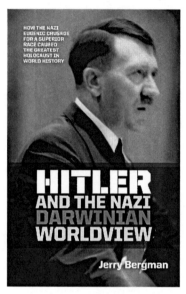

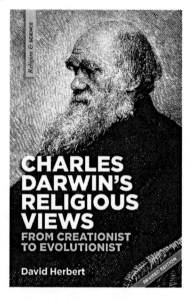

## HITLER AND THE NAZI DARWINIAN WORLDVIEW

How the Nazi eugenic crusade for a superior race caused the greatest holocaust in world history

*By Jerry Bergman*

THIS BOOK takes a fresh look at Germany's most influential Nazi leaders, showing that the rising influence of Darwinism, eugenics and race theory set the foundation for their pursuit of a "master race."

ISBN 978–1-894400-49–7

## CHARLES DARWIN'S RELIGIOUS VIEWS

From creationist to evolutionist

*By David Herbert*

A SPIRITUAL BIOGRAPHY that focuses primarily on the religious experiences of Charles Darwin's life—demonstrating how Darwin's rejection of the Bible led him to adopt the naturalistic assumptions that were foundational to his belief in evolutionism.

ISBN 978–1-894400-30–5

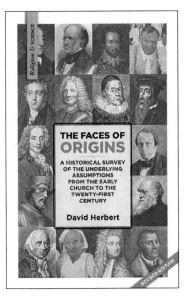

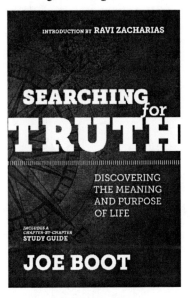

## THE FACES
## OF ORIGINS

A historical survey of the
underlying assumptions
from the early church to
the twenty-first century
*By David Herbert*

THIS IS NOT just another book
presenting evidence in favour
of creationism as opposed to
evolutionism. Herbert explores
the philosophical presupposi-
tions behind Western worldviews throughout history, with
a focus on origins.

ISBN 978–1-894400-45-9

## SEARCHING FOR
## TRUTH

Discovering the meaning
and purpose of life
*By Joe Boot*

BEGINNING WITH a basic understanding of the world, Joe
Boot explains the biblical
worldview, giving special attention to the life and claims
of Jesus Christ. He wrestles
with questions about suffering,
truth, morality and guilt.

ISBN 978–1-894400-40-4

*Deo Optimo et Maximo Gloria*
To God, best and greatest, be glory

www.joshuapress.com

CPSIA information can be obtained
at www.ICGtesting.com
Printed in the USA
FFOW03n1752131017
40957FF